THE HOLY VIRUS

IDENTIFYING THE HOLY VIRUS WITHIN THE HOLY BIBLE

**Written and Edited
by
Lional Christopher Parkinson**

**Cover Artwork and Drawing Illustrations
by
Lional Christopher Parkinson**

First edition - First printing
Printed in the United States of America.

Published by:
Grapevine Publications
P.O. Box 45057
Boise, Idaho 83711

For Ordering information see last page.

ISBN-10 # 0-9627989-3-2
ISBN-13 # 978-0-9627989-3-1

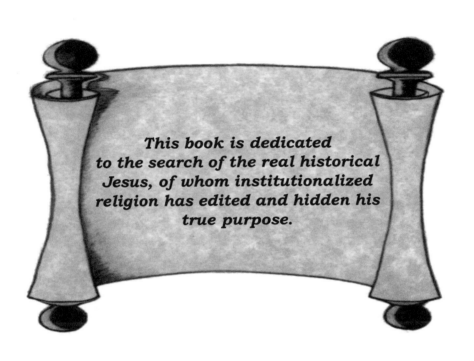

This book is dedicated
to the search of the real historical
Jesus, of whom institutionalized
religion has edited and hidden his
true purpose.

TABLE OF CONTENTS

Author
Lional Christopher Parkinson

For the first time an examiner has come to unlock the most significant mystery from the most influential figure in human history, how he thought, how he lived and most of all, how he defined his teachings and purpose in life. These insights will lift the conscience toward a far greater appreciation of who Jesus was, and unravel the most perplexing issues confronting his time era. The author focuses on resolving deadly religious psychological techniques left unchallenged from the dark ages, but still believed today by destructive religions bound in a quagmire of deception. The insights will leave the reader wondering why it has taken this long to discover these reasoned findings. The conclusions are so practical, you too will wonder how so many could be so taken in all these years. Drawing upon 13 years of experience in the field of Questioned Document work and working as an apprentice under his father, who was the leading instructor in this field and who also worked several years on the DEAD SEA SCROLLS, the author brings an enlightened perception not revealed in any commentary on the Bible.

Typically graduates from Biblical colleges continue to perpetuate the same doctrine passed down from their instructors - generation after generation. Does it seem logical that God would produce a book used as a guide for men to live by - yet it requires alleged experts to explain practically every sentence? And to follow, why are there so many disagreeing religions in the world, yet all claim the same heritage from the same Torah within the Bible? Is it reasonable to believe that God would inspire this human endeavor to formulate a book of the law with so many contradicting statements?

Many questions you have regarding the Bible will quickly be resolved. For many, this book will prompt further research. Much research is yet to be done - this book will be the catalyst.

QUALIFICATIONS OF THE AUTHOR

My father Keith Parkinson worked 30 years as an investigator and as the first Questioned Document Examiner for the State of Idaho. He was also one of the leading instructors in the field of Questioned Document work and sat on the Board of Directors for the World Association of Document Examiners.

My mother a Document Examiner as well, was also a handwriting Expert for 12 years. Being raised by two experienced instructors allowed me to learn both of these fields of study at a very rapid pace. I soon became the youngest court qualified Document Examiner in America. By the time I turned 19 years of age I had worked well over 50 criminal and civil cases.

From 1979 to 1993 it was my primary job as a Document Examiner to make comparisons and determine if documents whether handwritten or typed had been tampered with in any way, and also determine if questioned handwriting was genuine or not. In many cases I had to testify in court for the dead party who had written a family will, upon later, was questioned by a fellow family member. I had the unique opportunity to work criminal cases as an apprentice under my father who headed up the Questioned Document Department for the Bureau of Investigations in Boise, Idaho. For eight years I also handled civil and criminal cases in a private practice.

Studying for long periods of time and paying close attention to details is required as a Document Examiner. I was hired primarily by attorneys for my letter of opinion concerning the authenticity behind particular questioned handwriting and the authenticity behind the questioned document itself. By the time I joined (the World Association of Document Examiners) in the late 1980's, I had worked over 135 criminal and civil cases under the supervision of my father. The advantage of using a Questioned

Document Examiner is that the Examiner is trained not to have a vested interest or an association with any party concerning the questioned subject matter. The Examiner needs to think independent from all other predisposed minds and concentrate for long periods of time on making comparisons. Religious Scribes and Scholars are subject to personal institutional beliefs and payroll checks derived from the same institutions and are not professionally trained in spurious writings and spurious tamperings. Their field of expertise is essential to understanding literal translations, interpretations and transliterations of scripture.

One of the unusual courses I was forced to take involved Handwriting Analysis founded by Milton N. Bunker in 1929. This controversial system, known as Grapho-Analysis, uses stroke analysis to provide insight into personality traits and the evaluation of a writer's personal mental tendencies. Theoretically a person writes with their mind and not with their hand. All of us that write, leave habitual strokes across a page that are peculiarly characteristic to ourselves. These peculiarities differentiate us from most other authors. When found in sufficient numbers, these peculiarities become identifying similarities. These strokes are primarily caused by the mind and the eye working together in conjunction causing subconscious habitual memory. I found that learning this handwriting technique was valuable as a Document Examiner because this system devoted alot of time and energy in training the eye and mind toward identification purposes. So even though Questioned Document work is completely different from the study of Grapho-Analysis, they both share an intense study on the strokes made by authors for identification purposes.

In the early 1970s my father was asked to work on a

particular section of **The Dead Sea Scrolls.** I was very young at that time, but I was fascinated by looking at the handwriting of a particular scroll, thousands of years old, in my fathers examination room. Later when I was much older and qualified, as part of my training process, my father asked me to work on this same section of the Dead Sea Scrolls that he had worked 15 years prior. I was given an exact duplicate copy to work on and was given the same question posed to my father. *"How many authors are involved on this particular section of the Dead Sea Scroll submitted, if any? "*

Unlike religious biblical Scholars, Document Examiners are taught not to have predisposed beliefs or affiliations with religious parties concerning the examination of documents. Using this approach I am ultimately providing the reader a non-atheistic, non-Christian, non-Catholic, non-Jewish and non-Islamic opinion. So by providing a non-religious qualified opinion, the reader can be assured that the opinions rendered inside are without dogmatic influence. I can then appeal to minds predisposed toward logic, rather than religious or atheistic influence.

This book will address the what, where, when and how the Holy Virus originated and why it still continues unabated to this day. The other important issues dealt with include:

1. The actual purpose of Jesus and the final accomplishment behind his resurrection.

2. The hidden mystery behind the blood and flesh of Jesus.

3. The infallible Bible claim by Christianity.

PREFACE

THE HOLY VIRUS is an examination of the authors that composed the King James Holy Bible. The research will focus on the foreign Priests and Scribes appointed by Babylonian and Persian kings during the exile era of Israel in 586 B.C. to 444 B.C. The **HOLY VIRUS** focuses on the belief behind the insidious Old Testament blood covenant that eventually evolved into a human blood offering doctrine promoted by Paul within the New Testament (under the guise of a Holy merciful God). The Holy Virus was first introduced within the Torah of the King James Bible as "The Blood of the Covenant" upon Mount Sinai in Exodus 24:8. The Exodus story presented a nomadic tribe accepting the LORD'S Blood Covenant, upon which required the sprinkling of blood from freshly killed animals toward an entity referred to in the King James Bible as THE LORD. This blood covenant did not satisfy their conscience for long, so the Priests made a religious institution out of the ritual. The ritual served to sustain the psychological power Priests enjoyed over the people. The ripple effect is felt throughout the whole religious world today and has even influenced the secular judicial systems with its vindictive nature without so much as a whiff of suspicion. The Torah itself (a collection of five books allegedly written alone by Moses) becomes the main host and carrier for this trojan horse doctrine, from which it rides along its pages, unsuspected by main-line religions now known as Judaism, Islam, Christianity and Catholicism. As this blood doctrine spreads its toxic venom around the world influencing the minds and hearts of all those that enter into its religious portals - along comes a man labeled the King of the Jews, whose life defied the Jewish/Babylonian Priests and transcended them with his doctrine of life by evidence of his resurrection. A group of unknown authors in the New Testament blatantly revised this man's character by editing out his most important commandments and teachings by replacing him with a mythological substitute, taught by a Roman/Pharisee, purporting to be his Apostle. Using the Bible along with comparison examinations I will expose the Babylonian revised writings from the original authors and the true historical teachings of Jesus still left unedited within the New Testament King James Bible. The synopsis behind my research is to establish that the real historical Jesus never shed his blood on the cross for anyone's sins, as taught by modern Christianity, but rather Jesus took away these beliefs in blood offerings by evidence of his teachings and resurrection. The Torah was in part written by foreign occult authors utilizing occult tactics (mainly the implementation of blood offerings) for the purpose of manipulating peoples minds. The evidence of this Man's teachings and resurrection exposed these religious tactics and broke their psychological hold upon the conscience of mankind. Mankind didn't need a Saviour to shed his blood, but rather mankind needed the teachings from Jesus, so that man could regenerate himself from the inside, rather than depend on outward bloody sacrifices. By removing these occult beliefs, men could move forward towards a reliable knowledge of his Creator.

In my personal communications with Catholics and Christians, I have discovered there is a vast number of people having mutual concerns over their Bibles. Upon these personal discussions I was requested to examine their Bibles and release my findings according to their concerns. The purpose of this book is to uncover the original intent of the authors composing the Bible and for the first time this book will explain the most important mystery in the Bible. What the blood of Jesus actually means as recorded in;

Matthew 26:28? *"For this is my blood of the new testament, which is shed for many for the remission of sins."*

NOTE FROM THE PUBLISHER

You are about to set upon a path of discovery. The information found in the following pages will awaken any curious reader regarding the teaching in Christianity, Catholicism, Judaism and the Muslim religion. Long held beliefs that are thought to be from God are exposed as false - with sound evidence - right from the scriptures themselves.

This is not another "code discovery" within the text of the King James Bible or re-interpretation of scripture, but rather facts brought to light using dates, contradictions and mis-interpretations of various languages within the text.

But YOU have to read this book to make an informed decision - not take the word from some "authority" whom you have given the power. We all have a conscience with an ability to reason. This book is presented in such a way that you will soon recognize the fallacies and contradictions within the pages of the Bible. You will continue to recognize the value and good in the Bible - but you will also see what has been twisted to make Christ's message false and anti-Christian.

Portions of this book still have me wondering and wanting further research. I can only hope more answers will come. But what I have discovered herein has answered or confirmed many contradictions found to be unresolved in my reading of the scriptures. It also has answered one very large question: Why, with all the new converts to Christianity, are we not a kinder, safer and more loving world? Wisdom should be more evident with the advance of the spiritual life... I see that the opposite is paramount throughout the world. Hopefully this book will add both wisdom and sanity to a troubled world.

Phil

CHAPTER 1
THE HOLY VIRUS

THE FUNDAMENTAL RULE IN THE ENGAGEMENT OF RATIONAL THOUGHT IS THAT IF YOUR BASIC PREMISE IS WRONG, THEN ALL SPECIFICS THAT FOLLOW IN YOUR CHAIN OF REASONING ARE ALSO FLAWED. IN FACT, THEY ARE WORTHLESS. TO BUILD A CASE WITH AN ARRAY OF SEEMINGLY PERSUASIVE POINTS IS MEANINGLESS IF ONE'S STARTING POINT IS FLAWED.

1

The Bible is the most commercialized book in human history, but like all books **the facts** are always held hostage by the integrity and accuracy of the authors that composed it. The Bible covers a period in the development of Judaism which was transitional between Polytheism and Monotheism. The Biblical era 1700 B.C. to 70 A.D. is full of giants, monsters, demigods and superheroes with God like strength. Serpents and animals talk to humans and angels roam the earth, conveying the affairs of the LORD with people.

The Rabbinic era started around 444 B.C. (the time period of the Oral tradition of the Torah law along with the Persian rebuilt Temple in Jerusalem) to 500 A.D. (the closure of the Babylonian Talmud).

Judaic mythology came from many sources, much of the mythological material was elaborated on, from the two Talmuds, the Midrashic literature, and the mystical literature. Yet, more exists in the Apocrypha, the Dead Sea scrolls and additional texts written in Aramaic and Greek pertaining to Judaism. If there is any salvageable truth within the Bible, it would only rest on the hidden inner teachings of Jesus and the integrity behind the story of his resurrection. When it comes to history, one man's truth is another man's subjective fantasy, however, this book the Holy Virus is not based on any religion nor atheism, but rather on a neutral position that compares the historical facts and fictions evident in both these other realms.

The struggle between priests and prophets of the Old Testament is focused upon the battle of supremacy, as to who better knew the Creator of the universe and his laws. The strongest debate over God and his original laws took place near the time Israel went into captivity by the Babylonians in 586 B.C. The most damaging law being debated was the blood of the covenant first institutionalized in Exodus 24:8 as **THE BLOOD OF THE COVENANT** depicting an insidious blood ritual established under the guise of a Holy Merciful God. The Blood Covenant ritual required the sprinkling of blood from freshly killed animals (oxens) as a mark of their allegiance toward an entity later to be referred to as **"THE LORD"** in the Christian King James Bible.

Jeremiah of Anathoth was the last great Prophet during the final four decades of the Kingdom of Judah prior to their exile under the Babylonians. He started his prophetic ministry in 627 B.C. and continued through 586 B.C. Jeremiah was inspired to write down these words before the nation Israel was enslaved and exiled from Jerusalem to Babylon by Nebuchadnezzar the King of Babylon.

Jeremiah 7:21-24 *"Thus saith The God of Hosts, the God of Israel; Put your burnt offerings unto your sacrifices, and eat flesh.* *22* ***"For I spoke not unto your fathers, nor commanded them in the day that I brought them out of the land of Egypt, concerning burnt offerings or sacrifices."*** *23* *But this thing commanded I them, saying,* ***Obey my voice****, and I will be your God, and ye shall be my people: and walk ye in all the ways that I have commanded you, that it may be well unto you.* *24* *But they hearkened not, nor inclined their ear, but walked in the counsels and in the imagination of their evil heart, and went backward and not forward."*

The definition of Propitiation is a theological term describing an atoning sacrifice. Generally, Christians believe the death of Christ on the cross appeased the justice of God for all who believe in the blood sacrifice of the Son. In Jeremiah 7:21-24 God denies ever giving such laws and is disturbed by anyone believing his justice or anger needed appeasment through blood offerings. How much more disturbing it must be to the Creator, for people to believe his justice would be appeased through the blood offering of Christ. What he demanded from his people was this. **"Turn away from blood sacrifices and obey his voice."**

3

Implementing a blood offering ritual, as practiced by the Babylonian inspired Jewish Priests, made them self-centered. The purpose ultimately was to control Commerce by using occult practices already practiced under the worshiped gods of Babylon. Prior to Christianity, Rome was heavily influenced by the Babylonian Sun-god belief system. Later Rome took upon the dominate Babylonian religion of the Solar-god, while Israel was given the lesser Babylonian moon-god religion to worship as they were conquered by the Babylonians. This gave the Babylonian Scribes plenty of time to revise Jewish history and implement their own form of worship in the Jewish Temple well before Rome came and occupied the land. The Babylonian scribes most likely wrote Leviticus and revised a good portion of the Torah leaving all four main-line religions today infected with this Holy Virus doctrine. It was not necessarily the Jews that brought on this blood shed doctrine upon the world nor can they be blamed for crucifying Jesus. Rather it was the Babylonian revisionists disguising themselves as Jewish Scribes and Priests working their havoc in the Temple at the time. Today many orthodox Jews and Christians actively support the rebuilding of the Temple in Jerusalem. The Jews and Christians who agitate for this restoration do so, because they believe it is the LORD's will that Temple blood rituals be restored. Christians see the resumption of Temple sacrifices as a sure sign of the second coming of Christ. This book will focus on the central premise underpinning main-line religions that depend on blood-offering sacrifices of some type as their cornerstone of faith.

The world's religions are infected with this mutually shared deadly virus (A sort of Trojan horse doctrine), and unless properly exposed and eliminated, this virus will destroy the integrity of any religion that embraces this ritual.

By definition the words ("Occult and cult") are:

Occult: *Hidden from the eye or the understanding; inviable;*

4

secret; concealed;unknown.-------- *relating to mysterious or supernatural powers and activities such as witchcraft, astrology, alchemy, magic and necromancy.* **Webster Dictionary 1913 and Cambridge Dictionary of American English.**

Cult: *A group of people who share religious or spiritual beliefs, especially beliefs regarded by others as misguided, unorthodox, or false.* ***Encarta World English Dictionary***

THE TORAH

According to Exodus 2:1&2 Moses was born from the house of Levi and it has been taught in Christianity that Moses was the sole author of all five books of the Torah. Presently the books that make up the alleged Torah are these:

1. Genesis describes human life before the time of Moses.

2. Exodus describes Moses leading his people out of Egypt towards Mount Sinai.

3. Leviticus describes Moses and his people on Mount Sinai.

4. Numbers describes Moses and his people leaving Mount Sinai towards the promised land.

5. Deuteronomy reflects on the whole encounter of Moses and the LORD on Mount Horeb while heading toward the promised land of Canaan.

For the purpose of identifying the main conflict between the Priests and the Prophets found in the Old Testament, it became necessary for me to identify **THE BLOOD COVENANT OF THE LORD** established by the Priests from the **inspired Word of the Prophets**. I will use the title (THE LORD) to represent the corrupt Laws of the Priests as they opposed the Prophets of "GOD" who wanted to make changes as their conscience moved them. **The HOLY VI-**

RUS represents the Blood Covenant initiated in Exodus 24:8. This blood ritual and other atrocities against the Prophets are mentioned throughout the Bible. However, the Priests, according to my research were the final editors compiling the Torah of the Old Testament as you read it today.

The following comparisons are a few compelling reasons not to believe that Moses was the sole author of the five books that make up the Torah. The Torah is a collection of complex traditions and not a cohesive whole. In at least some cases it is possible to untangle the various threads and identify different authors working with a specific agenda. The birth of Moses starts out in Exodus 2:1&4 with Moses being born without siblings and mysteriously being hidden for three months for no apparent reason, just to be picked up in the river by the daughter of Pharoah, whereas in the Exodus 6:20 version Moses was born along with his brother Aaron to Amram (the father) and Jochebed (the birth mother) who was also Amram's aunt. One does not have to read much further to see why traditional Christianity selects the first version over the second version of incest.

1. Exodus 17:6 - On his way toward Mount Horeb, Moses was commanded **to smite the rock,** subsequently water came out and the people drank. Moses obviously obeyed the command of the LORD in this Exodus version, because he had done exactly as the LORD had ordered him to do, which was *"thou shalt SMITE the rock"* and the name of the place in the Exodus version was called Meribah.

Exodus 17:6 *"Behold, I will stand before thee there upon the rock in Hor'-eb; and **thou shalt SMITE the rock,** and there shall come water out of it, that the people may drink........"*

However, in Numbers 20:8 Moses was commanded

by the LORD to only **speak to the rock** and water would come out, but instead, Moses smote the rock twice in defiance of the LORD'S order. Subsequently, this action barred Moses and Aaron from leading the LORD'S congregation into the Promised land. Therefore both Moses and Aaron died prematurely by the hand of the LORD, Aaron on top of Mount Hor in Chapter 20:28 and Moses was killed and buried by the LORD in Deuteronomy 34:5-7.

Numbers 20:8&11 *"Take the rod, and gather thou the assembly together, thou, and Aaron thy brother, and* **SPEAK ye unto the rock** *before their eyes; and it shall give forth his water, and thou shalt bring forth to them water out of the rock:.........."* *And Moses lifted up his hand, and with his rod he smote the rock twice:*

Moses obviously obeyed the command of the LORD in the Exodus version, but disobeyed the command of the LORD in the Numbers version. Had this story been written by only one author the details mentioned above would have stayed the same and not conflicted.

2. Obviously **Moses** never wrote Deuteronomy Chapter 34, because this chapter describes Moses being buried in the past tense. This story records **Moses** in the **third person** and not as a story **written** "by" **Moses** in the first **person**.

In fact, the author of Deuteronomy 34:5-7 is obtaining his information from another previously written source not known or mentioned anywhere else within the Torah. Note:

Deuteronomy 34:5-7 *"So Moses the servant of the LORD died there in the land of Moab,* **according to the word of the LORD.** *⁶ And he buried him in a valley in the land of Moab, over against Beth-pe-or: but no man knoweth of his sepulcher unto this day. ⁷ And Moses was a hundred* *and twenty years old when he died: his eye was not dim, nor his natural force abated."*

Noting that in this passage Moses is not only spoken of in the third person, but also in the past tense.

1. The author is admitting that Moses is not the author of this section at all.

2. How did the information of Moses death arrive to this author of Deuteronomy, especially when the author admits he can't even locate the sepulcher of Moses?

3. How does the author know how old Moses was and who buried Moses when he obviously wasn't there at the time of the burial? The author is either making up this story or simply reading the death of Moses from another written source. The reason given for the early death of Moses and Aaron was that Moses and Aaron trespassed against the LORD at the waters of Meribah (found in Numbers 20:12 and Deuteronomy 32:51&52). Subsequently both were not permitted to lead the nomadic exodus tribe any further.

There are also two different patriarch's named Moses being portrayed within the Numbers version. One Moses is portrayed as a very meek personality in Chapter 12 and another Moses portrayed as the murdering conquerer in Chapter 31.

1. Numbers 12:3 **"Now the man Moses was very meek, above all the men upon the face of the earth."**

2. Numbers 31:14, 17, 18: *"And Moses was wroth...And Moses said unto them, "Have ye saved all the women alive? ...* **Now therefore kill every male among the little ones, and kill every woman, ... But all the women children ... keep alive for yourselves."**

3.   THE SABBATH

Concerning the Sabbath: there are three different

accounts displaying the psychological profile of the LORD penned by the Priests.

1. Numbers 15:32-35 *"And while the children of Israel were in the wilderness, they found a man that gathered sticks upon the Sabbath day.* [34]*"And they put him in ward,* **because it was not declared what should be done to him** [35] *"AND THE LORD SAID UNTO MOSES, THE MAN SHALL SURELY BE PUT TO DEATH: all the congregation shall stone him with stones without the camp."*

In this Numbers 15:32-35 version it was not determined what to do with a person that had violated the sabbath. So the scribes wrote a law as if it came directly from their LORD. In the following Exodus account, it had been already declared what to do with someone that violated the Sabbath law.

2. Exodus 31:12-16 *"AND THE LORD SPAKE UNTO MOSES saying:* [14] *Ye shall keep the Sabbath therefore; for it is holy unto you:* **EVERY ONE THAT DEFILETH IT SHALL SURELY BE PUT TO DEATH:** *therefore the children of Israel shall keep the Sabbath, to observe the Sabbath throughout their generations, FOR A PERPETUAL COVENANT."*

This is a perpetual law that applied zero tolerance and a death penalty. This law had clearly been declared in Leviticus; only the LORD declared that he personally would destroy everyone that defiled his Sabbath law. This indicates that the book of Leviticus and Numbers were written at a different time era than the Exodus and Deuteronomy versions. The author of Leviticus is relying on the reader to believe that the LORD was murdering the violators personally instead of relying on the community as a whole to stone the transgressors as written in the Numbers and Exodus versions. These of course are trivial dissimilarities, however, they contain the necessary contradictions to determine different authors at possibly different time eras.

3. Leviticus 23:30 *"and whatsoever soul it be that*

doeth any work in that same day, the same soul **WILL I DESTROY** *from among the people."*

I find it odd that the LORD would command the community to kill the poor man in the Exodus version, while emphasizing the destruction of the person by the LORD himself in the Leviticus version. At any rate, if we compare these three Old Testament examples with the writings accredited to Jesus in Mark 2:27 and Matthew 12:7, we will find a diametrically opposed opinion regarding the Sabbath.

Mark 2:27 **"And he said unto them, The Sabbath was made for man, and not man for the Sabbath:........"**

Matthew 12:7 *"But if ye had known what this meaneth,* **I WILL HAVE MERCY, AND NOT SACRIFICE, ye would not have condemned the guiltless."**

Jesus clearly violated the LORD'S sabbath by committing such acts as healing others in need and showing compassion toward others on that day. Jesus taught that the sabbath was a day made for man and that any man was above the Sabbath day law if the man determines it necessary to meet a pressing need for a fellow human or animal.

Luke 14:5 **"Which of you shall have an ass or an Ox fallen into a pit, and will not straightway pull him out on the sabbath day?"**

Matthew 12:1-3 *"At that time Jesus went on the Sabbath day through the corn; and his disciples were hungered, and began to pluck the ears of corn, and to eat. But when The Pharisees saw it, they said unto him, Behold, thy disciples do that which is not lawful to do upon the Sabbath day."*

Matthew 12:8 *"For the son of man is Lord even of the sabbath day."*

4.   In Exodus 16:13 &31- **the quail and Manna story** occurred near the 15th day of the 2nd month of the 1st year when Moses led the nomadic tribe out of Egypt.

Exodus 16:13 ***"And it came to pass, that   at evening the quails came up, and covered the camp: and in the mourning the dew lay round about the host."*** *" And the taste of it was like wafers made with honey."*

However in the Numbers account in chapter 11:31-33 the same quail and Manna story occurs near the 20th day of the 2nd month of the 2nd year with a different taste to the Manna and with a disastrous plague resulting from the quails for the people of Moses.

Numbers 11:8 & 31 & 33 **"And the taste of it was as the taste of fresh oil."** *"And there went forth a wind from the LORD, and brought quails from the sea, and let them fall by the camp, as it were a day's journey on this side, and as it were a day's journey on the other side, round about the camp, and as it were two cubits high upon the face of the earth. [33] And while the flesh was yet between their teeth, ere it was chewed, the wrath of the LORD was kindled against the people, and the LORD smote the people with a very great plague."*

Both versions are explaining how they received Manna and the quails for the very first time coming out of Egypt.   Both quail and Manna stories are so far apart in their traditions, neither story agrees to the same time, place, or results of the event.   In the Exodus version the quail story was a non-event compared to standing knee deep in quail for two days that resulted in a plague that killed the people in the Numbers version.   Both quail versions were preserved in the non-Davidic section of the book of Psalms. Psalm 105:40 only agrees with the Exodus version, while Psalm 78:27-31 agrees only with the Numbers version.

Exodus preserved in Psalm 105:40 *"The people asked, and he brought quails, and satisfied them with the bread from heaven."*

Numbers preserved in Psalm 78:27 *"He rained flesh upon them like dust, and feathered fowls like as the sand of the sea:"* [31]*"The wrath of God came upon them, and slew the fattest of them, and smote down the chosen men of Israel."*

Hense, the quail story is expressed by different authors at different locations at different times with different ending results. I should also mention that **the flesh** that rained on the people in Psalm 78:27 really meant (manna Bread), but the people craved the flesh of animals. Hense the plague came upon them for not accepting the bread with thanksgiving.

5. According to the authors of Deuteronomy, Moses was never aware of the existence of Mount Sinai, instead the authors of this book used **Mount (HOREB)** as the exact location where the Ten Commandments were delivered to Moses. Such as: Deuteronomy 2:1&2, 4:10, 5:2, 9:8, 18:16 and 29:1.

Deuteronomy 5:2&4 *"The LORD our God made a covenant with us in HOREB"* [4]*"The LORD talked with you face to face in the MOUNT out of the midst of the fire."*

The book of Numbers and Leviticus exclusively uses Mount (Sinai) as the location where upon the Ten Commandments were delivered to Moses, whereas Exodus tries to employ both locations.

Exodus 3:1 ***"Now Moses ....led the flock to the backside of the desert, and came to the mountain of God, even unto Horeb."***

Exodus 19:20. ***"And the LORD came down upon mount SINAI, on the top of the mount: and the LORD called Moses up to the top of the mount; and Moses went up."***

According to the authors of Numbers and Leviticus, Moses was never aware of the existence of Mount Horeb where the LORD gave him the Ten Commandments.

Numbers 3:1 ***"These also are the generations of Aaron and Moses in the day that the LORD spake with Moses in mount Sinai."***

The fact the authors of Exodus, Numbers and Leviticus named the Mountain "Sinai" from the authors of Deuteronomy who exclusively named the Mountain "Horeb" indicates that the different authors identified this mount at different time eras. If there was only one author of these books as alleged by the Jewish and Christian community, then logic dictates only one name would have been used throughout all the five books continuously also. Elijah in 1st Kings 19:8 mentions only the name **Horeb** as the Mount of God.

There appears also to be several different authors within the book of Exodus based on the LORD'S requirement to be seen face to face with Moses in Exodus 33:11, as compared to his requirement not to be seen face to face by any man nine verses later in Exodus 33:20.

Exodus 33:11 ***"And the LORD spake unto Moses face to face, as a man speaketh unto his friend. "***

Exodus 33: 20 ***"And he said, Thou canst not see my face: for there shall no man see me, and live."***

6. Within the Book of Deuteronomy there are two separate sets of Statues and Judgments that go totally contrary to one another. One version in Chapter 6 places all focus on recognizing God for who he is (as the Creator) whereas the Chapter 12 version focuses attention on killing others and making bloody sacrifices to the LORD. In Mark 12:29-30 it should be noted that Jesus only endorsed the Statutes and Judgements of Deuteronomy Chapter 6:1-9 as to any link to his Father God.

Deuteronomy 6:1-9 *"**NOW THESE ARE THE COMMANDMENTS, THE STATUTES, AND THE JUDGEMENTS,** WHICH THE LORD YOUR GOD COMMANDED TO TEACH YOU, THAT YOU MIGHT DO THEM IN THE LAND WHITHER YE GO TO POSSESS IT.* ⁵ *"**Hear O Israel: The Lord our God is one Lord: And thou shalt love the Lord thy God with all thy heart, and with all thy soul, and with all might. ⁶And these words, which I command thee this day, shall be in thine heart: ⁸And thou shalt bind them upon thine hand, and they shall be as frontlets between thine eyes. ⁹And thou shalt write them upon the posts of thy house, and on thy gates.**"*

The Statutes and Judgments within Deuteronomy Chapter 12:6 &15 turn toward killing anything the tribe desires to eat and towards animal sacrifices to the LORD.

Deuteronomy 12:1-6 *"**THESE ARE THE STATUTES AND JUDGEMENTS,** which you shall observe to do in the land, which THE LORD God of thy fathers giveth thee to possess it, all the days that ye live upon the earth.* ⁶ *"And thither ye shall bring your burnt offerings, and your sacrifices, and your tithes, and your heave offerings of your hand, and your vows, and your freewill offerings, and the firstlings of your herds and of your flocks."* ¹⁵ *"Notwithstanding thou mayest kill and eat flesh in all thy gates, whatsoever thy soul lusteth after..."*

The notion that all five books of the Torah were authored by Moses (as believed by some Biblical scholars) is inaccurate. The Torah was influenced by different traditions and different cultures. For example: King David and his sons, were not aware of the strict requirements listed in the books of Numbers and Leviticus concerning who was to perform the Priestly duties of blood-shed sacrifices at the tabernacle. Any stranger outside the appointed Aaronite clan would have been put to death. If the King of Israel didn't have access to this information in the book of Leviticus, then it probably didn't exist during his time era. The Priests were the final editors of most, if not all the Old Testament books. The Prophets did not have this advantage.

Numbers 3:10 *"And thou shalt appoint **Aaron and his sons, and they shall wait on their priest's office: and the stranger that cometh nigh shall be put to death.**"*

Leviticus 1:5 *"And he shall kill the bullock before the LORD: **and the Priests, Aaron's sons, shall bring the blood, and sprinkle the blood round about upon the altar that is by the door of the Tabernacle of the congregation.**"*

7. The Book of Genesis is certainly not exempt from different authors writing inconsistent stories within its pages. For example: Were the fowls of the Earth created from the waters, as one author records in Genesis 1:20, or were the fowls created from the ground as another author records in Genesis 2:19?

Genesis 1:20 *"and God said, **Let the waters bring forth** abundantly the moving creature that hath life, and **fowl that may fly above.....**"*

Genesis 2:19 *"**And out of the ground** the LORD God*

*formed every beast of the field, and every **fowl of the air;........**"*

In Genesis 1:29 the author defined **"Meat" as herb bearing seeds and fruit bearing trees,** yet immediately after the story of the great flood found in Genesis 9:3 carnal minded authors revised the word **"Meat"** as pertaining to every animal that moves.

Genesis 1:29 *"And God said, Behold I have given you every herb bearing seed, which is upon the face of the earth, and every tree, in the which is the fruit of the tree yielding seed; to you it **shall be for meat.**"*
Genesis 9:3 *"**Every moving thing that liveth shall be meat for you**; ...."*

Whereas, in the book of Leviticus the author has restrictions on some animals and no restrictions on others.
Leviticus 11:1-3 *"And the LORD spake unto Moses and to Aaron, saying unto them, Speak unto the children of Israel, saying, These are the beasts which **ye shall eat** among all the beasts that are on the earth."*

Leviticus 11:4 " Nevertheless these **shall ye not eat** of them that chew the cud, or of them that divide the hoof: as the camel, because he cheweth the cud, but divideth not the hoof; he is unclean to you."

While some would argue that these widely divergent viewpoints are mere conflicts and not contradictions merely reported as facts within the Bible. An entire overview provides a long term perspective not revealed by a short term view of events. When religions provide the explanation there is no contradictions within the Bible by not displaying the conflicts written within, it only leaves a deceptive notion impressed upon the mind of the reader.

THE LAW

The Torah (the original Book of the law of Moses) did not consist of the first five books of the Bible as presented today. In fact, the only books that mentions Moses writing "**THE LAW**" is the book of Deuteronomy 31:24.and Exodus 24:4&7. So the original Torah (the law of Moses) is entirely different from the five successive versions known today as Genesis, Exodus, Leviticus, Numbers and Deuteronomy. Defining the contents that comprised "**THE LAW**" from the contents that comprised the **book of the law** is essential before making comparisons and examining any edited evidence.

1. **Deuteronomy 30:10** *"If thou shalt hearken unto the voice of the Lord thy God,to keep his commandments and his statutes and his judgements **which are written in the book of the law.**"*

2. **Deuteronomy 29:21** *"........according to all the curses of the covenant that are **written in this book of the law.**"*

3. **Deuteronomy 31:24&26** *"And it came to pass, when Moses had made an end of the **writing of the law in a book**, until they were finished, That Moses commanded the Levites, which bare the ark of the covenant of the LORD saying, Take **this book of the law**, and put it in the side of the ark of the covenant...........*"

4. **Exodus 24:4&7** the author refers to Moses in the third person past tense and calls it the book of the covenant. Exodus 24:4&7 "**And Moses wrote all the words of the LORD............And he took the book of the covenant, and read in the audience of the people.**"

17

According to the book of Deuteronomy, the book of the law of Moses only consisted of the above listed contents labeled **1, 2** and **3.**

1. The commandments, statutes and judgements.

2. The curses of the covenant.

3. The Ten Commandments.

Deuteronomy 4:44 *"And this is* **THE LAW** *which Moses set before the children of Israel."*

THE COMMANDMENTS, THE STATUTES, AND THE JUDGEMENTS all rolled up into one Law.

"Hear O Israel: The Lord our God is one Lord: And thou shalt love the Lord thy God with all thy heart, and with all thy soul, and with all might."

Whenever Jesus spoke directly to Lawyers, Scribes and Pharisees he referred them back to Deuteronomy 6:4&5. For example Luke 10:26, Mark 12:28-30 and Matthew 22:40. **The Law** was defined there as *"The Great Commandment".*

"Hear O Israel: The Lord our God is one Lord: And thou shalt love the Lord thy God with all thy heart, and with all thy soul, and with all might." "On these two commandments hang all "THE LAW"and the prophets."

However, when Jesus taught **The Law** to his inner circle of friends and Apostles, **The Law** took on a different esoteric appearance.

Matthew 7:12 ***"Therefore all things whatsoever ye would that men should do unto you, do ye even so unto them: For this is THE LAW and the prophets."***

Jesus taught his Disciples by a different set of Commandments which made up **The Law,** because the law quoted by Jesus in Matthew 7:12 does not exist in the Torah. Neither was this law practiced in the Old Testament. Whereas, the The Law quoted by Jesus toward Lawyers, Scribes and Pharisees was always Deuteronomy 6:5. Jesus even dis-associates himself from the lawyers and their laws in Deuteronomy by referring to these laws as belonging to them only.

John 8:17 ***"It is also written in YOUR LAW"***

Luke 11:52 ***"Woe unto you, Lawyers! for ye have taken away the key of knowledge: ye entered not in yourselves, and them that were entering in ye hindered."***

Compare the way the book of Deuteronomy 1:42 starts out by God speaking to Moses in the first person present tense: ***"And the LORD said unto me."*** as opposed to the many edited in writings throughout Deuteronomy such as Deuteronomy 29:1, the author refers to Moses in the third person past tense.

Deuteronomy 29:1 ***"These are the words of the covenant, which the LORD commanded Moses*** to make with the children of Israel in the land of MOAB, beside the covenant which he made with them in HOREB.***"***

Very little of Deuteronomy is written in the first person present tense. Jesus had a problem accepting the entire book of Deuteronomy as the original book of the law of Moses and Jesus had suspicions over the way the Ten Commandments were interpreted by the lawyers and scribes. Jesus taught and warned about the Scribes of his day who taught and edited hearsay laws that were drafted onto the book of the law. Using New Testament quotes

19

from Jesus we can surmise a few of his thoughts concerning the original law from the later edited versions. The book of Deuteronomy is the only book of the Torah that states emphatically that Mount Horeb (not Mount Sinai) was the place the LORD spoke to Moses. Jesus even quotes a passage from Exodus chapter 3, where mount HOREB was used only once, referenced from the author of Matthew 22:32. Jesus also mentioned God speaking to Moses from the burning bush on Mount Horeb as part of the original book of Moses in Mark 12:26. Jesus never quoted any laws or any scriptures that pertained to Mount Sinai which is where the book of Leviticus and Numbers describes in horror detail the blood and burnt offerings.

Jesus always quoted from selected sections presented in the present tense first person form within Chapters 6 and 8 of Deuteronomy, rather than from the past tense third person sections of Deuteronomy. For example:

Matthew 4:4 *"**It is written**,man shall not live by bread alone, but by every word that proceedeth out of the mouth of God doth man live."* Deuteronomy 8:3.

Matthew 4:7 *"**It is written** again Thou shalt not tempt the Lord thy God."* Deuteronomy 6:7.

Matthew 4:10 *"**It is written**, thou shalt worship the Lord thy God, and him only thou shalt serve."* Deuteronomy 6:13.

Using the non-Jesus quoted section of the book of Luke in the New Testament, the author quotes a scripture out of Leviticus and renames the Book of the law of Moses to **" THE LAW OF THE LORD."**

Luke 2:24 *"And to offer a sacrifice according to that which is **said** in **THE LAW OF THE LORD**, a pair of turtle doves, or two young pigeons."* Leviticus 12:6-8.

Jesus distinguished the difference between the original law and the edited laws of Leviticus, Numbers and

Deuteronomy. In the mind of Jesus these versions were **HEARSAY** versions and were not the original **written** Law. For example Matthew chapter 5 presents a few direct quoted thoughts from Jesus.

1. Matthew 5:21 *"ye have HEARD that it was SAID by them of old time, Thou shalt not kill; and whoso ever shall be in danger of the judgment: But I say unto you, That whosoever is angry with his brother without a cause shall be in danger of the judge ment:............."*

2. Matthew 5:27 *"Ye have HEARD that it was SAID them of old time, Thou shalt not commit adul-tery: But I say unto you, That whosoever looketh upon a woman to lust after her hath committed adultery with her already in his heart."*

3. Matthew 5:31 *"It hath been SAID, Whosoever shall put away his wife, let him give her a writing of divorcement: But I say unto you, That whosoever shall put away his wife, saving for the cause of fornica-tion, causeth her to commit adultery: and whosoever shall marry her that is divorced committeth adultery."*

4. Matthew 5:33 *"Again ye have HEARD that it hath been SAID by them of old time, Thou shalt not foreswear thyself, but shalt per form unto the LORD thine oaths: But I say unto you swear not at all;..............................,"*

5. Matthew 5:38 *"Ye have HEARD that it hath been said, An eye for an eye, and a tooth for a tooth. But I say unto you, That ye resist not evil: but whoso ever shall smite thee on thy right cheek, turn to him the other also."*

6. Matthew 5:43 *"Ye have HEARD that it hath been SAID, Thou shalt love thy neighbor, and hate thy enemy. But, I say unto you Love your enemies, bless them that curse you, do good to them that hate you, and pray for them that despitefully use you, and persecute you;............................"*

In these examples Jesus takes on the hearsay teachings of the Ten Commandments and reveals the corrupted Levitical versions of the law in Leviticus chapter 24:20, 19:18 and 19:12. According to the authors of Leviticus 24:20 and 19:18, one was to love their neighbor as thyself up until the point one transgresses against his fellow neighbor or enemy, then it was all out war. In fact, Jesus strongly maintained that some of the laws contained in what was then called THE LAW (Torah) were deceptive and were not the laws of God at all. Even Moses was suspected by Jesus of editing in laws that were not God's. One example was the law of "divorse by writ", see quote in Deuteronomy 24:1 as referenced by Jesus in Matthew 19:8.

*"Moses because of the hardness of your hearts suffered you to put away your wives: **but from the beginning it was not so.**"*

Jesus clearly suspected something was wrong with the Ten Commandments. He lived and taught by a different set of lost or hidden Commandments; a set of Commandments that were edited out of the Old and New Testament King James Bible. Instead, we are given generic statements noted in the book of John.

*John 14:15 "If you love me keep **my commandments**".*

*John 14:21 "He that hath **my Commandments**, and keepeth them, he it is that loveth me: and he that loveth me shall be loved of my father, and I will manifest myself to him."*

*John 15:10 "If you keep **my Commandments**, ye*

22

shall abide in my love;..........."

Jesus establishes a different set of commandments for his Disciples from those in Deuteronomy 6:5.

John 15:12 ***"This is my commandment, That ye love one another as I have loved you."***

Deuteronomy 6:5 summed up everything in its entirety and it was these words to be placed upon the wrists of all the people and memorized by everyone.

Deuteronomy 6:8 ***"And thou shalt bind them for a sign upon thy hand, and they shall be as fronlets between thine eyes."***

Realistically how many laws can one write on their wrist anyway? The Ten Commandments listed in Deuteronomy 5:4 consists of 341 translated english words. The Torah as believed today consists of 200,000 english words divided into five separate books called Genesis, Exodus, Leviticus, Numbers and Deuteronomy. Much like the Internal Revenue Code book, the list grew longer and more burdensome as time went on, ***"but from the beginning it was not so.*** *"*

Jesus simplified the law for the lawyers during his day by simply quoting Deuteronomy 6:5. Jesus most likely knew **The original Law and the book of Moses** better than any Scribe of his day. Joshua was commissioned by Moses in Joshua 8:32 to write a copy of the law of Moses on large stones upon entering the promised land of Canaan. Since Christians are taught today the THE TORAH consisted of the five first books of the Bible, then how many stones would be required for Joshua to chisel and hammer out the whole copy of the Law as believed today? It would have been impossible for Joshua to do. Now try and imagine memorizing 200,000 words on your wrists as required in Deuteronomy 6:8. So obviously the original law was at one time only a simplified statement or two and not five books.

The Bible reader will find it difficult to distinguish the many different LORDs referred throughout their King James Bibles. For example:

The LORD referred in Deuteronomy 6:4&6 is different from the LORD referred to in Deuteronomy 12:27.

The LORD referred to on Mount Horeb in Exodus 3:14 is different from the LORD on Mount Sinai in Exodus 19:18.
The LORD called (Jah) in Psalm 68:4 is different from the LORD called (Jehovah) in Psalm 83:18.

The LORD referred to in Ezra 1:2 is different from the LORD in 2nd Samuel 24:1 referenced also in the book of 1st Chronicles 21:1.

The all powerful LORD that destroyed the Egyptian chariot army in the Red Sea in Exodus 14:28 is different from the weak inept LORD that could not drive out the chariot army in the book of Judges, because their chariots were made of iron.
Judges 1:19 *"And the LORD......COULD NOT drive out the inhabitants of the valley, because they had chariots of iron."*

All these LORDS when researched were different in character name such as: **"EH-YEH ASHER EH-YEH"** in Exodus 3:14, **"JAH or YAHWEH"** in Psalm 68:4, **"JEHOVAH"** in Psalm 83:18, **"MARDUK"** in Ezra 1:2 and **"SATAN"** in 2nd Samuel 24:1 and 1st Chronicles 21:1. The final editors of the King James Bible simply used the generic term LORD to illustrate all LORD'S are one and the same.

24

THE MOON-GOD OF LEVITICUS AND MOUNT SINAI

"In the fourteenth day of the first month at even is the LORD'S Passover." **LEVITICUS 23:5**

The god of Leviticus gives the Passover its date, which alone is fascinating, because the calendar of this Levitical god is based on the phases of the lunar moon. This cold hearted LORD that ruled the night, required the practice of animal blood and burnt offerings. It is through the sacrifices and consumption of these certain animals on this lunar date, that leads me to believe this was a moon worshipping cult, especially when the mount upon which these bloody rituals and invocations took place were practiced by other similar moon-cults named after a well known Babylonian moon-god called **SIN**. The Jewish calendar follows the lunar cycle of the moon, and each month is determined by the "arrival" of the new moon. On the Jewish Passover (known in Hebrew as **Pesach**), the Passover lamb was killed and consumed on the night of the full moon. This ritual was conducted on the 15th of the first lunar month of the Jewish calendar called Nisan, which falls within the months of March and April, then the remaining flesh was burnt the very next morning.

EXODUS *12:6 "And ye shall keep it up until the fourteenth day of the same month: and the whole ass embly of the congregation of Israel shall kill it in the evening."*

Exodus 12:10 *"And ye shall not let nothing of it remain until the morning, and that which remaineth of it until morning ye shall burn with fire."*

Jesus never taught the passover Sabbath to be practiced in this way. In Mark 2:27 Jesus taught the passover Sabbath was a day of rest made for mankind and not to be used for the purpose of serving institutionalized sacrifices in the form of animal blood-offerings. In Judaism the Hebrew word for 'sacrifice' is "**Korban**" which employs the meaning: *To Draw Near or Come close to God.* The Hebrew word for 'Altar' is "**Mizbe'ah**" from a word meaning *to slay.* The heritage of the altar incorporated the use of horns as tying posts at all four corners to keep the animal bound. To kill an animal for the sole purpose of invoking and drawing near to an entity that relates itself solely to the phases of the moon, causes me to question. What is the difference between "**Yahweh**", and the Canaanite moon-god **Yarih** or the Babylonian moon-god **Sin**?

All these lunar gods, along with their animal blood offerings rituals indicate the Exodus tribe of Exodus 24:8 was nothing more than another moon worshipping cult.

The Torah describes various Jewish offerings presented for each holiday, starting with those brought on **"Rosh Chodesh"** (the first of every lunar month) found in the book of Numbers.

Numbers 28:15 *"This is the **new moon burnt-offering**, for the year's **lunar months**. "And one kid of the goats for a sin-offering unto the LORD shall be offered,..........."*

26

There is a very peculiar Jewish Talmudic tradition about the purpose of the new **moon Sin offering.** For whom does this offering atone? The Jewish Talmud [Chulin 60b] explains that this is a *"Sin offering from God"*. The **Sin-offering** comes to atone for God, as it were, for making the moon smaller than the sun. According to the Jewish Midrash, the sun and the moon were initially created the same size. The moon complained to God, *"Is it possible for two kings to rule with one crown?"* and was punished by being reduced in size. For this reason, the Jewish people present a **Sin-offering** with the appearance of the new moon. Today, this ritual is merely celebrated as a festival moon dance. Although the history of this lunar ritual is not perfectly clear, the Israelites apparently adopted elements of marking time from both the ancient Canaanites and the Babylonians. Four months are known in the biblical text by older Canaanite names, while seven are mentioned in forms derived from Babylon. The actual lunar cycle is only about 29½ days, which resulted in a year of only 354½ days. Keeping the lunar calendar coordinated with the seasons of the year required adding a 13th month to the lunar calendar seven out of every nineteen years.

Numbers 26:6 *"It is a continual burnt offering, which was **ORDAINED** in **MOUNT SINAI** for **a sweet savor**, a sacrifice made by fire unto the LORD."*

According to the authors of Deuteronomy, Moses was never aware of the existence of Mount Sinai. In the Deuteronomy version **mount HOREB** was the chosen location for the covenant to be revealed. Such as: Deuteronomy 2:1&2, 4:10, 5:2, 9:8, 18:16 and 29:1.

Deuteronomy 9:8&9 ***"Also in Horeb...... When I was gone up into the mount to receive the tables of stone, even the tables of the covenant which the LORD made with you, then I abode in the mount forty days and forty nights ...."***

27

SIN THE MOON-GOD
OF MOUNT SINAI

SIN is most likely the name of the Babylonian moon god that has influenced terms we still read in the King James Bible such as:

1. Sinai - Sacred Mount consecrated and named after the moon-god **SIN** in Exodus 19:20. *"And the LORD came down upon mount Sinai, on top of the mount......"*

2. Sinate - an inhabitant of Sin.

3. The wilderness of Sin and the Desert of Sin - lying between Elim and Sinai - a wasteland, named after and consecrated to the Babylonian moon-god **Sin**. Exodus 16:1 and Numbers 33:11&12.

4. Sinitic Peninsula - the location where Manna and quails were sent to the Israelites in two different book versions of the Torah.

5. Sinim - susposed by some to be China, but more probably Phoenicia.

SIN the moon-god is one of the most worshipped gods of the Babylonian era. The land of Ur was consecrated to the moon-god SIN and this moon-god was primarily a Babylonian invention. It was Nebuchadnezzar who was a zealous worshiper of the moon-god SIN that conquered Jerusalem in 586 B.C. taking the Jewish survivors as his prisoners back to Babylon. This event is known as "the Babylonian captivity" or "Exile." I suspect the Torah was probably edited by Jewish and Babylonian Scribes be-

28

tween 620 B.C. to 457 B.C. While the book of Deuteronomy describes Mount Horeb as the only place where the LORD gives the law to Moses, the other Torah versions depict a nomadic tribe leaving an Egyptian culture of gods, to embrace a mountainous Sinaitic moon-god upon Mount Sinai, upon which a different sacred name was possibly adopted, before moving on to "the Promised land". This is evidenced by the traditional Jewish lunar ritual dates still practiced to this day. The Israelites had arrived in Canaan the promised land, where they lived for approximately two hundred years as a loose federation of tribes.

Historically Jesus endorsed the God on mount Horeb in Deuteronomy 6:4 referenced by Matthew 22:37-40.

There were at least two separate encounters with the LORD who demanded to be seen by Moses in Exodus 24:11 as opposed to Exodus 33:11, whom refused to be seen by anyone (including Moses) just nine verses later in Exodus 33:20.

Exodus 33:11 ***"And the LORD spake unto Moses face to face, as a man speaketh unto his friend."***

Exodus 33:20 ***"Thou canst not see my face: there shall no man see me, and live."***

Along with Jesus, Isaiah never endorsed the LORD that came down upon mount Sinai either, rather he was inspired to write these words against those that did worship the new moons of the LORD in Numbers 28:15.

Isaiah 1:13 &14 *"The **new moons** and sabbaths , it is iniquity......Your **new moons** and appointed feasts my soul hateth:....."*

THE HORNS OF THE ALTAR

The Brazen Altar of burnt offerings in Exodus 27 and the golden altar of incense in Exodus 30 both employed the use of horns and were both used on the Day of Atonement.

Exodus 27:2 *"And thou shalt make **THE HORNS** of it upon the four corners thereof: **HIS HORNS** shall be of the same: and thou shalt overlay it with brass."*

The Babylonian/Sumerian moon-Deity called Sin, for example, was depicted as a fierce bull with thick horns. The horns of the Jewish brazen altar possibly symbolized the moon-god they worshipped along with the sacrificed animal that best represented that moon-Deity. On the golden altar of incense (Exodus 30:10) the Jewish lunar ritual was acted out once a year by the Priest dipping his finger into the blood of the sacrificed bull or young calf and touching all the horns of the altar, thereby merging the atonement sin-offering along with the lunar Levitical moon-god. The Hebrew name for this lunar ritual is now known as **Yom Kippur (The Day of Atonement) observed on the 10th day of the 7th lunar month called Tishri which takes place in September-October.** Leviticus Chapter 16 deals with the ceremonies of this Annual Day of Atonement. Even the altar itself had blood atonements made for it.

Leviticus 16:18 *"**And he shall go out unto the altar that is before the LORD, and make an atonement for it**; and shall take the blood of the bullock, and the blood of the goat, and put it upon the horns of the altar round about."*

Leviticus 4:7 *"And the priest shall put [some] of the blood upon **THE HORNS OF THE ALTAR** of sweet incense before the LORD, which [is] in the tabernacle of the congregation; and shall pour all the blood of the bullock at the bottom of the altar of the burnt offering,.......*"

The size of the Brazen Altar, the use of the horns and the purification ritual are revealed in the following scriptures.

Exodus 27:1 & 2 *"And thou shalt make an altar of shit-him wood, five cubits long, and five cubits broad; the altar shall be foursquare: and the height thereof shall be three cubits. **And thou shalt make the horns of it upon the four corners thereof:** his horns shall be of the same: and thou shalt overlay it with brass."*

The horns were used as secure posts

Psalm 118:27 *"God is the LORD, which hath shewed us light: **BIND THE SACRIFICE WITH CORDS, even unto the horns of the altar.**"*

Blood sanctified and purified the altar

Leviticus 8:14 *"And he brought the bullock for the **sin offering**: and Aaron and his sons laid their hands upon the head of the bullock for the sin offering. 8:15 And he slew [it]; and Moses took the blood, and put [it] upon the **horns** of the altar round about with his finger**,** and **puri-***

31

fied the altar, and poured the blood at the bottom of the altar, and sanctified it, to make reconciliation upon it."

Blood placed upon the horns
Leviticus 9:8 *"Aaron therefore went unto the altar, and slew **the calf** of the **sin offering**, which was for himself. **9:9** And the sons of Aaron brought the blood unto him: and he dipped his finger in **the blood,** and put it upon **the horns of the altar,** and poured out the blood at the bottom of the altar:*

The Golden Altar of Incense

The altar of incense described in Exodus 30:1-10 had different dimensions compared to the Brazen alter of brass and was overlayed with gold including the horns.

Exodus 30:1 *"And thou shalt make an altar to burn incense upon: [of] shittim wood shalt thou make it."*

Exodus 30:2 *"A cubit [shall be] the length thereof, and a cubit the breadth thereof; foursquare shall it be: and two cubits [shall be] the height thereof: **the horns** thereof [shall be] of the same."*

Exodus 30:3 *"And thou shalt **overlay it with pure gold**, the top thereof, and the sides thereof round about, and **the horns** thereof; and thou shalt make unto it a crown of gold round about."*

Exodus 30:10 *"And **Aaron shall make an atonement upon the horns of it once in a year with the blood of the sin offering of atonements:** once in the year shall he make atonement upon it throughout your generations: it {is} most holy unto the LORD."*

Michelangelo's
THE HORNS OF MOSES

In 1513 Michelangelo carefully and purposefully carved two horns into the statue of Moses now located at the Church of S. Pietro in Vincola at Rome.

It is alleged by modern Christianity that Michelangelo mis-interpreted the original definition of the hebrew word **"qaran"** as 'shining horns' found in the Exodus 34:29&35 text, instead of interpretating the same translated version found in the King James Bible as *"the skin of Moses face shone."*

However, the King James Bible in Psalm 69:31 the word **"qaran"** is used to describe an Ox or **young bull with horns.**

Psalm 69:31 *" This also shall please the LORD better than an Ox or Bullock that hath* **horns (qaran)** *and hoofs."*

The Hebrew word **"qaran"** and its corresponding search number (7160) of the Strong's Hebrew dictionary has possibly dual meanings; however the primary definition of the word means: *A primitive root to shoot out horns; (figuratively, rays):-- have horns, shine.*

The Hebrew word **'qeren'** (7161) *derived from* **'qaran'** (7160); **a horn (as projecting)**; *by implication,* **a corner (of the Altar)**, *a ray (of light); (figuratively, power).*

From 347 A.D. to 420 A.D. Jerome, a Hebrew Scholar, Translator and Theologian of the Bible into Latin (known as the Vulgate Latin of the common people) is held responsible for translating Exodus 34:29, thus giving the revered Moses his horns. **Whether Jerome was mistaken, or courageously correct in his translation, can not be answered conclusively.** Given the uncertainties about the original text, and the possible modification caused by copyists and translators, Jerome saw the primary definition of the root Qaran in the Hiphil form meaning "horned," rather than the Qal form meaning rays of light. The meaning "horns" fits the context better. Later, the people were so afraid of the terrifying Sinaitic leader (Moses), in Exodus 34:30, that they would not go near him.

Possibly the Israelites could have been frightened by a radiant Moses. More likely though, they would have been afraid of a horned Moses, necessitating a mask, or veil.

The Hebrew **"masweh"** is no where else used in the Old Testament to cover the alarming disfigurement of Moses as employed in Exodus 34:30-35. More likely, Moses changed himself by utilizing this **"masweh"** (mask) and was not physically enlightened as Christians have been led to believe.

Keep in mind, this whole Exodus version was probably written by Babylonian Scribes from a different time era than the story refers to. These Scribes who enjoyed immense psychological influence over people by institutionalizing these blood-offering rituals, thereby portraying Moses and the LORD in their own image.

There is no mention of Moses face radiating or disfigured with horns from the first encounter with the LORD in Exodus 3. Neither is this unusual story mentioned in the Deuteronomy 10:1-5 version. In the New Testament the author of 2nd Cor 3:7 would lead the reader to believe Moses displayed a glorious shining face.

History records images of Moses displaying a horned hat and then horns: Aelfric 1025 AD, Moses with serpent 1225, Sluter 1404, Michaelangelo 1513, Freud 20th Century (Mellenkoff).

Artists have found ways to incorporate these horned symbols into their artwork down through the ages. One such example was "Pan" the Mythological Greek god called "The Horned God." In art, the horned God is depicted as half man and half animal "the Eternal Hunter," and Pan is the animal which is hunted. He is the beast who is sacrificed so that human life can live on.

So Jerome's interpretation of the Hebrew word

"Qaran" correctly fits the primary definition of the Hebrew word and his interpretation of the described text properly fits the described context of the story in Exodus 34. Therefore the Statue of Moses with horns upon his head, sculpted by Michelangelo in Vincola Rome, is probably a correct depiction based on the original written version of Exodus 34. Jerome has some worthy credentials as a Translator of the Hebrew scripture. Originally translating from the Greek Septuagint, he became dissatisfied with this second hand production. From 390-405 A.D. he gave all his attention to translating the Old Testament from the Hebrew which he had come to believe was the only inspired text. During this time and until his death in 420 A.D., he lived in Bethlehem. Biographers characterize him as a meticulous biblical Translator knowledgeable in both Greek and Hebrew. In Canonicity Controversies, Jerome championed the inspiration of only the Hebrew text.

Down through the centuries the blood-shed doctrine symbolized by the Horns of the Altar remains obscure, but the mythological male figure with horns upon the head has been portrayed in different time eras by different names and different faces such as: The Celtic God Cernunnos, Herne the Hunter, a spector of Britain, Janus the Roman god, Tammuz and Damuzi, the consorts of Ishtar and Ianna, Osiris, the Egyptian lord of the underworld, Dionysus, the Greek god, the green man, the lord of vegetation and the woodlands.

Whether or not Moses wore a mask with bull horns on his head or if his face shone is irrelevant. You can not cover past transgressions with the blood of animals or virgin born Saviours. This will only bring on more psychological condemnation on the human conscience. Deeply seated within this blood-covenant lunar ritual exists a never ending cycle of killing and guilt that is never satisfied.

LEVITICUS PARAPHRASED

The Holy Bible is proclaimed to be the infallible inspired word of God, yet over half the authors can not be identified. Now shielded behind the guise of infallibility, the killing of animals goes un-scrutinized within the Torah. In this demented lunar ritual, the Priests criminalizes the innocent animal to satisfy the psychological fears implanted by the Priests towards the nomadic tribe. Today no one wants to question this ritual for what it really is, because it would throw doubt upon the origins of all religions that embrace such related practices including the interpretational connection to the blood sacrifice of Jesus Christ. The following is a paraphrased example of the absurd logic written within the book of **LEVITICUS 5:7-10.**

Today I accidentally touched something that was 'ceremonially unclean,' but I didn't know it at the time. Fortunately one of the Aaronite Priests brought it to my attention, so now I find myself guilty of this offense. I don't have enough money to afford a lamb to be slaughtered for my trespass. However, I am told I can purchase two turtle doves for a shekel over at Aaron's wild bird Emporium. I am instructed that killing the two turtle doves will suffice for any atonements needed for this trespass. I can now take my two condemned doves to the Priest for slaughter. He wrings the head from the neck of one of the doves, but not severing it completely. He sprinkles the blood, and drains the rest. And then the priest burns the other turtle dove. Now I am forgiven.

 **THANK GOD**

Actual Leviticus 5:7-10

"And if he be not able to bring a lamb, then he shall bring for his trespass, which he hath committed, two turtle doves, or two young pigeons, unto the LORD; one for the sin offering, and the other for the burnt offering.

8 And he shall bring them unto the priest, who shall offer that which is for the sin offering first, and wring off his head from his neck, but shall not divide it asunder:

9 And he shall sprinkle of the blood of the sin offering upon the side of the altar; and the rest of the blood shall be wrung out the bottom of the altar: it is a sin offering.

10 And he shall offer the second for a burnt offering, according to the manner: and the priest shall make an atonement for him for the sin which he has sinned, and it shall be forgiven him."

By definition the word atonement means: *The act of atoning for sin or wrongdoing (**especially appeasing a DEITY**).*

In Exodus 30:15 we read another method this exodus tribe used to purge their conscience and atone for their souls as the author describes Moses receiving his instructions from the LORD.

Exodus 30:15 *"The rich shall not give more, and the poor shall not give less than half a shekel, when they give an offering unto the LORD, to make AN ATONEMENT for your **souls**."*

In the Book of Numbers 25:1-18 the author is describing a son of an Israelite Priest making AN ATONEMENT for the people of Israel by killing a fellow Israelite member for bringing home a condemned Moabite woman named Coz-bi in the sight of the congregation.

Numbers 25:11-13 *"Phin-e-has the son of El-e-a-zar the son of Aaron the priest and rose up and took a javelin in his hand and thrust both of them through, the man of Israel, and the woman through her belly. So the plague was stayed from the children of Israel. ...and made* **AN ATONEMENT** *for the children of Israel."*

In Numbers 31:50 we read the author describing Moses making **AN ATONEMENT** for the people after a battle using the spoils gathered from the people they had just murdered.

Numbers 31:50 *"We have therefore brought an oblation for the LORD, what every man hath gotten, of jewels of old, chains, and bracelets, rings, earrings, and tablets, to make* **AN ATONEMENT** *for our souls before the LORD."*

This was after they were instructed by the LORD to kill all the men, women and male babies from the Midianites who never even provoked this battle against them. The only charge against these Midianite people was that they worshipped a different god. This blood covenant on Mount Sinai began with shedding the innocent blood of animals as an atonement for their souls. Then it turned into giving the right amount of money unto the LORD for an atonement for their souls. Then the murder of an innocent fellow Israelite member as an atonement for their souls. Then it turned into an offering of jewels as an atonement for their souls.

A rational question needs to be addressed here. Why do animals and humans have to die every time someone else needs an atonement for their soul? As we break these actions down in numerical order we find the mindset of these unknown authors.

1. Slaughtering animals **atones** for peoples souls found in Exodus 29:36
2. Murdering a fellow Israelite **atones** for peoples souls found in Numbers 25:13
3. Slaughtering another tribe of people and offering the jewels they just stole off their dead bodies **atones** for peoples souls found in Numbers 31:50

It appears the atoning for souls is a never ending cycle of killing and death that is never quenched. A animal ritual that self perpetuates itself as no one questions this pathological disorder. Ultimately the way humans treat an animal is a precursor to the way he will treat his fellow man. The more we feel guilty of something the more we have to transfer that guilt onto something else by killing it to relieve our conscience. The power over other life is heady; and the desire to kill animals seems elemental to human beings. The thought is: " **I'll put my sin on that animal and kill the animal and my guilt is killed along with it. "I'm so guilty that I should be killed, so I'll kill that animal in my place."** For Christians, senselessly killing animals is no longer necessary. According to the New Testament authors and the Christian faith, Jesus is now the *human sacrifice* that satisfies or appeases the wrath of the LORD concerning their sin.

THE BLOOD ATONEMENT LAW OF LEVITICUS

LEVITICUS 17:11 *"FOR THE LIFE OF THE FLESH IS IN THE BLOOD: AND I HAVE GIVEN IT TO YOU UPON THE ALTAR TO MAKE AN ATONEMENT FOR YOUR SOULS: FOR IT IS THE BLOOD THAT MAKETH AN ATONEMENT FOR THE SOUL."*

Essentially it is upon this law the author of the book of Leviticus established the doctrine of killing to draw closer to their moon-god. Taking a closer look at this unusual killing practice as it is graphically described by the author in Leviticus 1:5-9.

Leviticus Chapter 1:5-9 - *The Priest's Barbeque.*

[5] "And he shall kill the bullock before the LORD: and the priests, Aaron's sons, shall bring the blood, and sprinkle the blood round about upon the altar that is by the door of the tabernacle of the congregation. [6] And he shall flay the burnt offering, and cut it into his pieces. [7] And the sons of Aaron the priest shall put fire upon the altar, and lay the wood in order upon the fire. [8] And the priests, Aaron's sons, shall lay the parts, the head, and the fat, in order upon the wood that is on the fire which is on the altar: [9] But his inwards and his legs shall he wash in water: and the priest shall burn all on the altar, to be a burnt sacrifice, an offering by fire, of a SWEET SAVOR unto the LORD."

Did an all-loving Creator dictate these words to Moses or were these words inspired by a band of hungry slobbering Priests with an appetite for a good barbeque?

Leviticus Chapter 7:34 - *The Priest feast*

"For the wave breast and the heave shoulder have I taken from the children of Israel from off the sacrifices of their peace offerings, and have given them to Aaron the priest and unto his sons by a statute for ever from among the children of Israel."

Did these words proceed out of the mouth of the living God, or were these words authored by a band of superstitious Priests satisfying their craving for meat under the guise of statutory law?

Analyzing this process again in Leviticus Chapter
1. The person making this offering unto the LORD must do it voluntarily.
2. The same person must perform or allow the killing of the animal himself under the instructions of the Levitical priests.
3. The priests wring off the head of the bird and wring out the blood round about the altar.
4. If this be an animal, the priests would cut it into pieces and burn it in the fire as a burnt offering atonement for the human. Then the priests would eat the remaining choice sections.

The author of Leviticus implies divine revelation given directly from the LORD on Mount Sinai. As it states in the very last verse in chapter 27:34. ***"These are the commandments, which the LORD commanded Moses for the children of Israel in Mount Sinai."*** This system of atonement has been adopted by the authors of the New Testament. However it has evolved, and has been adapted into what, according to the Catholic and Christian theologians, believe it to be. That Jesus Christ died as the final, whole sin sacrifice offering, unto the LORD to pay an atonement for all our sins, by perfectly fulfilling this lunar blood ritual found in Leviticus 17:11. To this day, Pastors and Priests have maintained the meaning of the altar at weddings and at the time they give their heart to Christ at the church altar by accepting the blood-offering sacrifice of Christ on the cross as their atonement. The thought is: to be washed in the precious blood of the Christ means to partake of this perfect sacrifice and thus take on, his righteousness and avert the wrath of **"The LORD" (the moon-god on mount Sinai).**

THE LAW OF THE LEVITICAL PRIESTS

Leviticus 3:17 *"It shall be a perpetual statute for your generations throughout all your dwellings, that ye eat neither fat nor blood."*

The authors initiating this blood offering cult never intended for the blood offering ritual to cover all transgressions for the soul. The ritual served to empower the Priests, using the Moon as a front to prohibit the consumption of fat and blood as practiced by the blood drinking vampire cults. The list below describes some of the transgressions not atoned for by this blood-offering ritual.

1. **Breaking the Sabbath. - Lev 23:30&31**
2. **Homosexuality. - Lev 18:22**
3. **Bestiality. - Lev 18:23**
4. **Sacrificing children to Molech. - Lev 20:2**
5. **Turning to spirits and Wizards. - Lev 20:6**
6. **Cursing one's Father or Mother. - Lev - 20:9**
7. **Adultery. - Lev 20:10**
8. **Taking a wife and her daughter. - Lev 20:14**
9. **Murder. - Lev 24:21**

How could Christ be the final blood-shed sacrifice for mankind as purported by Christians, when initially this Levitical blood-offering ritual never covered the above transgressions as defined by the Levitical authors? The New Testament Christian theology does not fit the original intent of the Levitical law they still purport to connect it to.

It was upon this blood offering law, written within the Leviticus that Judaism, Catholicism, Christianity and even Islam share a similar heritage towards atonement.

However, Christianity has taken this blood offering

law in a direction the Old Testament Hebrew scriptures never intended. The notion of an innocent, divine being, sacrificing himself as a blood offering to save others from their sins, is purely a Christian concept that is simply not supported in the original Old Testament Hebrew scriptures. Listed below are a few scriptures used to misdirect Christians back under the levitical law with a twist towards a human Saviour blood offering.

Matthew 26:28 *"For this is my blood of the new testament, which is shed for many for the remission of sins."*

Romans 5:9 *"Much more then, being now justified by his blood, we shall be saved from wrath through him."*

Revelation 12:11 *"And they overcame him by the Blood of the Lamb...."*

1 John 2:2 *"And he is the PROPITIATION for our sins: and not for ours only, but also for the sins of the world."*

1 John 1:7 *"But if we walk in the light, as he is in the light, we have fellowship one with another, and the blood of Jesus Christ his Son cleanseth us from all sin."*

1 Peter 1:18,19 *"For as much as ye know that ye were not redeemed with corruptible things, as silver and gold, from your vain conversation received by tradition from your fathers; but with the precious blood of Christ, as of a lamb without blemish and without spot."*

Hebrews 9:13-14 *"For if the blood of bulls and of goats, and the ashes of a heifer sprinkling the unclean, sanctifieth to the purifying of the flesh: How much more shall the blood of Christ, who through the eternal spirit offered himself without spot to God, purge your conscience from dead works to serve the living God."*

44

THE EGYPTIAN
 # CULTURE

In Egyptian culture, trying to understand the ever changing names of Egyptian gods, as they related to their Egyptians inventors, can be very taxing. The Egyptian names: Re, Ra, Osiris, Amun, Amen, Shu, Isis, Horus, Geb, Nut, Atum, Nu, Nephthys, Set, Aten and Serapis are just a few. The creator of all things was either Re, Amun, Aten, Ptah, or Khnum, depending on which version of the myth was currently in use. The heavens were represented by Horus, Bat and Hathor. Osiris was the earth god as was Ptah. Re, the sun god, took on many forms and transcended most of the Egyptian borders that contained the other gods. The moon-god was Thoth and Khonsu, and there was another controversial moon-god of Egypt that was called by the name of **"Yah"**- known as the Egyptian moon-god.

The name **"Jah"** used only once in the King James Version (found in Psalm 68:4) and is allegedly a transliteration of the word **"Yah"** or **"Yahweh"** which is merely a guess name on the pronunciation of the tetragrammaton. The pronunciation of the letter J is not used in the Hebrew language, therefore the letter Y is correctly used. The Canaanites of Ugarit worshiped the moon-god **"Yarih"** which is cognate to the Hebrew word **"Yareah"** which both means the moon. The word **"Yareah"** already incorporates the meaning of the moon into this Hebrew entity named **"Jah"** and the name "Jah" is still found in the last three letters of the phrase **Hallelu-jah**. Christians are taught this means **"Praise ye Yahweh,"** however, when analyzing the original definition of the Hebrew word **"Halal"** used in the phrase **Hallelu-jah** under Strong's Hebrew Dictionary #1984 the word actually means:

THE HOLY VIRUS

"SHINE ON YAH"

Halal: *A primitive root:* **to be clear** *(orig. or sound, but usually color);* **To Shine** *hence* **to make a show,** *to boast;and thus* **to be (clamorously) foolish**; *to rave,* **glory, give (light), rage,** *praise,* **shine.**

Strongs dictionary renders the word **"moon"** in Genesis 37:9 from the hebrew as **"Yareach #3394"**, showing a notable attempt to change the lettering of a word for the purpose of misleading examiners from seeing a connection between "Yareah" - the pale moon and "Yahweh" the guessed pronunciation for the TETRAGRAMMATON.

Psalm 68:4 is most likely describing the moon-god rotating around the earth while reflecting the suns rays back towards the earth, giving the moon a shiny illuminating appearance. Moon worship was attributed to the Egyptian moon-god **"Yah"**, the Canaanite moon-god **"Yarih"** and the Babylonian moon-god **"Sin", whose name most likely influenced the name of mount Sin**ai. Several professors of archeology claim that many stories in the Old Testament, including popular stories about Abraham, Moses, Samson etc, were actually made up for the first time by Scribes hired by King Josiah 7th century B.C. in order to rationalize a monotheistic belief in "Yahweh". Josiah was the King of Judah from (639-608) B.C. and as far as archeologists can tell, neighboring countries that kept many written records, such as Egypt and Assyria, have no writings about these stories of the Bible or its main characters before 650 B.C.

46

THE ALLEGED NAME OF THE LORD

The Tetragrammaton consists of four letters, i.e., **"Yud Kay Vav Kay"**. The Tetragrammaton as found in the Phoenician script and modern Hebrew " ⲊⲦⲎⲀ " " יהוה ".

When presented in the english alphabet the Tetragrammaton is spelled like this: **"YHVH"**.

According to Jewish rabbinic tradition, upon entering the Temple the name was pronounced by the high priest on Yom Kippur, the day of atonement. There is a Jewish tradition that the actual name of God, only known by the high priest, was actually 72 letters long.

Judaism - "*Hashem* or Ha-Shem" which means in Hebrew "*The name*" found in Devarim 16:16, Shemos 23:17 and Shemos 34:23. The pronunciation of the "*Hashem*" with the expression of Master represents the attribute of Divine Mercy. However, Judaism pronounces the Tetragrammaton as "*Adonai*" in substitution of "*Hashem* or Ha-Shem".

Christianity - "*Yahweh*" is believed to be the Tetragrammaton. The Tetragrammaton is replaced by "***The LORD***" with all capitals letters within the Old Testament King James Bible (except for "*Jehovah*" in Isaiah12:2 & Psalm 83:18).

Catholism - exclusively use "*Jahveh or Yahweh* "

Jehovah Witnesses - exclusively use "*Jehovah* "

Islam - exclusively use "*Allah* "

There is no evidence in scripture, in which Jesus ever uses the term "*Yahweh*" to refer to his Father the Creator. Christianity believes John 8:58 establishes that Jesus used "*Yahweh*" in scripture but, the original Greek word used in the book of John for "*I am*" is "ego-eimi" which simply means "designating oneself" and not as the Hebrew word **"Yud Kay Vav Kay"** which means "*The living, Self subsisting*".

John 8:58 "*verily, verily, I say unto you, before Abraham was, I am* ".

People today that follow sacred names always recite Acts 4:12 as their Biblical scripture to condemn anyone that doesn't pronounce the name of their LORD YAHSHUA or YAHWEH perfectly.

Acts 4:12 ***"Neither is there salvation in any other: for there is none other name under heaven given among men, whereby we must be saved."***

What these people leave out, is that this statement is merely a paraphrased decree made by an unknown author of the book of Acts describing Peter addressing the High Priests and Elders in Jerusalem over the healing of a lame man. Here, instead, are a few direct statements attributed to Jesus in the King James New Testament.

1. John 10:27 ***"My sheep hear my voice, and I know them, and they follow me."***

2. Matthew 7:21-23 *"Many will say to me in that day, Lord, Lord, have we not prophesied **in thy name?** and **in thy name** cast out devils? and **in thy name** done many wonderful works?* [23] **And then will I profess unto them, I never knew you: depart from me, ye that work iniquity***."*

3. John 8:19 ***"Ye neither know me, nor my Father: if ye had known me, ye should have known my Father also."***

1. According to Jesus in John 10:27, knowing the voice of God is more important than knowing the correct pronunciation of his name.

2. According to Jesus in Matthew 7:21-23, using names (like an encantation) is considered an act of iniquity.

3. According to Jesus in John 8:19, knowing the Father is far more important than knowing any pronunciation of his name. For example; the Pharisees knew the pronunciation, but they obviously didn't know the Father or Jesus.

In the Strong's Lexicon the hebrew word for **"name"** is "Shem" which means: *"as a mark or memorial of individuality."* So when one takes on a name, one essentially takes on **"the doctrine"** from which that name represents. **"YHVH"** = is allegedly translated as "**LORD**" in the King James Bibles today. The name **"EH-YEH ASHER EH-YEH"** in Exodus 3:14 (**EHYEH**) using the Paleo-Hebrew letters HYH was used at the burning bush and can not be connected to the tetragrammaton **"YHVH"**. **"YAHWEH"**is only a guess toward the pronounciation of YHVH.

"This hypothesis is not intrinsically improbable--and **in Aramaic**, *a language closely related to Hebrew, "to be" actually is* **Hawa**-- *but it should be noted that in adopting it we admit that, using the name in the historical sense,* **YAHWEH is not a Hebrew name.**" (Ency. Brit. 1958 Ed. Vol 12. page 996).

Aramaic is a language originating from Babylon and it was adopted by the Jews after they had been taken into captivity by Nebuchadnezzar in 586 B.C. Nearly all the existing manuscripts, including the Masoretic text and the Dead Sea scrolls, were all in the Babylonian/Aramaic alphabet. There is no evidence that Aramaic is pronounced like the ancient Paleo-Hebrew, and to take the Babylonian/Aramaic "**Hawa**" meaning "to be" and superimpose this upon HYH (Ehyeh) as the bases to invent **"YHVH"** and then finally the guessed name **"YAHWEH"** is playing linguistic games. The idea that the name of God must be spoken in Paleo-Hebrew or in Babylonian Aramaic is absurd. The word "JAH" found only once in the Bible is hardly enough evidence to even link this name to **"YAHWEH"**, rather it is by the doctrine or conduct of sacrificing animals on altars on lunar moon dates, that supports my theory this was a moon cult. Those that believe King David used this name in Psalm 68:4 are assuming King David was alive at the time Psalm 68:4 was written. Psalm 68:29 refers to a time the Temple had already been built, an event that did not exist during King David's time. Therefore, the author of Psalm 68:4 is not King David, rather instead the author came well after King David and is unknown.

Psalm 68:29 **"Because of thy Temple in Jerusalem shall kings bring presents unto thee."**

Psalm 68:4 *"Sing unto God, sing praises to his name: extol him that rideth upon the heavens by his name JAH......................"*

Jesus probably associated himself with the God of Deuteronomy 6:5 named **"EH-YEH"**on Mount Horeb and stated that he came in his Father's name. For example

John 5:43 *"I come in my Father's name ....,"* Jesus, is merely announcing by whose authority and Kingdom he speaks from and not from the point of a particular pronunciation. Neither John the Baptist nor Jesus ever used the term Yahweh, Jehovah or Ehyeh in the King James Bible. In every instance in the New Testament Jesus refers to God in the Aramaic language as *"Abba"* which means **father** for example:

Mark 14:36 *"Abba father, all things are possible unto thee........,"*.

Jesus also taught the Apostles the proper way to pray using only *"Abba"* as the example found in Matthew 6:9. *"Our father who art in heaven, Hallowed be thy name............"*

If Jesus wanted his Apostles to use a particular hallowed pronunciation other than the word *"Abba"*, certainly he would have included this within the model prayer he taught. According to Jesus, the hallowed name of the father is already incorporated within the remaining verses of the model prayer as a doctrine of conduct. The pronunciation of certain sacred letters was never taught by Jesus, but rather teaching others to apply the knowledge of the father was the key to keeping oneself and others **as one** in the name of the **"Holy Father"**.

John 17:11&12 **"Holy Father, keep through thine own name** *those thou hast given me,that they may be one, as we are one. While I was with them in the world,* **I kept them in thy name..."**

Conclusion: The name of God is rather a conduct of knowledge, rather than a linguistic pronunciation of letters. Jesus never worshiped Yahweh, by observing the sabbath new moons or by sacrificing animals on altars based on lunar moon dates, but rather Jesus defined the name of the father as living a conduct of Mercy and preserving other life. The idea of knowing God simply by the pronunciation of certain letters is absurd, but knowing God by practicing his commandments was key to showing knowledge in him. For example, according to Jesus: Mark 2:27 **"The sabbath was made for man, and not man for the sabbath"**. According to Jesus the sabbath was a commandment from God and certainly a day to violate the law if the situation required saving or feeding a starving lost animal or saving another man's life in jeopardy when the occasion arises. The point here is that the name of God is an applied conduct attributed to one of God's commandments. To use another example, a mute person would never be able to pronounce the names Yahweh, Jehovah, Ehyeh, Jesus, Yahshua etc, but they could still perform actions of mercy and compassion toward others, therefore through his conduct he fulfills the requirement Jesus sets out, while the Yahwist would condemn our poor unfortunate mute from ever entering into the congregation of the LORD according to the LORD in Deuteronomy 23:1.

"He that is wounded in the stones, or hath his privy member cut off, shall not enter into the congregation of the LORD ".

51

THE ABRAHAM AND ISAAC STORY

Reading the King James Bible, I have observed that it leaves a trail of two separate "psychological profiles" - one set of merciful personality traits best defined by the life of Jesus and John the Baptist, the other profile of inhumane personality traits defining **"YAHWEH The LORD created by the Priests."** For example: one personality trait identifying the LORD is best defined by his lust for burnt animal flesh (as the aroma sends a sweet savor of death from the brazen and golden altars) found in Leviticus 1:9,13,17; 2:2, 9; 3:5 and Numbers 29:36.

Numbers 29:36 *"But ye shall offer a burnt offering,* ***a sacrifice made by fire, of a sweet savor unto the LORD****: one bullock, one ram, seven lambs of the first year without blemish."*

Depending on which religion people adhere to, the ethical implications of the story of Abraham and Isaac, in the Bible and the Koran, clearly states that the LORD tempted Abraham to sacrifice one of his sons.

King James Bible Genesis 22:1&2 *"And it came to pass after these things, that God did* **tempt Abraham,** *and he said, Behold, here I am. 2 And he said, Take now thy son, thine only son Isaac, whom thou lovest, and thee into the land of Moriah; and offer him there for a burnt offering upon one of the mountains which I will tell thee of."*
Book of the Qu'ran 37:100-102 *"O my LORD! grant me a righteous (son)' So We gave him the good news of a boy ready to suffer and forbear. Then when (the son) reached (the age of) (serious) work with him, He said 'O my*

52

son! ***I SEE IN VISION** that I offer thee in sacrifice:* Do *as thou art commanded: Thou wilt find me if Allah so wills one practising patience and constancy."*

The Quran teaches that Abraham is the first Islamic prophet and the first Muslim. **"The Dome of the Rock"** near Jerusalem is considered the place where Muslims believe Abraham offered up Ishmael as a sacrifice unto his LORD (Allah). Muslims believe that Ishmael was the first son of Abraham with Isaac later born 13 years after Ishmael. However the Quran's version describes this event as a vision being communicated between Abraham, and a unnamed son, rather than an actual event taken place as described in the King James biblical version. Christians are taught in the King James Bible that Isaac was the son being sacrificed, while Muslims are taught Ishmael or Ismail was the son being sacrificed. In the King James Bible version, Isaac was not aware that it was he to be sacrificed until he was up on the mount, whereas in the Quran version the son was aware of this event through a vision communicated to him by Abraham his father.

Through archeological findings the evidence of King David is practically non-existent, and for Abraham, the Bible appears to be the only source of record. The conclusion is somewhat startling to Bible readers. There is no mention of Abraham, Isaac and Jacob in any of King David's psalms, and the Canaanites are portrayed in the Bible as immoral idolaters; most of the Israelites were in fact formerly Canaanites. Some of the stories such as Abraham's journey from Ur of the Chaldeans, the Patriarchs, the Exodus, Sinai and the conquest of Canaan, were apparently based on stories grafted into jewish history sometime after 640 B.C. The consolidation of the Israelites into a nation was not the result of wanderings in the desert and divine revelation, but came from the need to defend themselves against the Philistines who settled in the Canaanite coastal plain (more or less) at the same time the Israelites were establishing themselves in the hills. Thus the languages of the Philistines and the Israelis must have been very similar, because they conversed with one another on the battle field without any mention of interpretors. Thus the founders of Israel were Saul and David and not so much Abraham and Moses. It was apparently Saul who consolidated the hill farmers under his rule and created fighting units capable of confronting the Philistines. It was David who defeated the Philistines and united the hill farmers with the people of the Canaanite plains, thus establishing the Kingdom of Israel and its capital city. The story of Abraham and Isaac in the Bible was not a story about an atonement for sins, as it was a story about the LORD tempting Abraham to perform an act of murder. Allegedly the LORD intervened to keep Abraham from doing what allegedly the LORD commanded Abraham to do in the first place. The author of this Abraham and Isaac story in Genesis 22 has Abraham inaugurating the animal sacrifice ritual at the end, by sacrificing the ram allegedly provided by the LORD.

Comparing the differences between the Islamic Quran version and the Christian Biblical version explains why several professors of archeology claim some stories in the Old Testament (about Abraham, Samson and others) were made up by Scribes according to the religions they belonged to. I suspect that some portions of these books, that make up the Torah, were revised by Babylonian Scribes sometime after the exile of Israel in 586 B.C. This would have been the opportune time in which the true history of Israel could have been edited or changed, thereby giving Jews and Christians a distorted version of Jewish history within their Bibles. The King James Bible only records one book, or one historical version of the law, that was placed along side the ark of the covenant by Moses (recorded by the author of Deuteronomy 31:26 allegedly believed by mainline religions around 1400-1200 B.C).

Deuteronomy 31:26 *"**Take this book of the law**, and put it in the side of the ark of the covenant of the LORD your God......."*

Allegedly, 900 years later, the same alleged book of the law was discovered by Hilkiah the High Priest during King Josiah in 639-608 B.C. King Josiah's reaction in 2nd Kings 22:11 indicates that the rest of the books of the Torah were not yet written during his reign. The written contents of burning incense, and worshipping of other gods was the first time this King had ever heard of these laws. The King acted as if he had never heard of such laws before.

2nd Kings 22:8 *"...**I have found the book of the law** in the house of the LORD......."* **around 561 B.C.**

2nd Kings 22:11 *"**And it came to pass, when the king heard the words of the book of the law, that he rent his clothes.**"*

If the other books and traditions of the Torah had existed, then how could the Levitical Priests, whose main function was to impart the knowledge of the law, lose these alleged law books for so many years, especially when the version of the law was allegedly laid along side their own ark of the covenant? This leaves the location of the rest of the books **(Genesis, Exodus, Leviticus and Numbers)** - unaccounted for during the time of King Josiah. In light of this evidence I believe these other books of the Torah were mostly the edited works of authors soon after or sometime after King Josiah's era. It bears repeating again that in the early works of Samuel, we are told that "David's sons were ruling priests." *(2 Samuel Chapter 8 verse 18)*. This is one of many indications that the authors of the Samuel knew nothing of the book of Leviticus. It was a law, formulated later by the self interest of revisionist Priests, that only Levites (from the tribe of Levi) were allowed to be priests. There is an even narrower interpretation in the book of Numbers, formulated by one small faction of Levites, that stated that only Levites, who were linear descendants of Aaron, were allowed to be priests. The author of Samuel knew nothing of such matters, and allowed David's sons, from the tribe of Judah and also of 'mixed origins' (Moabite-Israelite) to serve as priests.

The Babylonian Kingdom goes back as far as 1792-1750 B.C. during which time King Hammurabi ruled the first dynasty. The Babylonians were nortorious Sun and Moon-god worshippers. It is recorded that Abraham came from the land of Ur which makes Abraham a Babylonian by origin. It makes sense the Babylonian revisionists would insert one of their own patriarchal figures (such as Abraham) and build a lesser main-line religion (Judaism) around one of their own Babylonian gods. By controlling the history of Israel, Babylon could then control their future worshipping practices. By the time John the Baptist and Jesus came on the world stage, both had to face this impossible task of calling people out of a Babylonian inspired culture under Roman occupation. Babylon had centers of worship at Eridu, Nippur, Erech, Ur and other places that can be dated from the 4th and 3rd millenniums B.C. Babylon records give evidence of an elaborate worship system of animal sacrifices at these temples similar to that written within the book of Leviticus. One document records the same exact animals being offered in sacrifice by the Babylonian King Gudea as described in the book of Leviticus. Whenever a nation was taken over by Babylon or especially the Persians, such as in the case of Israel in 586 B.C. and 539 B.C.- history was often destroyed or revised by the Babylonian/Persian revisionists. This leads me to believe many sections within the Torah were never written by Moses in 1500 to 1270 B.C., nor were they written in 1,000 B.C. (during the time of King David). Nor was the Torah written prior to 650 B.C. before the time of King Josiah.

CONCLUSION: The story of Abraham in the King James Bible comes to us (most likely) from the Babylonian Scribes, just as the story of Moses receiving the law of burnt offerings and sacrifices on Mount Sinai did. Even though Moses may have initiated some kind of sacrifice system to satisfy the manipulating carnal desires of his fellow priests, Moses certainly did not receive such laws from God. Penned by the Babylonian revisionists, the myth makers inserted an iron clad patriarchal figure (Abraham), inaugurating animal sacrifice rituals well after Abraham's time. If the Creator of Heaven and Earth denied ever ordering Moses to perform burnt offerings and sacrifices upon Mount Sinai (as recorded by Jeremiah in 7:22-23), why then, would the same Creator order any child sacrifice on Mount Moriah? The same logic can be applied to the story of Noah who built an altar and sacrificed one of every clean beast and one of every fowl to the LORD as a sweet smelling savor upon leaving the ark in Genesis 8:20 & 21. This story depicts the same altar smelling LORD found in the book of Leviticus and causes me to ask questions.

1. How could these animals possibly multiply on the face of the earth, if one of every kind was immediately sacrificed on the altar by Noah upon walking off the ark?

2. Why would the LORD go to all the trouble to deliver these animals from a horrible flood, just to smell the burnt carcasses on the altar upon touching dry ground?

3. Why does the LORD always enjoy the sweet aroma of animals being burnt to death? Does a loving merciful God create life, for the purpose of stabbing it to death, so as to smell a sweet aroma from its dead carcass?

Genesis 8:20&21 *"**And Noah builded an altar unto the LORD; and took of every clean beast, and of every clean fowl, and offered burnt offerings on the altar.** And the LORD smelled a sweet savor;.............."*

CHAPTER 2

THE RACIST LAWS
OF THE LORD

Chronologically, The book of Ruth stands as the era dividing point between the priests (whom edited the Torah) and the different authors of the Davidic dynasty written within the 1st and 2nd books of Samuel. Ruth was the grandmother of King David and the life of Ruth consisted of violating the laws of the LORD in Deuteronomy. The Moabite people were barred, according to the word of the LORD, from ever entering into the congregation, as stated by the occult author in Deuteronomy 23:3. We have read what happens when one brings home a Moabite woman to meet the folks. In Numbers 25:8, one is suddenly met with a javelin in the stomach. In Deuteronomy 23:1-3 we read the hate that exists in their LORD which decides who is allowed within the LORD's congregation and who is condemned. These laws also condemned the handicapped as well. Deuteronomy 23:1-3 ***"HE THAT IS WOUNDED IN THE STONES OR HATH HIS PRIVY MEMBER CUT OFF, SHALL NOT ENTER THE CONGREGATION OF THE LORD.*** *A BASTARD SHALL NOT ENTER THE CONGREGATION OF THE LORD, EVEN TO THE TENTH GENERATION. AN AMMONITE OR* **MOABITE SHALL NOT ENTER INTO THE CONGREGATION OF THE LORD**; *EVEN TO THE TENTH GENERATION SHALL THEY NOT ENTER INTO THE CONGREGATION OF THE LORD* **FOREVER.**"

King David's Father (Jesse) was half Israelite and half Moabite (Gentile) and the **Moabites** and the handicapped were hated more than any other people mentioned by this Exodus cult. This type of merciless personality trait reveals a distinct psychological profile that exists only in the LORD found in Deuteronomy 23:1-3 but does not exist in the New Testament profile of Jesus, who himself was partly a Moabite descendant and who healed the handicapped with compassion.

In Deuteronomy 7:2 the author depicts the rage of the LORD with uncontrollable hatred:

Deuteronomy 7:2 *"Thou shalt smite them, and utterly destroy them; thou shalt make no covenant with them, nor show mercy unto them: Neither shalt thou make marriages with them; thy daughter thou shalt not give unto his son, nor his daughter shalt thou take unto thy son."*

We also read the hate for any foreign babies as the author reveals his own personality traits within the Psalms.

Psalm137:9 *"Happy shall he be, that taketh and dasheth thy little ones against the stones."*

In the book of Ruth, beginning in the fourth Chapter verse 10 through 22. Boaz an Israelite, and the Grandfather of King David and according to the book of Ruth, Boaz purchased *(Ruth a Moabite 4:10)*. They had a son by the name of O-bed. O-bed begat Jesse and Jesse begat David who later goes on to become the King Of Israel. This made King David a mixed breed condemned Moabite, according to the authors of Deuteronomy.

When one considers the racist law in Deuteronomy to its ultimate conclusion, any descendent of King David would have been condemned, including the future King "Jesus the son of David". The only reason King David wasn't stoned by the congregation, concerning his moabite status, might be because this law or section of the book of Deuteronomy 23:1-3 was edited in much later than King David's era. There is no evidence that this part of the book of the law ever existed during the time of King David. Neither did Chapter 17:14-20, because this section commands the Israelites not to put any foreign king over themselves that has multiplied horses, wives, gold and silver etc. Deuteronomy 17:18 states emphatically that the King was suppose to keep an exact copy of the book of the law of Moses in his hand at all times.

Deuteronomy 17:18 *"And it shall be, when he sitteth upon the throne of his kingdom, that he shall write him a copy of this law in a book out of that which is before the priests the Levites."*

Obviously these requirements were edited in well after King David's time, because King David nor King Solomon never knew of such laws. Supposably the book of the law laid dormant along side the ark of the covenant which was in the possession of the Levite Priests according to the order of Moses in Deuteronomy 31:25&26 around 1450 B.C.

Deuteronomy 31:25&26 *That **Moses commanded the Levites, which bare the ark of the covenant of the LORD** saying, "Take this book of the law, and put it in the side of the ark of the covenant of the LORD your God, that it may be there for a witness against thee."*

Four hundred years later after King David, out of no where, as if by magic, the alleged book of Moses appears out of the house of the LORD and is read to Josiah the 16th King of Judah.

2nd Kings 22:8 & Chronicles 34:14 *"And Hilkiah the high priest said unto Shaphan the scribe, **I have found the book of the law** in the house of the LORD......."*

The unknown authors of the book of Kings and the book of Chronicles most likely back dated this finding of the book of the law to the time of Josiah's reigned in (639-608 B.C.). The authors wrote about this event well after the time the Israelites were captured and exiled to Babylon. Therefore some of these writings were subject to Babylonian editors under the Persian Kings. The last story in the book of Kings extends to the release of Jehoiachin from Babylonian imprisonment in 561 B.C. and the last story in the book of Chronicles extends to the time King Cyrus declares the restoration of the second Temple of Israel in Jerusalem in 537 B.C. - making the book of Kings and Chronicles most likely written between 537 B.C. to 440 B.C. Jeremiah's activities were well over by 586 B.C. where he migrated to Egypt according to the King James Bible. So Jeremiah was not the author of these books, nor did he prophesy anything within these books as alleged by the author of 2nd Chronicles 36:22. Jeremiah was most likely dead before 561 B.C. Later on, the book of Jeremiah is taken over by another author subject to the Babylonian King. **Some of these stories in the book of Kings and Chronicles where the book of the law magically appears, were revised and edited by Babylonian revisionists under the successive Persian Kings.** For example the name of the king of Judah in 1st Kings 15:1 is Abijam, but in 2nd Chronicles 13:1 the name of the same king magically adds "**Jah**" at the end of his name to become Abi**jah**. In 1st Kings 15:25,16:14, 16:20, 16:27 the names Nadab, Elah, Omni, and Zimri were edited out of the book of Chronicles, yet the book of Kings specifically states their acts are re-corded there. In most cases during the postexilic times, *the Book of Moses* is changed to *"the book of the LORD"* found in Nehemiah 8:8, 8:18 and 9:3 - and with a little Babylonian imagination, mount Horeb is transformed into Mount Sinai. Leaving the book of Deuteronomy as the only book that mentions mount Horeb throughout. Coin-cidentally, mount Sinai was the place where **SIN** (the Babylonian Moon-god) was worshipped by Nebuchadnezzar, the same Babylonian king who initially conquered and ex-iled the Israelites from Judah to Babylon in 586 B.C.

Nehemiah 9:13 *"**Thou camest down also upon mount SINAI, and spakest with them from heaven......**"*

The edited versions of the Torah are introduced to the Jewish exiles by two Babylonian leaders named Ezra and Nehemiah around 440 B.C. Nehemiah worked inside the court of the Persian King Artaxerxes and he was also directly involved with the restoration of the city in Jerusa-lem. Ezra was vitally interested in the rebuilding of the 2nd Temple and he served as the leading priest and main oracle for the book of the law of the LORD. This event of reading the book of the law of the LORD took place just a couple days before Yom Kippur (the Levitical day of Atonement). This outdoor spectacle took place in Jerusalem after Judah/Israel had been exiled and indoctrinated into the Babylonian culture for approximately 150 years. In Nehemiah 9:36&37 Ezra tries to convince the returning Israelites that their LORD subdued them with Babylonian and Persian kings because of their sins.

Nehemiah 9:37"*.....the kings whom thou hast set over us because of our sins: also they have dominion over our bodies, and over our cattle, at their pleasure, and we are in great distress.*"

Nehemiah 9:3 "*And they stood up in their place, and read in THE BOOK OF THE LAW OF THE LORD their God one fourth part of the day; and another fourth part they confessed, and worshiped the LORD their God.*"

In 1000 B.C. the Priests of King David, many of whom were moabite sons were not aware of the law in Deuteronomy 23:1-3, as they filled these same offices. One must wonder who, or what doctrine enlightened Boaz, (David's grandfather) concerning his unconditional love for Ruth by marrying a condemned Moabite woman given these racist regulations. One must wonder also just what a Moabite half-breed was doing sitting on the throne establishing a dynasty in Judah. There is no record within the Bible that indicates that King David was aware of the condemning laws of the LORD within the Book of Deuteronomy nor was he aware of the exclusive animal sacrificing laws written within the book of Leviticus and the book of Numbers.

King David instead wrote Psalms that condemned such primitive mindless practices.

Psalm 50:16&17 "*For thou desirest not sacrifice;*

64

else would I give it: thou delightest not in burnt offering. The sacrifices of God are a broken spirit: a broken and contrite heart, O God thou wilt not despise."

Psalm 116:17 *"I will offer to thee the sacrifice of Thanksgiving."*

Psalm 34:18 *"The Lord is nigh unto them that are of a broken heart; and saveth such as be of a contrite spirit."*

Around 940 B.C. Solomon was alleged to have sacrificed 22,000 oxen and 120,000 sheep on completion of the 1st Temple when dedicating the House of the LORD as recorded by our unknown Babylonian author in 1st Kings 8:63. Solomon had no knowledge of the law that condemned him in Deuteronomy, yet we are told he practiced the sacrifices that were reserved only for the Levitical Aaronite tribe. Mathematically, if one were to sacrifice 142,000 oxen and sheep as recorded by our Babylonian scribe in 1st Kings, they would have found this feat impossible on one brazen altar. The Brazen altar would have to be used approximately 387 times a day for a whole year to reach this number of 142,000. Even if Solomon used the inner court for additional sacrifices, the author is not considering the enormous clean up problems one encounters in sacrificing 142,000 large animals on an altar in a few short days. Therefore this story of Solomon sacrificing 142,000 oxen and sheep upon completion of the first Temple is highly suspect. Even Solomon recognized how evil it was to sacrifice animals on altars in his statement.

Ecclesiastes 5:1 *"Keep thy foot when thou goest to the house of God, and be more ready to hear, than to give* **THE SACRIFICE OF FOOLS***: for they consider not that they do evil."*

Soon after Solomon's time era, Hosea wrote these inspired words: Hosea 6:6 *"**FOR I DESIRED MERCY AND NOT SACRIFICE***; ...."*

THE HISTORICAL PROCLAMATION OF KING CYRUS

The author of Ezra 1:1&2 and 2nd Chronicles 36:22&23 records King Cyrus of Persia proclaiming the LORD GOD of heaven gave him the kingdoms of the earth and charged him to rebuild the 2nd Temple of Israel in Jerusalem.

Ezra 1:2 *"Thus saith Cyrus king of Persia,* **the LORD GOD of heaven hath given me the kingdoms of the earth; and he hath charged me to build him a house at Jerusalem, which is in Judah.***"*

In 1879 a Persian clay cylinder was unearthed at the excavation site of Babylon (Nineveh, Iraq.) This persian clay cylinder is now located in the British Museum, in London. The artifact records the Persian King Cyrus proclaiming all foreign inhabitants who were previously deported to Babylon to return back to their former habitations, carrying with them the images of their gods. At this time King Cyrus allowed 42,300 Jews to leave Babylon and return back to Jerusalem, found in the book of Nehemiah Chapter 7. The actual written artifact records the decree of King Cyrus assuming the title of **" King of Babylon "** and paying homage at the Temple of the Babylonian god Marduk in this proclamation. The following quotes are the translated excerpts from this historical proclamation contained on the Persian clay cylinder found in Iraq. A replica of this proclamation is also found in the United Nations building in New York.

*" I am Kurash {**"Cyrus"**} **King of the world , King of Babilani**...... When I entered Babilani as a friend and when I established the seat of the government in the palace of the ruler under jubulation and rejoicing,* **Marduk, the great LORD***, inducred the magnanimous inhabitants of Babilani*

*to love me, and **I was daily endeavoring to worship him....
I also gathered all their former inhabitants and returned them to their habitations.** Futhermore, **I resettled
upon the command of Marduk, the great LORD**, all the
gods of Kiengir and Akkade whom Nabonidus had brought
into Babilani to the anger of the lord of the gods, unharmed,
in their former temples, the places which make them
happy.*"

This command from the persian King Cyrus to re-
settle the foreign inhabitants and restore their former gods
to their former temples coincides with the same command
given by the LORD GOD of Heaven given to King Cyrus
recorded in the Bible found in 2nd Chronicles 36:22&23
and Ezra 1:2. However, the actual excavated finding records
the great LORD Marduk (the mythological solar god of
Babylon), giving this decree to King Cyrus. This would
have included resettling the Jews back to Judah in 537
B.C. by rebuilding their 2nd Temple in Jerusalem. After
years of delay this Temple eventually saw its completion in
the year of 516 B.C.

**In conclusion: The LORD GOD of heaven (men-
tioned in the book of Ezra 1:1&2) - is Marduk, the mythological solar LORD of Babylon. The actual historical cylinder mentions Marduk the great LORD allegedly giving
the decree to King Cyrus. The King James Bible leaves
out the actual name " Marduk" and inserts the generic
title " The LORD GOD of heaven" in its place.**

Therefore the 2nd Temple in Jerusalem was a Temple
fashioned around the image of Babylon by sacrificing animals in accordance to the newly installed puppet Priesthood pretending to be the perfectly restored religion of
Israel. By personally appointing Babylonian Governors,
Priests and resources, King Cyrus and the successive kings
of Persia could curtail any future rebellions caused by any
past reflecting beliefs. According to the King, this Jewish

religion and its temple had to be adapted to the local Babylonian god who conquered the land. The truth is that when Persian kings *"restored " gods to their temples*, the restoration was not to what they were in the past, but rather, in the image of the local god that best suited the king. This was best accomplished by paying off the appointed Priests and leaders with the gold and silver vessels of the previous Temple, which is exactly what we see in Ezra 1:11. In Ezra 5:14 King Cyrus returned all the gold and silver over to his newly appointed Persian Governor of Judah (Sheshbazzar). The thought was by sending in waves of Babylonian scribes, prophets, priests and money from Babylon, this would ease the transition for a rebuilt Temple in Jerusalem.

Ezra 1:11 *" All the vessels of Gold and of Silver were five thousand and four hundred.* ***All these did Sheshbazzar, the prince of Judah*** *bring up with them of the captivity that were brought up from Babylon unto Jerusalem."*

Ezra 5:14 *" And the vessels also of gold and silver of the house of God, which Nebuchadnezzar took out of the Temple that was in Jerusalem, and brought them unto the Temple of Babylon, those did Cyrus the King take out of the Temple of Babylon, and they were delivered unto one,* ***whose name was Sheshbazzar, whom he had made Governor."***

By 516 B.C. the temple was complete and known as the temple of Zerub**babel**. Named after another persian appointed Jewish governor in those days.

THE DAVIDIC COVENANT CHALLENGED

The Davidic Covenant is found in Jeremiah.
Jeremiah 23:5 "Behold, the days come, saith the Lord, that I will raise unto David a righteous Branch, and a King shall reign and prosper, and shall execute judgment and justice in the earth."
This Davidic covenant is also found in the Psalms.
Psalm 132:11 "The Lord has sworn in truth unto David; he will not turn from it; Of the fruit of thy body will I set upon the throne."

As stated before this condemned half-breed dynasty did not go unchallenged. The King James Bible records Ezra reading Deuteronomy 7:3 in open public concerning the violation of the law by King David and King Solomon for marrying foreign women. Around 430 B.C. Ezra reads these words:
Ezra 9:2 *"FOR THEY HAVE TAKEN OF THEIR DAUGHTERS FOR THEMSELVES, and for their sons: so that the* **HOLY SEED** *have mingled themselves with the people of those lands:* **YEA THE HAND OF THE PRINCES AND RULERS HATH BEEN CHIEF IN THIS TRESPASS."**

Nehemiah 13:26 **"Did not Solomon king of Israel sin by these things?"**

Ezra neglected to tell his returning Judahite audience that Moses himself was married to a foreign Ethiopian woman in Numbers 12:1, but when one has an agenda on their mind, one only notices the newly edited laws pertaining to that agenda. By discrediting the kings of Israel, Ezra, could then smooth the transition for the Persian kings

69

that occupied the land and the newly Jewish rebuilt Temple. Ezra, the Babylonian oracle continues on to convince the returning Judean exiles, that their slavery under foreign kings was solely due to their sins and the sins of their former Israeli kings.

Nehemiah 9:37 *".....the kings whom thou hast set over us because of our sins:"*

So Ezra, finished by dredging up the racist law in Deuteronomy 23:1-3.

Nehemiah 13:1 *"On that day **they read in the book of Moses** in the audience of the people; and therein was found written, that the Ammonite and **THE MOABITE SHOULD NOT COME INTO THE CONGREGATION OF THE LORD FOREVER."***

Initially, the Babylonians were planning to take over Judah clear back in the days of King Hezekiah 726-697 B.C. So it was not the violations of the LORD's law committed by King David and Solomon that Judah, but rather through the relentless pursuit of the Babylonians to steal all the treasures of the kingdom of Judah, whom the Jewish King Hezekiah foolishly revealed to Babylonian spies bearing gifts for this sick king in Isaiah 39.

Isaiah 39:3&4 *"They are come from a far country unto me, even from **Babylon**. All that is in mine house have they seen: there is nothing among my treasures that I have not showed them."*

THE BIRTH OF LEVITICUS

Rebuilding the second Jewish Temple of Israel was a minor accomplishment next to restoring the Jewish community to its newly revised Babylonian/Persian law book. The Babylonian Priests, sent by the successive Kings of Persia, were responsible for this restoration task. It was the Babylonian scribes and leaders that took over the leadership of the Jewish community. The aramaic language took over the Hebrew language as the primary language during this Persian period. The successive kings of Persia sent specially trained Scribes such as Ezra and Nehemiah (noted in the Bible from 464 to 424 B.C.). Both of these men would have been trained under the Persian scribal chancellary of Babylon. It was during this time period of Ezra and Nehemiah that the book of Leviticus, and possibly the contradictory traditions mentioned in Numbers were originated. The book of Leviticus had already existed in part through Babylonian practices and law. There was such an emphasis by Ezra to cause the people to understand through translation the detailed meaning of all these alleged laws of the LORD, that only the book of Leviticus and parts of the book of Numbers devotes all its pages to such laws given in such graphic detail referenced in Nehemiah 8:7 & 8. Practically every chapter of Leviticus and most of the chapters of the book of Numbers starts with the LORD speaking to Moses in the third person. **"And the LORD spake unto Moses saying,"** The long elaborate list of rules and regulations graphically details every sacrifice on the altar as the Priests explain it to the Jewish exiles in Nehemiah chapter 8 through 10. All of these rules were allegedly written down by the hand of the LORD for Moses on mount Sinai. Even though the origin of Leviticus is most likely Persian, it would be more appropriate to call this book, **" The book of Babylon"**. Jesus discerned the

71

difference between the Babylonian revised writings in the Old Testament from those of the Prophets. Jesus systematically quoted only those sections attributed to **Isaiah** and a few selected sections attributed to **King David** in the Psalms. Not all of the book of Isaiah was written by Isaiah and not all of the Psalms were written by King David, but according to Jesus, the list below methodically reveals which writings he believed belonged to the prophet Isaiah and which ones belonged to King David.

Luke 20:42 ------------------ **Psalm 110:1**----------**King David**
Luke 20:17 ------------------ **Psalm 118:22**--------**King David**
John 10:34 ------------------ **Psalm 82:6**----------**King David**
John 12:13 ------------------ **Psalm 118:25&26**---**King David**
John 13:18 ------------------ **Psalm 41:9**------------**King David**
Matthew 27:37 ------------- **Psalm 22:18** -------- **King David**
Matthew 21:16 ------------- **Psalm 8:2**-------------**King David**
Matthew 13:35 ------------ **Psalm 78:2** ----------**King David**

Mark 7:6 --------------------- **Isaiah 29:13**-----------**Isaiah**
Luke 19:14 ------------------ **Isaiah 56:7**------------**Isaiah**
Luke 8:10 -------------------- **Isaiah 6:9**--------------**Isaiah**
Luke 4:18 -------------------- **Isaiah 61:1**------------**Isaiah**
John 6:45 -------------------- **Isaiah 54:13**-----------**Isaiah**
John 12:38 ------------------ **Isaiah 53:1**------------**Isaiah**
John 12:40 ------------------ **Isaiah 6:10**------------**Isaiah**

Other Old Testament quotes from Jesus

Luke 7:27 -- Malachi 3:1, Mark 11:17 -- Jeremiah 7:11, Mark 14:27 -- Zechariah 13:7, Mark 13:14--Daniel 9:27, Matthew 12:40 -- Jonah 1:17.

Jesus would never quote from any Old Testament writings that were revised during the time the Babylonians and Persians conquered Judah. Not unless he wanted to establish just how corrupt the passage was in the first place.

And even though Jesus would at times quote passages from a few reliable Prophets in the Old Testament, he admits the Prophets errored in understanding the full personality profile of the Creator. This is why Jesus endorsed John the Baptist as the greatest prophet of all, even over Moses.

Luke 7:28 " *For I say unto you, Among those that are born of women* **there is not a greater prophet than John the Baptist***: but he that is least in the kingdom of God is greater than he.*"

THE THREE LAWS THAT CONDEMNED JESUS

Just being part Moabite was the first reason why Jesus was condemned by the LORD. Breaking the Sabbath law was the second reason why Jesus was condemned to death by the Temple Priests of Jerusalem. The third reason is found in Matthew 26:65-66 *".....He hath spoken blasphemy; .... He is guilty of death."*

Apparently Jesus claimed to be the Son of the Highest sitting on the right hand of power. In those days that was considered blasphemy and worthy of the death penalty according to Leviticus 24:16 *"And he that blasphemeth the name of the LORD, he shall surely be put to death, and all the congregation shall stone him......."* The perception of the Pharisees was that they were collectively the son of God, through their Abraham, Isaac, and Jacob bloodline as was written in their Exodus law.
Exodus 4: 22 ***"And thou say unto Pharaoh, thus saith the LORD, Israel is my son, even my first-born."***

The Roman/Jewish establishments, during the time of Jesus, could not accept another King claiming to be the Son of God. This is due in part because the Romans had their version of the son of God called the Babylonian pontiff named Tiberias Caesar. The Priests of the Temple worshipped him out of religious obligation. Prior to the arrival of Jesus, Israel did not have a King for several hundred years. Jesus announced his status just as the Davidic covenant required. So to break this all down, Jesus (the Son of God) was a three-time condemned criminal, who broke the laws of the LORD. He was, in the eyes of the Pharisees and Saducees, nothing more than a half-breed, sabbath breaking, blasphemer.

The crucifixion of Jesus should not be looked upon as an atonement for sins in the form of a final blood-shed sacrifice. Instead the crucifixion should be looked upon and remembered as the most horrible example of what can happen when a society follows after the wrong set of laws given to them by a Babylonian animal blood offering cult. The end result was a society consumed in condemnation which left the world with the sad display of mistakenly crucifying the promised King.

Jesus's mix-breed status was mentioned only once in the New Testament and this is found in John. This may have been due to the physical features of Jesus, as he possibly was a darker shade in skin color than the regular Jew. We can get a slight indication of this fact as his fore-father King Solomon who described himself in this way in the Song of Solomon.

Song of Solomon 1:5-6 *"I am black, but comely, O ye daughters of Jerusalem........Look not upon me, because I am black..............."*

John 8:48: *"Then answered the Jews, and said unto him, Say we not well **that thou art a SAMARITAN, and hast a devil?** "*

Jesus never denied being a Samaritan. After all, he was the promised son of a condemned half-breed Moabite. So Jesus responded in John with these words:

John 8:49 ***"Jesus answered, I have not a devil; but I honor my Father, and ye do dishonor me."***

The origin of Samaritans, and these racist statements, possibly came about when gentiles were brought into Israel and interbred with the Israelites back in the time era of the Kings. See 2 Kings17:24.

As discussed before, these are the three reasons the Pharisee's condemned Jesus to death. However, they could not execute him within a Roman occupied territory according to their Levitical law by stoning someone. So they

75

needed to find a Roman law Jesus actually broke. This is the final reason why Jesus was condemned to the cross. This law is written briefly in John.

John 19:12 *"**every one who makes himself a king sets himself against Caesar.**"*

Pilate could not find any reason to crucify Jesus under Pharisee/Jewish law. This is because Pilate only had legal jurisdiction under Roman law. So under the pressure of the Priests who ruled over the Jewish Temple (according to the Levitical law), Pilate recognized they had a valid Roman law they could use against Jesus. So Jesus was crucified under the law of Caesar for claiming to be a King. This explains the accusation nailed upon the cross over his head that stated in Matthew.

Matthew 27:37 ***"THIS IS JESUS THE KING OF THE JEWS."***

It was believed back then, if there is only one God that rules the Universe, then there must be only one King that rules the earth. For any one to state, **"I am the son of God."** would have been calling Caesar a fraudulent king and liar.

In a last ditched effort, Pilate tried to release Jesus under a Jewish feast custom because he knew the Jewish Priests delivered Jesus to Pilate out of envy. The result was the Jewish Priests swayed the crowd towards crucifying Jesus and releasing a well known murderer by the name of Bar-ab-bas back into their community. Pilate washed his hands of this kind of execution.

In churches today, Christians are still pleading the blood to be upon them, in the form of Jesus sacrificing himself to save them from the wrath of a revengeful LORD. Christians claim there is power in the blood of Jesus and they have even written songs to this effect. History records what happened to the Jewish people that pleaded the blood of Jesus be upon themselves for the crucifixion in Matthew 27:25

"Then answered all the people, and said His blood be upon us, and on our children." History records within decades after the crucifixion of Jesus, these same people in Jerusalem were grossly starved out by the Romans, even to the point of having to eat their own new born children as their only source of food.

To recap: The wicked Chief Priests and leading Elders of Jerusalem saw Jesus violating these four written laws.

1. Jesus was a half-breed gentile condemned Moabite. The Old Testament law forever barred him from the congregation of the LORD, found in Deuteronomy 23:3.

2. Jesus broke the Sabbath law by healing and picking corn on the Sabbath day recorded in Matthew 12:1-2 and Matthew 12:12. The Old Testament law applied zero tolerance. The law required only death as the resolution. These occult laws are found in Exodus 31:11-16, Exodus 35:1-3, Numbers 15:32-36 and Leviticus 23:30.

3. Jesus declared himself the Son of the Highest in Matthew 26:64. The Chief Priests and Elders reasoned that Jesus was to be put to death based on his blasphemist statement. The occult law is found in Leviticus 24:16 *"And he that blasphemeth the name of the LORD, he shall surely be put to death........"*

4. Jesus broke the Roman law under Tiberias Caesar recorded in John.

John 19:12 *"Every one who makes himself a King sets himself against Caesar."* In other words, sedition.

Luke 23:2, *"And they began to accuse him, saying, We found this fellow perverting the nation, and forbidding to give tribute to Caesar, saying that he himself is Christ a King."*

During the time of Jesus, Tiberias Caesar was not only the acting Emperor of Rome, but Tiberias Caesar was also elected to the position of Pope (the Pontiff of Rome). And before the time of Tiberias Caesar, Julius Caesar (in 63 B.C.) was also elected to the position of Pontifex Maximus (The Pontiff of Rome). Thus they both vested themself all the powers and functions of the Babylonian Pontiff. **Today, the pope or Pontiff of Rome, as a leader, can be traced back (via Roman paganism) to Babylon rather than to an Apostolic successor from Jesus.** This might explain why the Chief Priests in Jerusalem said to Pilate which king they were worshipping, and which god they were making animal sacrifices at the Temple in Jerusalem, recorded in the Book of John:

John19:15 "..........*Pilate saith unto them, Shall I crucify your King? The chief priests answered, **We have no king but Caesar.***"

By verifying Caesar as their king, they were also verifying the Roman/Babylonian Sun god (and all the other gods) that Caesar worshipped. So the animal sacrifices performed in the Jewish Temple were merely directed toward the Babylonian gods. Jesus would not go along with these occult practices, therefore it became a conflict of doctrines that needed to be settled on the cross. The Pharisees and Saducees were simply doing what the law of the LORD required of them (penned within their own Torah by the Babylonian scribes).

The violations of the law required the death penalty, in fact, one could not even substitute animal sacrifices for these so-called alleged crimes. There was no way around these laws without the death penalty being administered. No exceptions were written for these violations and no exceptions were given.

There was no reconciling the two doctrines together, one doctrine had to be exposed as the fraud while the other one continued on.

Jesus never died on the cross for the purpose of paying for anyone's sins as Christianity teaches. Rather, in order to take away the sin of the world, it became necessary to overcome the Temple bloody sacrifice doctrine by evidence of the resurrection. This established that bloody sacifices never came from the Creator. The resurrection of Jesus served to crucify both the blood covenant of the LORD and the notion that Caesar was the son of God, thereby destroying the psychological effect and ideological contamination these two belief systems brought upon the world. The following are just a few New Testament examples concerning Jesus teaching against the laws of the LORD (of the Torah) found in Matthew Chapter 5: verses 21,27,31,33,38,43. These are just six laws Jesus changed in this chapter alone.

1. Mat 5:21 *"ye have heard that it was said by them of old time, Thou shalt kill; and whosoever shall be in danger of the judgment:* **But I say unto you, That whosoever is angry with his brother without a cause shall be in danger of the judgement:............................"**

2. Mat 5:27 *"Ye have heard that it was said by them of old time, Thou shalt not commit adultery:* **But I say unto you, That whosoever looketh upon a woman to lust after her hath committed adultery with her already in his heart."**

3. Mat 5:31 *"It hath been said, Whosoever shall put away his wife, let him give her a writing of divorcement:* **But I say unto you, That whosoever shall put away his wife, saving for the cause of fornication, causeth her to commit adultery: and whosoever shall marry her that is divorced committeth adultery."**

79

4. Mat 5:33 *"Again, ye have heard that it hath been said by them of time, Thou shalt not forswear thyself, but shalt perform unto the LORD thine oaths:* **But I say unto you, Swear not at all; neither by heaven; for it is God's throne:..............."**

5. Mat 5:38 *"Ye have heard that it hath been said, An eye for an eye, and a tooth for a tooth:* **But I say unto you, That ye resist not evil:..................."**

6. Mat 5:43 *"Ye have heard that it hath been said, Thou shalt love thy neighbor, and hate thine enemy.* **But I say unto you, Love your enemies, bless them that curse you, do good to them that hate you, and pray for them..............................."**

This is just one example of many in Matthew chapter 5:38-48 *"Ye have heard that it hath been said, an eye for an eye, and a tooth for a tooth:* **But I say unto you, that ye resist not evil: but whosoever shall smite thee on thy right cheek, turn to him the other also."**

In Leviticus the Law of the LORD reads like this:
Leviticus 24:20 **"Breach for breach, eye for eye, tooth for tooth: as he hath caused a blemish in a man, so shall it be done to him."**
Here the Levitical law advocates revenge on anyone and everyone, while Jesus is teaching not to resist evil with revenge. Anyone that accepts the whole Bible in its entirety will take on the same pathological personality traits of those that wrote it. When they feel like forgiving someone they will quote a scripture made by Jesus, but when they feel revenge upon someone they will quote the author of Leviticus 24:20.

THE TRUE PURPOSE OF Jesus AND THE CROSS

IF JESUS DIDN'T DIE ON THE CROSS FOR ANYONES SINS, THEN WHY DID HE BOTHER GOING TO THE CROSS AT ALL?

Contrary to what Christianity states, the true purpose of Jesus was never to die on the cross as an atonement for anyone's sins. Instead Jesus came to take away the bloody sacrifices of the law initiated by Moses and the carnal priests. (The Blood Covenant) was later expanded upon by Babylonian revisionists by changing the location of the exodus story to mount Sinai and introducing blood sacrifices as a part of daily Temple requirements. This was after Israel was exiled to Babylon in 586 B.C. The resurrection of Jesus was the only sign Jesus could use to disrupt this harmful practice at the Temple. Blood offerings were nothing more than acts of murder in the eyes of the Creator. By 33 A.D. Jesus put an end to all blood offerings practiced at the Temple by exposing these fraudulent doctrines perpetrated to be the laws of the Creator. **Mankind didn't need the shed blood of a Saviour on a cross for the atonement of their sins, but rather mankind needed the essential teachings of Jesus shed upon their hearts to find the peace their conscience searched for.** Through this knowledge, mankind could regenerate his own conscience from the inside, rather than depending on outward animal or human bloody sacrifices.

Christianity now twists the real gospel of Jesus into a clever counterfeit gospel. Christianity is oblivious to this fact and will defend the Levitical blood offering doctrine to their last dying breath, simply because Christianity desperately believes a Saviour must shed his blood to appease the revengeful rage of the LORD, thereby presenting God with a severe flawd human trait.

When Jesus had thrown out the animal merchants from the Temple in John 2:13-16, he was confronted by the religious leaders who had a logical question on their minds. They asked Jesus this question recorded in the book of John.

John 2:18. *"What sign showest thou unto us, seeing that thou doest these things?"*

The following verse Jesus makes the most challenging and important statement that has ever changed the course of human history.

John 2:19 *"Destroy this temple, and in three days I will raise it up."*

By putting out this sign (the resurrection), the religious leaders (now influenced by hundreds of years of Babylonian culture) could see beyond any doubt, that Jesus had full authority to dispute the corrupt laws of the LORD practiced at the Temple. It was only fitting the resurrection would take place where the blood covenant had gained it's strongest foothold - in Jerusalem, where the Temple was rebuilt by the Persian kings. Jesus purposefully confronted the Blood covenant doctrine practiced at the Temple for the purpose of removing its psychological impact. The Blood covenant was nothing more than a deceptive diversionary law set up to keep the truth from those that would never receive the original Commandments. The resurrection simply reinforced the teachings and Commandments of Jesus. The resurrection also served to expose Caesar as a fraud along with the Babylonian culture that invented the Sun and Moon gods. Jesus certainly did not fulfill the Levitical animal blood offering laws as spun by some of the authors in the New Testament, but rather Jesus came to take away and replace these evil practices with his teachings and Commandments. If the laws of **"Yahweh the LORD"** were true, there would have been no conflict between Jesus and the Priests concerning the atonement for sins. Animal sacrifices were the clear choice of action at the Temple in Jerusalem. So then, with the reputation of both doctrines hanging on the cross, only one doctrine could be proven correct. The self appointed Apostle Paul preserved the blood covenant cult, along with its LORD, by modifying the crucifixion into a final Christ blood offering religion known now as Catholicism, and Christianity. By twisting the teachings of Jesus - into a final blood-shed offering, Paul reconstructed his former Babylonian blood-offering religion by connecting his Christ back to the animal blood sacrifices written within the book of Leviticus, thereby prolonging the days of the Babylonian LORD in the New Testament.

John the Baptist instead taught the Baptism of repentance, which was the ritual of turning away from these destructive practices of the Temple. This ritual was personally endorsed and practiced by Jesus. Clearly Jesus had not committed sin to be baptized as Christians today are baptized. Jesus instead endorsed the Baptism of John, because it was the only correct ritual that best identified itself with preserving life. Christianity has twisted the meaning of water baptism to mean: you are to be baptized in the shed-blood of Christ as your personal Saviour on the cross.

Jesus was asked again this question by the Chief Priests, scribes and elders.

Mark 11:28 *"By what authority doest thou these things?"* Jesus responded by challenging the practicing religion of that day to answer his question first in the following verse in Mark.

Mark 11:30 **"The Baptism of John, was it from heaven, or of men? answer me."**

Of course the Priests declined to answer this question from Jesus. The doctrine of John the Baptist is defined in Luke as stated by the father of John the Baptist' Zechariah.

Luke 1:76 *"And thou, child, shalt be called the prophet of the Highest: for thou shalt go before the face of the Lord to prepare his ways;* **TO GIVE KNOWLEDGE OF SALVATION UNTO HIS PEOPLE BY THE REMISSION OF THEIR SINS, THROUGH THE TENDER MERCY OF OUR GOD,...."**

It was the knowledge of God's MERCY and not the offering of innocent blood that mankind could find the peace he strived for. No animal sacrifices, no Priests, no altars in this doctrine - just the teachings of Mercy that came from Jesus.

John the Baptist refers to Jesus as the Lamb of God that taketh away the sin of the world. John 1:29. **"........ Behold the Lamb of God that taketh away THE SIN of the world."** John was not referring to Jesus as a sacrificed lamb on the altar for the purpose of paying the price for others sins. Rather John was referring to the passive nature of Jesus as his teachings and evidence of his resurrection would eventually take away the **bloody sacrifice beliefs** out of the world. The Baptism of John was the required ritual to purify one's self from the blood soaked sacrifice beliefs made on the altars of death. The water was symbolic in that it washed away the bloody sacrifice beliefs by simply accepting the proper teachings of life. This is what separated John's teachings from the Pharisee's. Though for Christianity, the human race had to actually move into the realm of *human sacrifice* to finally appease their LORD. Senselessly killing animals was no longer sufficient to satisfy their conscience. According to the Christian faith, Christ is the *human sacrifice* that satisfies the LORD. So Christians are now told they must be baptized under this bloody sacrifice belief.

The Bible's Genealogy of Jesus

On the following page is a side by side comparison of two separate authors giving us different genealogies of Christ. When it comes to relying on the authors for the correct genealogy of Jesus, we find a completely different list of fathers leading back to King David. Both the Matthew version and the Luke version disagree and are incomplete. The author of the Matthew version has 26 fathers between Jesus and King David, while the author of Luke has 41 fathers between the two, with the bloodline coming down through Nathan instead of Solomon. It will then be suggested by Christian apologetics that one list is 'the genealogy of Mary' which might pass for an explanation if it were not for the fact that both genealogies in both gospel accounts are of the genealogy of Joseph as stated. Furthermore, it was not customary to denote a person's lineage through any genealogy but the father's line. Every genealogy in the Bible is through the line of fathers and sons since this was a very patriarchal society. This would be quite odd to give 'the genealogy of Mary' without mentioning Mary but instead giving the genealogy of Joseph, which is what one finds in both accounts. It appears both authors fell short in accuracy and integrity. Both authors recorded their versions possibly to divert the reader towards an alleged virgin birth myth in Isaiah 7:14 - probably in order to get around that condemned, half-breed ancestry bloodline of King David. It became necessary for both authors to sever the Davidic covenant God had promised King David by simply introducing the Holy Spirit as the father of Jesus instead of Joseph the biological father. By editing history in this way, the New Testament authors could turn the unacceptable half-breed condemned Messiah into the unblemished purebred lamb that needed to be sacrificed on the cross for everyone's sins, thereby pro-

The genealogy of Jesus according to the author of Matthew:

Matthew 1:6-16

King David	E-li-ud
Solomon	El-e-a-zar
Reho-boam	Mat-than
Abi-jah	Jacob
A-sa	Joseph
Je-hosh-a-phat	Jesus
Jeho-ram	
Uzziah	
Jo-tham	
Ahaz	
Hezeki-ah	
Ma-nas-seh	
Amon	
Jo-si-ah	
Jech-o-ni-ah	
She-al-ti-el	
Zerub-babel	
A-bi-ud	
E-li-a-kim	
A-zor	
Sa-doc	
A-chim	

The genealogy of Jesus according to the author of Luke:

Luke 3:23-31

King David	Ze-rub-babel
Nathan	Rhe-sa
Mat-ta-tha	Jo-an-na
Me-nan	Judah
Me-le-a	Joseph
E-li—a-kim	Sem-e-i
Jo-nan	Mat-ta-thi-as
Joseph	Ma-ath
Judah	Nag-gai
Simeon	Es-li
Levi	Na-hum
Mat-that	Amos
Jo-rim	Mat-ta-thi-as
El-i-e-zer	Joseph
Jo-se	Jan-na
Er	Mel-chi
El-mo-dam	Levi
Co-sam	Mat-that
Ad-di	He-li
Mel-chi	Joseph
Ne-ri	Jesus
She-al-tiel	

26 fathers listed between them

41 fathers listed between them

viding a perfect human blood sacrifice to the Babylonian/ Levitical god. A reasoned question that comes to mind is: **Why did these authors of Matthew and Luke even bother to mention any genealogy, if both authors believed Jesus had no biological father?**

THE BIRTH OF JESUS

The death of King Herod is important in its relation to the birth of Jesus. Before I address the virgin birth event, I will need to first determine if the real birth of Jesus actually took place in history. The eclipse of the moon mentioned by Josephus gives us a precise time frame from which we can determine the date of King Herod's death (The Antiquities of the Jews, Ant., XVII, vi, 4). Josephus the historian tells us a lot about this King. Born in 73 B.C., Herod was a builder of temples to the gods - one at Rhodes, for instance, to the god Apollo (Jos., "Ant." XVI,v,3). Apparently Herod died of a medical condition a little while after an incident involving several young intellects and a high priest during a fast day.

Ant., 17:6:4 " ***Herod deprived this Matthias of the high priesthood, and burnt the other Matthias, who had raised the sedition, with his companions, alive. And that very night there was an eclipse of the moon.***"

The Jewish new year is always the nearest new moon to the 21st of March. Now a lunar eclipse always happens at a full moon which is always on the 14th day of the Jewish month. The only fast on the 13th day of the Jewish month is the 'Esther Fast' which takes place during the Purim festival. This occurs during the last Jewish month of the year, known as ' ADAR. ' Josephus also gives the length of King Herod's reign as 37 years from the time he was appointed by the Romans, somewhere near 40 B.C. which places the death of King Herod in the spring of 4

B.C. There are only two recorded moon eclipses in the period of 7 B.C. to 6 A.D.

1. A partial eclipse occurred on the 13th of **March in 4 B.C.** at 2:45 PM

2. A total eclipse occurred on the 23rd of **March in 5 B.C.** at 7:45 AM.

According to Josephus, Herod died before the Jewish Passover of that year (Ant.17.9.3). Jesus was probably born many years prior to King Herod's death. In Matthew 2:16 the order went out from King Herod to destroy all male babies from 2 years of age and under, thereby making this order at least 2 or 3 to 12 years prior to King Herod's death in 4 or 5 B.C. Just exactly how many years prior to his death is difficult to determine, but an accurate birth year of Jesus can be determined somewhere between 7 B.C. to 16 B.C. This is because the Bible does not indicate what year King Herod originally spoke to the wise men or Magi who originally came to see the young child at birth. This range would also give us an age for Jesus being crucified somewhere between the age of 40 to 49 in the year of 33 A.D. Another way to possibly confirm this range of 40 to 49 is to work backwards by determining the date the Temple was declared to be 46 years old in John 2:20.

"Then said the Jews, Forty and six years was this temple in building, and wilt thou rear it up in three days?"

The reign of King Herod was from 37 B.C. to 4 or 5 B.C. According to Josephus (Jos., "Antiquities" XV, xi,1) the construction of the Temple in Jerusalem began in the eighteenth year of Herod's reign which would make it approximately 19 B.C. We get 27 A.D. if we add the 46 years onto 19 B.C. (when the temple was first constructed as stated by the author of John 2:20), thereby giving the age

88

of Jesus approximately 34 to 43. By adding another 6 years to 27 A.D. makes Jesus 40 to 49 years of age in 33 A.D. at the time of the crucifixion.

Jesus was declared 30 years of age in Luke 3:23, also in chapter 3 the author inserted a false genealogy concerning Jesus. Previously in this same chapter of Luke 3:1-3 John the Baptist begins preaching the Baptism of repentance in the 15th year reign of the Roman Emperor Tiberius Caesar. Tiberius Caesar was declared 'Pontifex Maximus' (the Pontiff of Rome) in March of 15 A.D. History records Tiberius Caesar reigned from 14 A.D. to 37 A.D. and died in 37 A.D. smothered by Marco in his bed near Micenum. The correct age of John the Baptist was probably 43 when he began preaching in 29 A.D. according to the 15th year of Tiberius Caesar. One should not assume that Jesus was 30 years of age during the time John the Baptist was preaching in Luke chapter 3 verse 1. The author, claiming Jesus was 30 years of age in Luke 3:23, inserted an inaccurate genealogy of Jesus working backward to King David using his son Nathan in 3:31, instead of using his son Solomon in Matthew 1:7. The reader is left with a deceptive inserted section along with a deceptive genealogy. The only Gospel account that accurately fills in the time frame where one can determine the accurate birth year of Jesus is called The Gospel of the Holy 12. It states in Lection 5:14 that *Joseph, Mary and Jesus stayed in Egypt for 7 years prior to King Herod's death in 4 or 5 B.C.* The Gospel of the Holy 12 also explains how Elizabeth hid her son John the Baptist in the mountains from the Romans during this time of King Herod's paranoia - a piece of history that is edited out of all other Biblical versions. The Gospel of the Holy 12 gives us an approximate date from which we can determine how old Jesus was in 11 B.C., which was around 2 years of age. Given the fact that King Herod's order to kill all male children went out approximately 2 years after the initial visit with the Wise men, would narrow the time line in which **Jesus was born approximately in 12 or 13 B.C.** Using the historian Josephus and the written account from The Gospel of the Holy 12, we are given the most detailed and accurate record concerning the actual birth and resurrection dates of Jesus. **This makes Jesus, at the time of the crucifixion, approximately 46 or 47 years of age in 33 A.D.**

THE STONE OF VENICE

The microletters on the Lapis Venetus also offers archaeological evidence in support of the conclusion that Jesus was born approximately in 12 B.C. and the census was the census mentioned in Luke 2:2.

Luke 2:2 ***"And this taxing was first made when Cyrenius was governor of Syria."***

Publius Sulpicius Quirinius (rendered in greek *Kyrenios*, sometimes Grecized as ***Cyrenius***, c. 51 B.C. - A.D. 21) was the Roman governor of Syria in Luke 2:2.

A census is mentioned on an ancient tombstone called "Lapis Venetus" (stone of Venice). The tombstone was for a Roman officer who, under the orders from Quirinius, made a census of Apamea, a city in Syria. Using the microletters on the tombstone itself Dr. E. Vardaman deciphered the date to be 10 B.C. The text reads: "LA CONS P.S.QVIRINI" which means: "year one of the consulship of P.S. Quirini." L is abbreviated = year, A = one. In the greek number system, the first letter represented 1, the second letter represented 2, etc. "CONS" = Consulship and "P.S.QVIRINI" = Quirinius/Cyrenius mentioned in Luke 2:2. Quirinius is also mentioned by Josephus and by Dio, both of whom state that **Quirinius in 12 B.C. was a Roman consul as a favorite of Augustus Caesar who made the decree mentioned in Luke 2:1.** Historically, the Roman census was taken every 17 years and in every case would take about 2 years to complete the census.

Luke 2:1 ***"And it came to pass in those days, that there went out a decree from Caesar Augustus, that all the world should be taxed."***

Luke 2:5 ***"To be taxed with Mary his espoused wife, being great with child."***

ISAIAH 7:14
THE VIRGIN BIRTH

According to the book of Isaiah (around 742 B.C.) king Ahaz of Judea was under threat of attack by an alliance by Rezim, the King of Aram, and Pekah, the king of Israel. The Prophet Isaiah then attempted to calm the king down, so he prophesied to the king in the controversial scripture Isaiah 7:14. Matthew 1:23 refers the reader directly to this scripture, whereas Luke 1:31 only hints towards this passage in Isaiah 7:14 by using the exact words quoted in Isaiah 7:14. For comparison purposes, using the Jewish translated version and the King James version, here are the two Isaiah 7:14 renditions.

Isaiah 7:14 Jewish Hebrew Translation: ***"Therefore the Lord, of his own, shall give you a (SIGN), Behold the young woman is with child, and she will bear a son, and she shall call his name Emanuel."***

Isaiah 7:14 King James Version: ***"Therefore the Lord himself shall give you a (SIGN); Behold a virgin shall conceive, and bear a son, and shall call his name Im-man-u-el."***

THE FIRST SECTION of this scripture in Isaiah 7:14 was based on a sign that would be given by the Lord for a particular time frame that was meant to be fulfilled. Jesus denies giving any other sign but the one he chose to give in Matthew 16:4 and in John 2:19. The only **SIGN** Jesus chose to give the Jews during his time era was the sign of his resurrection.

John 2:19 *"Destroy this temple and in three days I will raise it up."*

Matthew 16:4 *"A wicked and adulterous generation seeketh after a SIGN;* **and there shall NO SIGN be given unto it, but the sign of the prophet Jonah."**

Luke 11:30 *" For as Jonah was a sign unto the Nin-e-vites so shall the son of man be to this generation."*

Jesus never refers anyone back to Isaiah 7:14, because he knew this particular sign never referred to him in the first place. Besides who would have believed it, if he had said: *"I was born of a virgin"*, I am sure the Pharisees would have broken some ribs laughing over such a statement. How would one go about proving they were born of a virgin anyway? That would have been impossible to prove then, as it would be today. The virgin birth story is simply a mythological man-made invention for the sole purpose to preserve an occult unblemished blood offering sacrifice. There are no virgin birth declarations or teachings coming from Jesus directly. Even the self appointed apostle Paul whom Christians today believe is the greatest apostle of all, taught that Joseph was the biological father of Jesus. Paul wrote these two statements found in 2 Tim 2:8 and Romans 1:3.

2 Tim 2:8 *"Remember Jesus Christ risen from the dead, descended from David as preached in my gospel."*

Romans 1:3 *"Concerning Jesus Christ our Lord, which was made of the seed of David according to the flesh."*

The author of the book of Mark records no such virgin birth event either. So the first section of this prediction in Isaiah 7:14 does not fit the sign Jesus actually gave to the Jews to establish the authenticity behind his doctrine. The only answer is that the child referred to in Isaiah 7:14 was born 732 years before Jesus. The sign from the Lord in Isaiah 7:14 was only for Ahaz whom it was spoken to at that time.

THE SECOND SECTION in Isaiah 7:14 is based on the word used in the original language. The Hebrew word "ALMAH" used in this section really defines a general age group and specifically means a "young woman" or "young maiden" of child bearing age. Anyone fluent in Hebrew knows that "ALMAH" is not the proper word to use if one refers to a virgin exclusively. Isaiah was well aware of the proper word for "Virgin," which is "BTULAH", because Isaiah used that word specifically to mean virgin in Isaiah 23:4, Isaiah 23:12, Isaiah 37:22, Isaiah 47:1, Isaiah 62:5. So Isaiah knew the difference between "ALMAH" and "BTULAH."

For example, in Isaiah 62:5 *"For as a young man marries a virgin (BTULAH), so shall your sons marry you; and as the bridegroom rejoices over the bride, so shall your God rejoice over you."*

THE THIRD SECTION of this scripture in Isaiah 7:14 is based on the actual name that this child was given. Hebrew names are often times given certain meanings attached to the name itself. The pronunciation of the name is very important, as is the meaning. For example: in this third section the name Emanuel allegedly means "God with us." Whereas the name Jesus is pronounced differently and has a different meaning. In the Matthew 1:20-21 account, Joseph was instructed by the angel of the Lord to name the child "JESUS." Whereas in the Isaiah 7:14 scripture the "young woman" exclusively names her son "Emanuel." So we are dealing with two separate names with two separate meanings. There are two separate children being named by two separate people. This is because we are dealing with two separate births at two separate time eras approximately 742 years apart. There is no getting around the two separate names. The name Emanuel eludes to a generic word that describes a title not a personal name. Reading on into the next verse in Isaiah.

Isaiah 7:15&16 *"Butter and honey shall he eat, that he may know to refuse the evil, and choose the good.* **For before the child shall know to refuse the evil, and choose the good, the land that thou abhorrest shall be forsaken of both her kings."**

This section is so vague and meaningless that it appears to have no structured value applied to comment on. Jesus probably ate butter and honey, but who didn't back then? In Isaiah 22:7 it states: *"....for butter and honey shall every one eat that is left in the land."*

Ahaz was king over the southern kingdom. The two kingdoms referred to in this scripture did not exist during the time of Jesus. Only Roman occupation dominated this era and Tiberias Caesar never forsook the land. Therefore Isaiah is not talking about a future event 742 years into the future. Therefore the additional scripture evidence here just does not support a future virgin born Christian Messiah.

Conclusion: The real historical Jesus was neither a virgin born man nor was he a blood shedding saviour in the sense Christians believe in today. Jesus provided the world with a very simple doctrine to live by and if applied would reconcile mankind back to his Creator. The virgin birth account written in Matthew and Luke can not be supported by Isaiah 7:14. Therefore there is no scripture in the Old that stands by itself as a viable scripture supporting a virgin birth. The people clearly declared Jesus the son of David in Luke 18:38, Mat 9:27, Mat 15:22, Mat

21:9, Mat 22:42 and these scriptures indicate a biological direct reference to Joseph being his father. Instead Christians should examine Isaiah chapter 9 and 11 to find the true historical Jesus. At least there they will find interpretational connections leading back to King David.

PROVING JESUS EXISTED HISTORICALLY

The burden of proof falls exclusively on the Creator to reveal himself to whomever he wishes to reveal himself to. My research indicates the authentic Jesus of history was a real living man and he was a revolutionary thinker. Jesus never once promoted the Old Testament LORD whose psychopathic profile mimicked the personality traits of the Babylonian revisionist. They worshipped a god that:

1. Demanded a blood offering for the atonement of sins. Leviticus 17:11
2. Loved the sweet aroma of burnt animals on the Altar. Leviticus 1: 9,13,17.
3. Hated Ammorites and Moabites to the death. Deuteronomy 23:3.
4. Hated and excluded all handicapped people from entering the congregation of the LORD. Deuteronomy 23:1
5. Demanded instant death on anyone who broke his Sabbath day law. Leviticus 23:30

From a pure psychological level, Jesus exists. However, from a archeologist point of view, there is no conclusive first hand evidence dating back to the time of Jesus to support his existence. Only second and third hand hearsay from various historians do we begin to see circumstantial support. ie; Thallus, Josephus, Justin Martyr (150 A.D.), Tacitus, Phlegon, Origen and Suetonius. Personally I would much rather focus on the character and wisdom behind

the teachings of Jesus, rather than to examine the historical statements of second and third hand historians. Even
if one could dredge up enough first hand historic evidence,
one is faced with establishing the credibility of that evidence. The reason for the lack of first hand evidence is
that Jerusalem was destroyed by the Romans in 70 A.D.
Therefore most first hand objective evidence from Jewish
records would have been destroyed along with the Temple.
The story of Masada stands as perfect evidence of how bru-
tally determined Rome was in destroying Jerusalem and
the remaining Jews. The Romans would have suppressed
any hard historical evidence of Jesus left inside Jerusalem
and would have revised history or reconstructed Jesus the
same way the Babylonians did with the Jewish history in
Jerusalem from 586 B.C to 450 B.C. Therefore there is no
solid objective evidence such as coins or artifacts with Jesus
on them dating to the exact time of Jesus. We can however have first hand knowledge of his teachings if we discern him from the unedited sections within the King James
Bible. For example Jesus taught that God requires to be
PERCEIVED and **UNDERSTOOD** through proper **KNOWL-
EDGE**. Jesus taught these following statements to his disciples in Mark 3:11&12, also found in Matthew 13:13-15
and Matthew 6:33.

Mark 3: 11&12 *"And he said unto them, Unto you it
is given to know* **the mystery of the kingdom of God**: *but
unto them that are without, all these things are done in
parables: that seeing they may see, and not* **PERCEIVE**;
and hearing they may hear, and not **UNDERSTAND**; *lest at
any time they should be converted, and their sins should be
forgiven them."*

Jesus says *"Seek"* *first the Kingdom of God and his
righteousness ...."* Matthew 6:33

Miracles and evidence will not change the psychological profile of an Atheist, only the search for a life preserving God. **The Creator acts on Conduct** and it is upon

this action God reveals himself to others. Besides, how could any historian prove to an Atheist the existence of God in a materialistic world - then or now? To "believe" using the terms Jesus taught, one must apply his definition of knowledge and to apply this knowledge one must **"search"** for that exclusive knowledge.

Searching and applying the commandments of Jesus initiates change and not belief. Belief alone doesn't change an individual only applied knowledge. Having knowledge is different from applying knowledge and in this case, it is the difference between being forgiven or not. The Kingdom of God is a perceived kingdom, unlike the moon-god Yahweh that came down and presented himself on a Babylonian mountain with smoke and fire. A person practices what they perceive and applied knowledge reinforces that perception. It was upon this ideological foundation Jesus taught the *"mystery of the Kingdom of God"*.

There were two events in the New Testament I always met with a skeptical mind concerning the validity behind the stories. One was the roving star that guided the wise men to Bethlehem to find the baby Jesus found in Matthew 2:9. The other was the story about dead people rising out of their graves at the time of the crucifixion found in Matthew 27:52 & 53. Back when I questioned the validity of such events I encountered such a enity of light in person. This enity of light passed over me and my father while we were both sitting down in the family room. This light had all the capabilities of stopping abruptly and moving in any direction it so desired. The encounter with the entity of light was brief and left me with the impression this entity was a living personality having the awareness of its own existence and intelligence. I could see back then, how a star could appear, stop, disappear and then reappear at another location guiding men to Bethlehem as written in Matthew 2:9. So now when I doubt the validity of dead people rising out of their graves at the time of Jesus's crucifixion, I simply remind myself of that entity of light that kindly defied my skeptical mind with its presence.

THE RESUSCITATION THEORY

It has been suggested by some modern day authors that Jesus was resuscitated after the crucifixion. This would be a viable theory except for the fact that no historical accounts support this theory nor does the reality of the situation. Let's say, for the sake of argument, that Jesus survived the incredible beating he endured prior to the crucifixion. He then had to endure the crucifixion itself and the Roman spear in the side. Just the fact of being laid in a full length shroud from head to toe soaked in 50 pounds of ointment would have killed a perfectly healthy man within 12 minutes through suffocation, a little known fact that is never addressed by the resuscitating theorists. According to scripture Jesus was so badly beaten prior to being crucified, the Romans had to have someone else carry his cross. So Jesus was in no way in the same physical condition as the other two Zealot thieves that were crucified along with him. Some theorist have also suggested that nearby friends soaked a reed with some kind of knock out drug and gave it to Jesus on the cross, thereby fooling the the Romans into thinking Jesus was dead just to be resuscitated later. This would be a viable theory if it were not for the fact that it was the Roman soldiers recorded in the Bible as mocking him by offering Jesus vinegar on a reed instead of his nearby friends offering him a knock out drug. The Roman crucifixion of Jesus was a Roman death sentence (for the claim that he was a King). No one was allowed to come close to a sentenced crucified man while he was on the cross, except for the authorized Roman soldiers involved with the crucifixion.

Luke 23:36 *"And the soldiers also mocked him, coming to him, and offering him vinegar."*

CAESAR'S TRIBUTE

Another misinterpretated scripture by modern day Christian authors is the loaded question posed to Jesus by the Jews concerning paying tribute to Caesar in the form of a confession tax found in the book of Mark.

Mark 12:14 *"Is it lawful to give tribute to Caesar, or not?"*

Mark 12:17 *"Render to Caesar the things that are Caesar's, and to God the things that are God's."*

Much like most questions presented to Jesus during his time era, this one was designed to entrap Jesus using his personal teachings, thereby trying to make him into an enemy of the STATE and Caesar. The response given by Jesus was brilliant as recorded in Mark 12:17. Jesus understood Rome had their own kingdom venue and God has his, the response from Jesus made people contemplate just who rightfully owns and creates everything? Did Caesar create the metal out of the ground that formed the denarius coin or did God? Did Caesar create his real body and face that appears on the denarius coin or did God? Jesus's answer implied that everything belongs to the Creator, but if you really perceive Caesar to be God then render those things unto him. His response divided people into two separate venues and it was this kind of reasoning that the people marveled at him in verse 17. Jesus never endorsed human slavery on any level, especially slavery found in the form of tribute confessions made under the threat of the Roman sword. Tiberias Caesar was an egotistical high priest who claimed to be the son of God and anyone that challenged that statement would have been in violation of the STATE. Around the time of Jesus both Julius and Tiberias (The Caesars) became the Babylonian Pontiffs of Rome. On the front side of the denarius coin appears the image of Tiberius Caesar himself with the inscription "*TI CAESAR DIVI*" which means (Tiberius Caesar the Divine). On the back side of the coin is an image of Tiberius on his throne of power which reads "*PONTIF MAXIMUMS*" which means (the POPE or High Priest of Rome). Given at that time the Babylonian culture controlled Rome at its highest office, how much more the Babylonian culture had controlled the religions they previously conquered and revised to their specifications such as in the case of Judah and Judaism. During the time of Jesus one was either forced to worship the Roman Sun god through the High Priest of Babylon (Caesar) or the lesser Babylonian moon-god that Babylon had previously provided for Judah and Judaism through Neuchadnezzar and the successive kings of Persia.

CHAPTER 3
THE PSYCHOPATHIC PROFILE
OF THE LORD

For the purpose of identifying the conflict between the two doctrines found within the Old Testament, it was necessary for me to first identify and separate the pathological profile of the priests and scribes that invented the Old Testament "**LORD**" from the word of the Creator which inspired the Prophets. The psychopathic profile of the priests and scribes was to establish power and maintain it. Anyone that opposed or violated their power structure was destroyed. The corruption of The Torah required the invention of the LORD, so the priests and scribes deemed it necessary to institutionalize the sacrifice of animals as the ceremony used in the worship of their invention. The following laws reflect the psychopathic traits the priests imposed upon the LORD they created in their own image.

101

1. Demanding a blood offering for the atonement of sins. Leviticus 17:11.
2. Loved the sweet aroma of burnt animals on the Altar. Leviticus 1:9,13,17.
3. Hated Ammorites and Moabites to the death. Deuteronomy 23:3.
4. Hated and excluded all handicapped people from entering the congregation of the LORD. Deuteronomy 23:1
5. Demanded instant death on anyone who broke the LORD'S Sabbath law. Leviticus 23:30

In Jeremiah 7:3 the word of God inspired Jeremiah to declare these words.

Jeremiah 7:3 *"Thus saith the God of Hosts, the God of Israel,* **Amend your ways and your doings**, *and I will cause you to dwell in this place.* ⁶ *If you oppress not the stranger, the fatherless, and the widow,* **and shed not IN-NOCENT BLOOD in this place,** *neither walk after other gods to your hurt."*

Jeremiah 7:22-23 **"For I spoke not unto your fathers, nor commanded them in the day that I brought them out of the land of Egypt, concerning burnt offerings or sacrifices."** ²³ **"But this thing commanded I them, saying, Obey my voice, and I will be your God, and ye shall be my people: and walk ye in all the ways that I have commanded you, that it may be well unto you."**

Jeremiah 7:22 in the original Hebrew - *Ky l(-dBrTy (t-(btyke wl(cWytye Bye hcy(hcy(y (te m(ru mcrye)l-Dbry)lh wzbx*

A common 'apologetic' dodge is to insist that animal sacrifices were not ordered when the Israelites came out of Egypt, but rather later. However, the issue isn't when, but whether or not The Creator ordered any animal sacrifices or burnt offerings at all. The law books specifically state that the LORD required the "law of sacrifices" in Exodus 24:7 and the "order of sacrifices" in Leviticus 7:37 (which were the alleged Laws of Moses allegedly received from the LORD while on Mount Sinai).

In Leviticus 7:37-38 we read:

Leviticus 7:37-38 *"This is the law of the burnt offering, of the meat offering, and of the sin offering, and of the trespass offering, and of the consecrations, and of the sacrifice of the peace offerings;* [38] ***Which the LORD commanded Moses in mount Sinai, in the day that he commanded the children of Israel to offer their oblations unto the LORD, in the wilderness of Sinai."***

During the time of Jeremiah, the Temple priests were converting to foreign occult practices, thereby saturating the Jewish Temple with foreign influences. According to Jeremiah 7:22 in 627 B.C. to 586 B.C. - just before Israel went into captivity by the Babylonians, the Creator denies giving any commands concerning burnt offerings and sacrifices over to Moses and the Levite priests. This begs the question. Why would the LORD require the same blood shedding sacrifices laid out in the book of Levitcus as already practiced by the priests of Egypt and especially Babylon? No matter how much Judaism and Christianity wants to argue their faith on this matter, the truth of the matter is this: under the pretense of atonements, innocent blood has to be shed to appease the revengeful nature of their jealous LORD. Their revengeful LORD simply can not find it within himself to forgive anyones transgressions without first seeing the blood-shed of the innocent first. The desire to satisfy one's rage for revenge becomes paramount over actually changing others through proper teaching. In order to justify a Messiah blood-offering doctrine, Christianity had to justify the Old Testament Levitical blood-offering rituals of innocent animals. Christianity can not see the error in ripping the entrails out of animals, splattering their blood around the base of the alter and sprinkling the blood upon the horns of the altar, while at the same time rip the carcass into pieces and burn the pieces for a sweet smelling savor unto their LORD. To the rational mind this sounds like a brutal sick ritual out of a horror movie, yet Christianity believes this was a normal Old Testament religious practice that evolved into a human Saviour sacrifice of Jesus Christ.

In Jeremiah 18:18 there is an obvious conflict between the words that are coming out of the Prophet Jeremiah and the words of the Priests trying to preserve the written law of their LORD. For example in Jeremiah 18:18 the Priests released this statement:

Jeremiah 18:18 **"Then said they, Come, and let us devise devices against Jeremiah; for the law shall not perish from the Priest, nor counsel from the wise, nor the word from the Prophet. Come, let us smite him with the tongue, and let us not give heed to any of his words."**

In Jeremiah 20:1-2 Jeremiah is struck by Pas'-ur (the son of Im-'mer, the priest), who was also chief governor in the house of **the LORD.** Jeremiah was thrown into prison for words spoken against the Priests.

God, through His Prophet Isaiah (740-680 B.C.) referred to these blood offering practices as acts of Murder when he stated these words in Isaiah 1: 11-15.

Isaiah 1:11-15 *"To what purpose is the multitude of your sacrifices unto me?   I am full of the burnt offerings of rams, and the fat of fed beasts;* **and I delight not in the blood of bullocks, or of lambs, or of he goats. When you come to appear before me, who hath required this at your hand, to tread my courts?"** [13] *Bring no more vain oblations; incense is an abomination unto me;* [15] *And when you spread forth your hands, I will hide mine eyes* *from you: yea, when you make many prayers, I will not hear:* **your hands are full of blood."**

Isaiah 66:3 **"HE THAT KILLETH AN OX IS AS IF HE SLEW A MAN;** *HE THAT SACRIFICETH A LAMB, AS IF HE CUT OFF A DOG'S NECK ; HE THAT OFFERETH AN OBLATION, AS IF HE OFFERED SWINE'S BLOOD; HE THAT BURNETH INCENSE, AS IF HE BLESSED AN IDOL. YEA THEY HAVE CHOSEN THEIR OWN WAYS, AND THEIR SOUL DELIGHTETH IN THEIR ABOMINATIONS."*

Isaiah was instructed to teach the Baptism of repentance. This is known as a free offer of Mercy to all. In Isaiah these words were stated:

Isaiah 55:7-8 **"Let the wicked forsake his way, and the un-righteous man his thoughts: and let him return unto the God of Hosts, and he will have MERCY upon him; and to our God, for he will abundantly pardon. For your thoughts are not my thoughts, neither are your ways my ways saith the God of Hosts."**

The God of Jeremiah and of Isaiah stated very clearly that he never spoke of, or commanded any animal sacrifices. In fact, he condemned and abhorred these practices as acts of murder. God simply required repentance and to obey his voice. Yet modern Christianity and Catholicism would have you believe that their Christ is the perfect blood-offering sacrifice that the LORD had ordained from the foundation of the world for your sins. They would have you believe that the Bible is infallible and inerrant and contains no diametrically opposed contradictions or doctrines that run opposed to their superstitious blood shedding belief. To validate the blood-shed offering of Christ, it became necessary to make it a mandatory law - for to do otherwise is to drain the meaning out of the whole book of Leviticus and to break the interpretative connection to their mythological Christ.

The Prophet Micah (740-735 B.C.) condemned these superstitious practices as he compared the two doctrines together in this statement:

Micah 6:6-8 *"Wherewith shall I come before the Lord, and bow myself before the high God? Shall I come before him with burnt offerings, with calves of a year old? Will the Lord be pleased with thousands of rams, or with ten thousands of rivers of oil? Shall I give my first born for my transgression, the fruit of my body for the sin of my soul? He hath showed thee, O man, what is good; and what doth the Lord require of thee, but **to do JUSTLY, and to love MERCY, and to WALK HUMBLY with thy GOD?** "*

OR

Hosea 8:13 *"They sacrifice flesh for the sacrifices of mine offerings, and eat it; but God accepteth them not; now will he remember their iniquity, and visit their sins: they shall return to Egypt."*

MERCY by definition means: **Compassion that forbears punishment even when the law or justice demands it.** Blood offering sacrifices drain all meaning out of Mercy, and Mercy drains all meaning out of blood sacrifices. The two doctrines are mutually exclusive of one another. The two can not co-exist together in the same venue. King David recognized this truth late in his life. Ignoring the existence of the Mosaic law along with its blood sacrifices shows up in the psalms of David.

Psalm 50:8-14 *"I will not reprove thee for thy sacrifices or thy burnt offerings, to have been continually before me. I will take no bullock out of thy house, nor he goats out of thy folds: for every beast of the forest is mine, and the cattle upon the thousand hills. I know all the fowls of the heavens: and the wild beasts of the field are mine. If I were hungry, I would not tell thee: for the world is mine,* and the fullness thereof. Will I eat the flesh of bulls, or drink the blood of goats? **Offer unto God thanksgiving; and pay thy vows unto the Most high.**............"

Psalm 51:14-17 *"Deliver me from blood-guiltiness, O God, Thou God of my salvation. [16]* **For thou desirest not sacrifice;** *else would I give it: thou delightest not in burnt offerings. [17]* **The sacrifices of God are a broken spirit: a broken and a contrite heart, O God, thou wilt not despise."**

Psalm 40:6 reads: **"Sacrifice and offering thou didst not desire;** *mine ears hast thou opened: burnt offering and sin offering hast thou not required."*

By making a comparison between the New Testament author of Hebrews 10:6 and the Old Testament author of Psalm 40:6, I found the New Testament author of Hebrews 10:5 deliberately misquotes this Davidic Psalm 40:6. He edits out the words *"mine ears hast thou opened"* and edits in *"but a body hast thou prepared me."* By doing this the New Testament author of Hebrews twisted the scripture back under the Levitical blood offering covenant in which he refers the reader to the blood-offering of Jesus Christ as the propitiation for our sins. I suspect this act of over editing an Old Testament Psalm by a New Testament author was not an innocent mistake. The purpose was to divert the reader away from the original meaning of the Psalm. Here are the two scriptures together.

Old Testament - Psalm 40:6 *"Sacrifice and offering thou didst not desire;* **mine ears hast thou opened........."**

New Testament - Hebrews 10:5 *"Sacrifice and offering thou wouldest not,* **but a body hast thou prepared me...."**

Hebrews 9:13 *"For if the blood of bulls and of goats, and the ashes of a heifer sprinkling the unclean, sanctifieth to the purifying of the flesh: How much more shall the blood of Christ, who through the eternal spirit offered himself without spot to God, purge your conscience from dead works to serve the living God."*

Here the New Testament author of Hebrews 10:5 is altering the animal blood offering doctrine into a Christ blood offering doctrine. The author's doctrine is still relying on a superstitous blood-sacrifice to appease the anger of the LORD which is nothing more than a giant step backwards.

Ezekiel taught repentance for the remission of sins in the days of King Josiah around 600 B.C. to 586 B.C.

Ezekiel 18:20 states: ***"The soul that sinneth, it shall die. The son shall not bear the iniquity of the father, neither shall the father bear the iniquity of the son:*** .... [21] *But if the wicked will* **TURN FROM ALL HIS SINS** *that he hath committed, and keep all my statutes, and do that which is lawful and right, he shall surely live, he shall not die.* [22] ***All his transgressions that he hath committed, they shall not be mentioned unto him: in his righteousness that he hath done he shall live."***

No superstitious animal sacrifices required here, just turning away from one's past errors was enough.

Another example of over editing was performed by a scribe pretending to be Jeremiah in:

Jeremiah 33:17,18: *"For thus saith the LORD; David shall never want a man to sit upon the throne of the house of Israel;* ***Neither shall the priests the Levites want a man before me to offer burnt offerings, and to kindle meat offerings, and to do sacrifice continually."***

By making a quick reference back to Jeremiah 7:22, the contrast between these two authors becomes obvious. The author of Jeremiah 33:17-18 is making a prediction that never came true and we can see today how inaccurate this author really was. The God of Jeremiah hated animal sacrifices, as he so stated in Jeremiah 7:22.

Jeremiah 7:22 ***"For I spoke not unto your fathers, nor commanded them in the day that I brought them out of the land of Egypt, concerning burnt offerings or sacrifices."***

1. The last King to sit on the throne of Judah was Zedekiah (597-586 B.C.) who was a direct relative of the King of Babylon whose real name, according to the author of 2nd Kings 24:17, was actually Mattaniah.

2. The animal sacrifices ceased when the Romans finally destroyed the Jewish Temple in 70 A.D. Looking back, after the fact, helps when you have 2000 years to see which author was real and which one was the impostor.

The Babylonian authors under the Persian kings would paint a nicer modified version of King David as opposed to other Babylonian authors by editing and removing certain historical sections to hide murders committed by King David. One such example occurs in comparing the Chronicles version against the Samuel version of history. For example, according to the author of 2 Samuel 8:13, David killed 18,000 Edomites in Edom and then stationed his troops there. In the edited Chronicles version in 1 Chronicles 18:13 it was Abishai, not David, who killed those 18,000 Edomites and stationed his troops in Edom. The author of Chronicles edits out the murder of Uriah the Hittite, so King David could obtain his wife Bathsheba. The author edits out and covers up the murder of the first child that was conceived between David and Bathsheba. Whereas the author of 2 Samuel 12:15 writes that the murder of the first child was an act of God for punishing King David for murdering Uriah. Recalling the law of God in Ezekiel.

Ezekiel 18:20 *".... The son shall not bear the iniquity of the father, and the father shall not bear the iniquity of the son."* or the Deuteronomy version in 24:16 quoted again in 2 Kings 14:6 *"....The fathers shall not be put to death for the children, nor the children be put to death for the fathers; but every man shall be put to death for his own sin."*

Obviously God did not kill this child, besides, shortly thereafter David and Bathsheba had yet another son and named him Solomon. So if killing the first child was a punishment for King David, then what redeeming lesson did King David learn from this punishment? If one was to believe the edited version of Samuel, then what was the point of the LORD killing the first child, especially when killing the first child goes against God's own laws? Christians have a hard time reconciling the God that says: *"The children shall not be put to death for the sins of the fathers"* and then are told in their infallible Bibles that God turns right around and kills an innocent child for the sins of the father (King David). So Christianity has to create an apologetic spin machine to cover up all the over editing committed by the Babylonian authors within the King James Bible so as to present it infallible. All the books that wrote about the time of King David and King Solomon such as: 1st & 2nd Samuel, 1st & 2nd Kings, 1st & 2nd Chronicles have undeniably unknown authors of Babylonian origin written between 450 B.C. to 550 B.C. However, there are many Psalms that convey the actual thoughts of King David and there is the book of Ecclesiastes and the Songs of Solomon that convey Solomon's personality traits. Neither of which endorsed the killing or sacrificing of animals as mentioned by the unknown authors from Babylon.

THE KINGS

The following list reveals the names of the kings in chronological order. The first three Kings of Israel reigned allegedly from 1050 B.C. to 931 B.C.

1.King Saul ------- 1050 B.C.
2.King David -------1011 B.C.
3.King Solomon

The King James Bible relates these stories in the books of Kings and Chronicles as: After the death of king Solomon in 931 B.C., the united tribes of Israel split into two kingdoms. The northern kingdom called "ISRAEL" with its capital at Samaria set up its own religion. The southern Kingdom of "JUDAH" with the capital remaining at Jerusalem. After two hundred years in 722 B.C. the northern kingdom fell to the Assyrian Empire, and by 732 B.C. many Israelites were taken into captivity. Most who stayed intermarried and were later known as the despised Samaritans.

The southern kingdom lasted a little over 300 years with reforms coming from kings such as Hezekiah and Josiah along with the preaching prophets such as Jeremiah, Isaiah and Ezekiel. In 586 B.C., the Babylonian Empire under Nebuchadnezzar conquered Judah and destroyed their Temple. Many Israelites (now called Jews) were taken away to Babylon. Daniel served as a high-ranking official under Neuchadnezzar, and Daniel received visions of world kingdoms to come. In 539 B.C., the Medes and the Persians conquered Babylon. The new king, Cyrus, allows the Jews to return to their land and in 520 B.C. work resumes on the restoration of their Temple. This became known as the temple of Zerubbabel. the Jewish governor in those days.

Many Jews remained in the east and never returned, and even those that did return to Jerusalem felt like they were still in exile from God. The Jews had lost their independence and had no king. In 450-435 B.C., leaders such as Ezra and Nehemiah encouraged the Jews to embrace their new religion and Temple which were under the successive kings of the Persians. Prophets ceased after this time. When Alexander the Great conquered the Persians, the Jews fell under control of the Greeks. They revolted in 168 B.C., and had a century of independence before Pompey claimed the land for the Roman Empire. The Jews hope now rested in the prophecies of a Davidic king to come, the Messiah.

The Kings of Israel - Northern Kingdom

1. 933 Jeroboam 1 (933-911) B.C. 20 years
2. 911 Nadab (911-910) 2 years
3. 910 Bassha (910-887) 24 years
4. 887 Elah (887-886) 2 years
5. 886 Zimri (886) 7 days
6. 886 Omri (886-875) 12 years
7. 875 Ahab (875-854) 22 years
8. 855 Ahaziah (855-854) 2 years
9. 854 Joram / Jehoram (854-843) 12 years
10. 843 Jehu (843-816) 28 years
11. 820 Jehoahaz (820-804) 17 years
12. 806 Joash / Jehoash (806-790) 16 years
13. 790 Jeroboam 2 (790-749) 41 years
14. 748 Zechariah (748) six months
15. 748 Shallum (748) one month
16. 748 Menahem (748-738) 10 years
17. 738 Pekahiah (738-736) 2 years
18. 738 Pekah (748-730) 20 years
19. 730 Hoshea (730-721) 9 years

End of the Northern kingdom in 721 B.C.

The Kings of Judah - Southern Kingdom

1. 933 Rehoboam	(933-916) B.C.	17 years
2. 915 Abijam	(915-913)	3 years
3. 912 Asa	(912-872)	41 years
4. 874 Jehoshaphat	(874-850)	25 years
5. 850 Jehoram	(850-843)	8 years
6. 843 Ahaziah	(843)	1 year
7. 843 Athaliah	(843-837)	6 years
8. 843 Joash	(843-803)	40 years
9. 803 Amaziah	(803-775)	29 years
10. 787 Uzziah / Azariah	(787-735)	52 years
11. 749 Jotham	(749-734)	16 years
12. 741 Ahaz	(741-726)	16 years
13. 726 Hezekiah	(726-697)	29 years
14. 697 Manasseh	(697-642)	55 years
15. 641 Amon	(641-640)	2 years
16. 639 Josiah	(639-608)	31 years
17. 608 Jehoahaz	(608)	three months
18. 608 Jehoiakim	(608-597)	11 years
19. 597 Jehoiachin	(597)	three months
20. 597 Zedekiah	(597-586)	11 years

End of the Southern kingdom in 586 B.C.

ISAIAH 53

Isaiah 53 is often referred to by Christians as the foretold scripture that validates Jesus as their blood-shed offering to the LORD for their sins. Chapter 53 requires a thorough examination of the preceding chapters that lead up to it and those chapters that follow. This Chapter also requires a verse-by-verse commentary analysis to determine if Jesus is really the suffering Servant of God or not. The question we are attempting to answer is this: Who is the Suffering Servant in Isaiah 53 - the Righteous Remnant of Israel or Jesus? Is this Chapter speaking about the same Jesus referred to in John 12:38 of the New Testament, as this author quoted Isaiah 53:1?

John 12:38 *"Lord, who hath believed our report? and to whom hath the arm of the Lord been revealed?"*

As I attempt to examine this chapter verse by verse, I will be examining one of the most relied upon Old Testament scriptures that has held Christians hostage to a 2000 year old human blood offering cult. Isaiah Chapter 41 begins to describe who the suffering servant really is. In the original Hebrew texts, there are no chapters listed in numerical sequence. So Chapter 53 starts actually at Chapter 52:13 *"Behold, MY SERVANT....."* **The singular Servant,** referred to by Isaiah in the preceding chapters, is always described to us as **a plural collection of servants called Israel.**

Isaiah 41:8 *"But thou, Israel, art MY SERVANT."* This is always referring to a faithful remnant of prophets, teachers, evangelists devoted to the cause of bringing the light of God's teachings to the Jews and Gentiles.

114

Isaiah 42:1 *"Behold **MY SERVANT**, whom I uphold; **mine elect......"***

Isaiah Chapter 43:10 *"Ye are **(MY WITNESSES)**, saith the Lord; and **MY SERVANT** whom I have chosen..."*

Isaiah Chapter 44:1 *"Yet now hear, **O Jacob MY SERVANT**; and **Israel, whom I have chosen:"***

Isaiah 49:3 *"Thou art **MY SERVANT O Israel,** in whom I will be glorified."*

Isaiah 49:6 *"And he said, It is a light thing that thou shouldest be **MY SERVANT** to raise up the tribes of Jacob, and to restore the preserved of Israel: I will also give thee for a light to the Gentiles, that thou mayest be my salvation unto the end of the earth."*

All of these prior chapters flow into Chapter 53 as a plural, remnant of devoted people (called Israel or Jacob) with one common mission - to bringing the light of God's saving knowledge to the rest of the people of Israel and to the Gentiles. God wanted to deliver his people from their oppressors during the time of their captivity by using his Servant Israel (the righteous remnant). The people went into captivity because the Temple priests practiced and believed in foreign blood-shed sacrifices. If it had not been for this, the righteous remnant of Israel would have been totally destroyed as stated in Isaiah.

Isaiah 1:9 *"Except the God of hosts had left unto us a very small remnant, we should have been as Sodom, and we should have been like unto Gomorrah."*

Isaiah 54:7-8 again refers to the collective plural body of Israel, not to the Messiah (the son of David). It reads: *"...This is the heritage of **the (servants)** of the Lord, and*

their righteousness is of me, saith the Lord."
The knowledge came to the people in the very next chapter of Isaiah 55:7-8. So we have strong indications that the Servant, referred to in Isaiah, is "Israel" both before and after chapter 53. So why do so many Christians believe that chapter 53 is referring to the futuristic blood-offering sacrifice of Jesus? A good clue for this problem is that the King James version has changed some of the Hebrew verbs from the past tense into the future tense, thereby giving a misleading time frame from which an accurate determination can be made. For example, compare Isaiah 53:2 of the Jewish Hebrew translation to Isaiah 53:2 of the King James Version. A comparison of these two renditions reveals a significant difference. The main reason for confusion, I believe, is that certain key words in some verses, have been suspiciously altered from the original Hebrew to the King James version. The reader is thereby misled.

1. Isaiah 53:1 **Hebrew Version** - *"Who WOULD have believed our report, and to whom WAS the arm of the Lord revealed? "*

Isaiah 53:1 **King James Version** - *"Who has believed our report? and to whom IS the arm of the Lord revealed? "*

2. The Hebrew past tense version is more accurate because the arm of the Lord was already revealed to the Gentile nations in Isaiah 52:10 ***"The Lord has revealed His Holy arm to the eyes of all the nations;.........."*** Since Israel has already been established as the Servant in the preceding chapters, this verse is referring to Israel not Jesus.

Isaiah 53:2 **Hebrew Version** - *"And he CAME up like a sapling before it, and like a root out from dry ground; he HAD no features and no splendor; and we SAW him that he HAD no appearance; and how COULD we desire him? "*

Isaiah 53:2 **King James Version** - *"For he SHALL grow up before him as a tender plant, and as a root out of a dry ground: he hath no form nor comeliness; and when we SHALL see him, there is no beauty that we SHOULD desire him."*

Again the past tense version in the original Hebrew is giving the only logical choice (Israel) as the only Servant being talked about here - not Jesus.

3.   Isaiah 53:3 **Hebrew Version** - *"He WAS despised and forsaken by men; a man of pains, and accustomed to illness, and as one from whom we would hide our faces; he WAS despised, and we HAD no regard for him."*

Isaiah 53:3 **KJV** - *"He is despised and rejected of men; a man of sorrows, and acquainted with grief: and we hid as it were our faces from him; he was despised, and we esteemed him not."*

Both renditions are referring back to Isaiah 49:7 which says: *"Thus saith the Lord, the redeemer of Israel, His holy one, to Him who is despised of men, to Him who is abhorred by nations, to Him who is a slave of rulers."* Conclusion - Israel, not Jesus, is talked about here. The Hebrews rendition refers to the servant as accustomed to illness. This certainly does not refer to Jesus. No where does the New Testament refer to Jesus as ever being a slave to rulers, struck down with illness, or abhorred by nations.

4.   Isaiah 53:4 **Hebrew Version**: - *"Indeed he BORE our illnesses, and our pains - he HAS carried them, yet we HAD regarded him plagued, smitten by God, and oppressed."*

Isaiah 53:4 **KJV**: - *"Surely he hath borne our griefs,*

*and carried our sorrows: yet we did esteem **him stricken, smitten of God, and afflicted.***"

Here the KJV reverts back to the past tense, not the future tense. So the only one that can fit this verse is Israel - not Jesus. Besides, Jesus was never plagued or ill. It would be foolish to believe that the Messiah, who healed people at will, walked around hacking and coughing all the time with the plague. Israel was plagued many times for their iniquities, and in most cases it was because they ate the blood-shed sacrifices they made to their gods. Examples of this are found in Psalms and numbers.

Psalm 106:28 *"They joined themselves also unto Baal-peor, and ate the sacrifices of the dead. Thus they provoked him to anger with their inventions: and the **PLAGUE** broke in among them."*

Numbers 11:33 *"And while the flesh was yet between their teeth, the wrath of God kindled and God smote the people with a great **PLAGUE.**"*

5.   Isaiah 53:5 **Hebrew Version** - *"But he WAS pained (BECAUSE OF) our transgressions, crushed (BECAUSE OF) our iniquities; the chastisement of our welfare was upon him, (and with his wounds) we (WERE) healed."*

Isaiah 53:5 **KJV** - *"But he was wounded (FOR) our transgressions, he was bruised (FOR) our iniquities: the chastisement of our peace was upon him; and with his stripes we ARE healed."*

There is a significant difference between these two renditions. The Hebrew translated version states that the Servant was pained (Because of) the transgressions and iniquities of the gentile nations. Again these two renditions are written in the past tense. Jesus is yet to come for another 700 years. So Israel is the Servant here being pained and crushed - not Jesus.

6. Isaiah 53:6 **Hebrew Version** - *"We all (Went) astray like sheep. we have turned, each one on his way, and the Lord inflicted upon him (or, accepted his prayers for) the iniquity of all of us."*

Isaiah 53:6 **KJV** - *"All we like sheep **have gone** astray; we have turned every one to his own way; and the Lord **hath laid** on him the iniquity of us all."*

Israel never taught the Gentile nations the saving knowledge of God. Instead, Israel turned toward the evil practices of the gentiles. Hence they became victims of the very harsh judgments of the Gentiles from which their iniquities derived. Both renditions are referring to the Servant in the past tense. Israel is the Servant here - not Jesus.

7. Isaiah 53:7 **Hebrew Version** - *"He was oppressed, and **he was afflicted,** yet he would not open his mouth; like a lamb to the slaughter he would be brought, and like a ewe that is mute before his shearers, and he would not open his mouth."*

Isaiah 53:7 **KJV** - *"He was oppressed, and he was afflicted, yet **he opened not his mouth:** he is brought as a lamb to the slaughter, and as a sheep before her shearers is dumb, so he openeth not his mouth."*

Israel was often referred to as oppressed sheep in the scriptures. Psalm 44:11 is an excellent example. ***"Thou hast given us like sheep appointed for meat; and hast scattered us among the heathen."*** Israel is being referred to in Psalm 44:11 just like Israel is being referred to in Isaiah 53:7. Again I have to say that both the Hebrew and KJB renditions are in the past tense - not in the future. Israel is the one getting slaughtered here like sheep in verse 7 - not Jesus.

8. Isaiah 53:8 **Hebrew Version** - *"From imprisonment and from judgment he was taken, and his generation who shall tell? For he was cut off from the land of the living; BECAUSE OF the transgression of my people,* **a plague came upon THEM."**

Isaiah 53:8 **KJV** - **"He was taken** *from prison and from judgment: and who shall declare his generation? For* **he was cut off** *out of the land of the living:* **FOR the transgression of my people was he stricken."**

The translated Hebrew version describes the Servant in the plural noun form **(them)** which would rule out Jesus as the Servant in Isaiah 53:8 also. In both renditions the past tense is used. Therefore Israel is the Servant - not Jesus.

9. Isaiah 53:9 **Hebrew Version** - *"And he gave his grave to the wicked, and to the wealthy* **in his deaths,** *because he committed no violence, and there was no deceit in his mouth."*

Isaiah 53:9 **KJV** - *"And he made his grave with the wicked, and with the rich in his death, because he had done no violence, neither was any deceit in his mouth."*

The Hebrew language here indicates that the Servant in verse 9 is a tribe of non-violent people that suffered several deaths. Jesus died only once. Israel is the Servant here - not Jesus.

10. Isaiah 53:10 **Hebrew Version** - *"And the Lord wished to crush him,* **He made him ill, If his soul would acknowledge guilt,** *he shall have descendants (or, he shall see progeny), he shall prolong his days, and God's purpose shall prosper in his hand."*

Isaiah 53:10 **KJV** - *"Yet it pleased the Lord to bruise him, he hath put him to grief: when thou shalt make his soul an offering for sin, he shall see his seed, **he shall prolong his days,** and the pleasure of the Lord shall prosper in his hand."*
The original Hebrew translation describes a Servant in the past tense by God. Yet the servant was promised children, a long life and prosperity if he repents. This verse is again referring to Israel - not Jesus. Why would Jesus need his days prolonged when he was already the Son of God. The Hebrew version says the servant was made ill. Jesus was not ill, nor did he ever have children, and why would he need to acknowledge guilt? This verse does not fit Jesus. Israel is the servant here.

11. Isaiah 53:11 **Hebrew Version** - *"From the toil of his soul he shall see {and he shall} be satisfied, **with his knowledge my Servant will vindicate the righteous before the multitudes, a**nd their iniquities he shall carry."*

Isaiah 53:11 **KJV** - *"He shall see of the travail of his soul, and shall be satisfied: **by his knowledge shall my righteous servant justify many,** for he shall bear their iniquities."*
In both renditions the Servant justifies others through his teaching knowledge - not through a blood-shed sacrifice. Both renditions are in the future tense. Therefore both Israel and Jesus could be this servant. For that matter, a strong argument could be referring to John the Baptist as much as Jesus since he possessed the Knowledge of Salvation according to Luke 1: 76-78. Conclusion: Israel, Jesus or John the Baptist could be referred to here.

12. Isaiah 53:12 **Hebrew Version** - *"Therefore, I will allot him a portion among the multitudes, and with the mighty he* *shall share booty, because he has bared his soul to death, and with transgressors he was counted; he bore the sin of many, and he will { continue to} intercede for the transgressors."*

Isaiah 53:12 **KJV** - *"Therefore will I divide him a portion with the great, and he shall divide the spoil with the strong; because he HATH poured out his soul unto death: and he was numbered with the transgressors; and he bare the sin of many, and made intercession for the transgressors."*

Both renditions describe a servant who will share the spoils of war. The Hebrew word for Booty is **"shalal"**. This word is used throughout the Hebrew Bible to describe the spoils of war in a literal sense. The past tense used in the KJV indicates the servant has already poured out his soul unto death, and was already numbered among the transgressors. So this event had already taken place. It is not referring to or predicting a blood-shed sacrifice 700 years out into the future as the Christians now mistakenly believe it does. Depending on which religious affiliation one belongs to whether it be Jewish or Christian, it has been my experience that those who know the original Hebrew continue to disagree on the identity of the Suffering Servant in Isaiah 53. The Jewish scholars agree with my assessment because they have a personal bias against Jesus as being their Messiah according to their criterias. So they will tell you that Israel is the Suffering Servant - not Jesus. Whereas the Christians and Catholics will disagree with my assessment because they badly need an Old Testament scripture to help them establish the notion that Christ died on the cross for their sins. First and foremost, question everything - even your own conclusions. Use Reason that always leans toward solid objective evidence. Do not assume anything until all evidence and all points of arguments have been exhausted and even then the evidence may not be enough. Using independent thinking and allowing scripture to interpret scripture is a good starting approach. Knowing Latin, Greek and Hebrew is worthless unless one strives to interpret these scriptures with an unbiased mind.

THE LATTER PROPHETS

The Prophets such as Isaiah, Micah and Amos reiterated that the sacrifice of animals was an abomination in the sight of God and Jeremiah and Hosea were equally vocal about these evils perpetrated upon these creations of God. The message from the latter Prophets did not stand out in clear relief because their teachings did not break from Judaism to form a separate belief system. Instead, their prophetic message was absorbed into mainstream Judaism and became still another current running through the history of Israel. Consequently, the warnings against sacrificial blood offerings failed to co-exist with the destructive priestly power structure that was still developing complex rituals of slaughter at the Temple. Not only did the the prophets point out that animal sacrifices were invented by evil priests, they also faced their people with the fact that the violence done to sacrificed animals was reflected in the violence that the humans were willing to inflict upon one another.

PERSONAL THOUGHTS

In the early 1970s Keith Parkinson (my father) was asked to work on a particular section of the Dead Sea Scrolls requested by an Egyptian organization, to determine how many authors were involved in a particular section of the Scrolls. On October 6th 1973 Anwar Sadat of Egypt and the nation of Syria coordinated a surprise attack against Israel known as the Yom Kippur war. Subsequently due to these events, communications between my father and this Egyptian organization were severed. In that particular case study, a thorough understanding of the known author's handwriting strokes, sufficient in number to identify the author in the particular questioned section of the scroll was required. This involved carefully categorizing similarities and peculiarities known only to be made by the one author, until a sufficient, reliable pattern was established, before determining if there were any other authors involved within the questioned section.

When it comes to religion, one man's truth is another man's subjective fantasy, however, these studies are based on no religion nor Atheism, but rather comparing the facts and fictions evident in both these realms. I belong to no church, yet having an awareness that Jesus was a real person with a believable doctrine, I approach this study case with only the interest to clarify the historical note worthy teachings of Jesus. 1 John 4:16 *"God is love, and he who abides in love abides in God, and God abides in him."* The author of this verse, speaks as one of the Apostles, defining God as *"love"*. Love for others is a distinguishable personality trait that separated Jesus from the teachings of the Priests of the Temple. All religions claim the LORD/GOD is a great merciful GOD. None seem to recognize that the LORD of the Old Testament has the same defective personality traits created by their own imaginations, **because any doctrine that has to rely on killing the life of any man or animal for the atonement of others is of the lower occult order.**

PSALM 22

Psalm 22 is another scripture that Christians like to point to and use when backing up their belief that Jesus Christ died on the cross for their sins. Since there are no statements in Psalm 22 that directly refers to the person suffering for anyone's sins, there is not much for me to say. On the surface I think there is a compelling argument that needs to be raised here that supports an argument of a crucified man mentioned in this Psalm. However reason tells me that without actually examining the original questioned document in person, there is not enough evidence to support this conclusion. The first verse tells us that psalm 22 is a psalm of King David and by definition the word **Psalm** means: *A sacred song or poem made towards a Deity.* It is theorized that David, or the author of this psalm, in his suffering, was lifted by the spirit beyond his own experience to mysteriously describe some of the future sufferings of the Messiah.

One needs to ask a reasonable question first. If this was a future prediction of the crucified Messiah, then why didn't the author just write a clear concise future prediction and call it such in the original text? By not doing this, it leaves the door wide open for people's imaginations to fill in gaps that scripture might not have implied. Hiding a vague prophecy of a man suffering in Psalm 22, without addressing the identity issue of the man (by name or position) is confusing to the reader. This is what's causing the debate between Jews and Christians. To start out with a logical approach, one needs to ask logical questions.

1. Why would one bury a vague obscured prophecy within a song or poem?

2. Is the author worried about his writings being edited if he makes his future prediction too obvious?

3. Why didn't the author just come out and say. "This is what the future Messiah will suffer, when it will happen, why and where the Messiah is going to suffer these atrocities?"

When an author doesn't write a clear and concise statement, like this one in Psalm 22, the readers, with predisposed beliefs, will always read into the author's thoughts that might never had existed in the original author's mind. In John 2:19, the only sign Jesus would allow to establish his legitimate authority, was the sign of his resurrection (three days and three nights in the belly of the earth) similar to the story of Jonah spending three days and three nights in the belly of a great fish found in Jonah 1:17. Whether or not the Jonah story was true or just urban legend, Jesus used this story as a point of reference that the hearers could judge his integrity. This one sign Jesus chose to give the Jews, is far more important than a three thousand year old Psalm buried in the Old Testament that could be debated for another thousand years. If one wishes to believe this psalm is referring to Jesus, then there is no harm in believing this, as long as one understands this psalm is not stating the man is dying for anyone's sins then, now or in the future. I can not find any place in the New Testament where Jesus tells the Apostles directly or indirectly that psalm 22 referred to himself.

Christianity would have you focus on verses 16 through 18 in an attempt to establish their argument while disregarding the other verses that appear to be very awkward to attribute to Jesus. Such as these:

Psalm 22:6 *"But I am a worm, and no man;......."*
Psalm 22:12 *" Many bulls have compassed me: strong bulls of Bashan have beset me round."*
Psalm 22: 20 *"Deliver my soul from the sword; my darling from the power of the dog."*

Psalm 22: 21 *"Save me from the lion's mouth: for thou hast heard me from the horns of the unicorn."*

However, the following scriptures are compelling to examine within Psalm 22 that do indicate Jesus as the suffering man within the King James Version.

Psalm 22:16 *"...they pierced my hands and my feet."*
Psalm 22:17 *"I may tell all my bones.............."*
Psalm 22:18 *"They part my garments among them, and cast lots upon my vesture."*

These are strong reasons to believe christians are correct in their assumptions that Psalm 22 is referring to Jesus.

Did King David of Psalm 22, ever have his hands and feet pierced in verse 16? And if he did suffer his hands being pierced, how could he possibly use his hands and feet afterward as a King?

Did David ever have a particular concern over the condition of all his bones in verse 17?

Did David or the author of this psalm have his garments gambled away as written in verse 18? These are all questions that appear on the surface to be difficult to attribute to King David. At best, here are some weak explanations.

1. Psalm 22:16 - " ....*they pierced my hands and my feet."* In a true crucifixion the wrists and ankles are pounded through, not the hands and feet.

2. Psalm 22:17 - *"I may tell all my bones."* This verse is too vague to comment on, not to mention it could apply to a lot of starving cases after many days of being chased by dogs, lions or one's enemies.

3. Psalm 22:18 - *"They part my garments among them,*

127

and cast lots upon my vesture." Sounds like any ordinary mugging in a bad neighborhood to me.

Comparing the Hebrew translation against the King James version, we can begin to see why there is such a difference of opinion on Psalm 22, especially with verse 16.

The King James version of Psalm 22:16
"*For dogs have compassed me: the assembly of the wicked have inclosed me:* **they pierced my hands and my feet.**"

The Jewish version translated from the Hebrew of Psalm 22:17 -"*For the dogs have surrounded me: a band of evildoers encompassed me:* **like a lion {they are at} my hands and my feet.**"

Using the King James Bible version, the focal point of this whole examination is found in Psalm 22 verse 16 referring to the phrase: "*they* **pierced** *my hands and my feet.*" The implication here is that the word translated into English resembles and describes a method of crucifixion that probably did not exist during the time of King David. Five hundred years after the era of King David, the Persians were the first to employ the use of crucifixions (Herodotus 1:128.2; 3:125.3; 3:132.2; 3:159.1). For example: Herodotus tells us that King Darius (mentioned in the Bible in Daniel 6:1-28) had 3000 Babylonians crucified in about 519 B.C. thereby implying that the Davidic Psalm 22 is a future prediction. That is if it is truly talking about a crucifixion. However before we assume this is truly referring to a crucifixion or not, we need to focus on the word 'pierced'. This one word might shed some light on whether this is a true future prediction of a crucifixion or not.

128

Originally the phrase **"karu yadai v'raglai"** which, according to Christians, translated into English meaning - "they pierced my hands and my feet". This is attested by two Hebrew manuscripts from the Dead Sea Scrolls and ten Hebrew manuscripts from the Masoretic text. The oldest known Hebrew manuscripts of Psalm 22 were discovered among the Dead Sea Scrolls at Khirbet Qumran and Nahal Hever. Both the Qumran text (4QPsf) and the Hebrew text (5/6HevPs) reads "they pierced". However they use two different spellings. Remember as you read these Hebrew words, they are always read from right to left. Also remember we are not examining the actual documents in person. Rather we are accepting the definition of these translated words from people that have a personal interest in the final translation. This puts us at a disadvantage. What are the personal beliefs of these people that have direct access to these documents? These are all logical questions as we read these translations.

1.4QPsf;3 manuscripts of the MT "Karu" (vav-resh-kaph)

2. 5/6 HevPs;7 manuscripts of the MT "Ka'aru" (he-resh- kaph)

I can not find any evidence that the Hebrew word **"Ka'aru"** even exists in the Hebrew language, so I will have to default to the word "Karu" to strengthen the christian argument. The word Karu/Ka'aru comes from the root Karah (Kaph Resh Hey). In modern Hebrew this word means "to dig." However in the original older Hebrew this word has additional variable definitions applied to it. For example referring back to Psalm 40:6, if you remember how the author of Hebrews 10:5 edited out the section in Psalm 40:6 **"mine ears hast thou opened"** and replaced it with **"but a body hast thou prepared for me."** Well another Hebrew translation is: "mine ears hast thou digged for me." However translated for the English reader in the King James version it reads "mine ears hast thou opened." Therefore, based on the variable nature of the original word "Karu," I can not agree with the Christian interpretation. They insist it means "pierced" however, it does imply a word which is close - "dug or digged." Translated like this into English properly, it would look like this: "They dug into my hands and my feet." The Jewish argument refers to this word being changed from the word "Ka'ari" (Kaph-aleph-resh-yod) which means "like a lion." On the surface this does not fit the context. Here is what it would look like if that argument was correct: "Like a lion my hands and my feet." or those that believe in the "Ka'ari" version inserted words inside brackets that never existed in the original Jewish writings.

Such a case in point "Like a lion {they maul} at my hands and feet." or "Like a lion {they are at} my hands and my feet."

"Karu" (**vav** resh kaph) -------- means "pierced"
"Ka'ari" (**yod** resh aleph kapf) --- means "like a lion."

These two Hebrew terms are practically identical except for Karu ends with the Hebrew letter "**vav**" and "Kaari" ends with the Hebrew letter "**yod.**" If the original author of Psalm 22:16 wrote "Karu" or "Ka'aru" he used a poor choice of words to describe a crucifixion. A more logical word in Hebrew that means "pierced" would have been "Daqar" found in Zech 12:10 "........... *and they shall look upon me whom they have* '*pierced,*'............".

Another important question that comes to mind is: Why did the author of the King James version correctly translate the Hebrew word "Ka'ari" in Isaiah 38:13 as: "**as a lion,**" yet incorrectly translated the word as "pierced" in Psalm 22:16?

Isaiah 38:13 *".......**as a lion,** so will he break all my bones:......"*

Conclusion: The whole investigation comes down to which word is actually being used in the original manuscripts. I would prefer to examine the actual documents in question to see for myself which word is actually being used in the fragmented scrolls. For me there is not a sufficient amount of evidence to conclude that the entire Psalm 22 is a future description of Jesus. **There is nothing in this 22nd Psalm that would remotely indicate the Man suffering was dying for anyone's sins as Christians are suggesting.** Neither is there enough evidence to indicate that Psalm 22 is referring to King David personally. Perhaps Psalm 22 may only be an imaginary poem written in the form of a song for a musician as stated in the psalm itself.

The Jewish rejection of Christ

Psalm 22 was written to the chief musician upon Aije-leth Sha-har for the purpose of translating it into a song or poem. The Jewish interpretation is correct concerning Psalm 22, however I believe it is a mistake for the Jewish community to reject Jesus entirely. Due to all of the editing involved in the New Testament, one has no choice but to reject the mythological Christ that died on the cross for the sins of others. The editors of the New Testament have gone to a great extent to hide the true historical Jesus from the recorded pages of history. The history of Rome does record a man that was crucified, but they could not produce the body (or the bones) of this man after the fact. The recorded evidence would point to an actual resurrection. If this be the case, the next best thing for Rome would be to cover up the purpose of the resurrection, by spinning a new reason for the crucifixion, (such as twisting the crucifixion of Jesus into a blood-offering doctrine).

The Jewish concept of **"Moshiach"** or **"Messiah"** means "The anointed one", and refers to a mortal human being. The Jewish Messiah concept has little, if anything, in common with the Christian concept of **"Jesus Christ"** as the (Savior) Messiah. Within Judaism, the Messiah is a mortal human being and a descendant of King David. Judaism today is correct in rejecting the Messiah written about by those books attributed to Paul in the King James New Testament. However it is my firm opinion that the Jewish criterias concerning the true historical Jesus is flawed. Besides the five books that make up the Torah, Judaism relies heavily on the following scriptures as being Messianic in nature and they also make up their whole Messianic concept. Following are the specific scriptures, that explain why Jews do not believe in Jesus as their Messiah today.

1. Isaiah chapters 2, 11, 42, 59:20
2. Jeremiah chapters 23, 30, 33, 48:47, 49:39
3. Ezekiel 38:16
4. Hosea 3: 4-5
5. Micah chapter 4:3
6. Zephaniah 3:9
7. Zechariah 14:9
8. Daniel 10:14

1st. He must be one of their own. In other words he must be 100% Jewish. This means that the blood line of both the father and mother must come from the Abraham, Isaac, and Jacob tribe found in Deuteronomy 17:15 and Numbers 24:17.
2nd. He must be a member of the tribe of Judah. Genesis 49:10.
3rd. He must be a direct male descendant of King David and King Solomon. 1st Chron. 17:11, Psalm 89:29-38, Jeremiah 33:17-18, 2 Samuel 7:12-16,

1st Chronicles 22:10, 2nd Chronicle 7:18. However this criteria goes totally contrary to the first two requirements just mentioned.
4th He must re-gather the Jewish people from exile and return them to Israel. Isaiah 27:12-13, Isaiah 11:12.
5th. He must rebuild the Jewish temple in Jerusalem. Micah 4:1.
6th. He must bring world peace. Isaiah 2:4, Isaiah 11:6, Micah 4:3.
7th. He must influence the entire world to acknowledge and serve one God. Isaiah 11:19, Isaiah 40:5, Zephaniah 3:9.

The first two requirements (mentioned above labeled 1st and 2nd) are flawed from the beginning, because even King David, being part Jew and part Moabite, could not fulfill the strict requirements of being the Judah King of Israel. The word of the LORD, in Deuteronomy 23:3, forever banned him and all his descendants. In part the Pharisees accused and rejected Jesus on the grounds of this mixed breed Samaritan background found in John 8:48. So the Jews, with all honesty, should have rejected King David, King Solomon and all his descendants (based on the same criteria founded on the Racist word of the LORD) in **Deuteronomy 17:15.**

Deuteronomy 17:15 *"Thou shalt in any wise set him king over thee, whom the LORD thy God shall choose:* **one from among thy brethren shalt thou set king over thee: thou mayest not set a stranger over thee, which is not thy brother.** *"*

It would have been impossible for any descendant of King David to fulfill the Judah bloodline requirements back then, let alone, any man today to prove he is the Jewish anointed ruler with 2000 years tacked on to this age old requirement. Because of this flawed Jewish requirement, no man could have fulfilled the bloodline requirements and no one did. This is due in part, to the fact that this particular requirement was written by corrupt priests.

Other examples of divergence exists between the **Christian King James Version Translation and the Jewish Hebrew Translation of Daniel.**

Daniel 9:25   **The Christian KJV** - *"Know therefore and understand, that from the going forth of the commandment to restore and to build Jerusalem unto **the Messiah** the Prince shall be seven weeks, and threescore and two weeks: the street shall be built again, and the wall, even in troublous times. 26 after threescore and two weeks shall **Messiah** be cut off, but not for himself: and the people of the prince that shall come shall destroy the city and the sanctuary; and the end thereof shall be with a flood, and unto the end of the war desolations are determined."*

Daniel 9:25   **The Jewish Hebrew Text** - *"And you should know and understand that, from the emergence of the word to restore and build Jerusalem until **an anointed ruler**, [shall be] seven weeks; and [in] sixty-two weeks it will be restored and be built, street and moat, but in troubled times. 26 And after the sixty-two weeks, **an anointed one** will be cut off, and [he] will be no more; and the city and the Sanctuary will be destroyed by people of the coming ruler, and his end will come about like a flood; and by end of the war, there will be desolation."*

In Daniel 9:25-26 there is a divergence of opinion between Christianity and Judaism concerning who the Man in Daniel 9:25 was. Jews would argue that to be officially anointed King, one needed to go through the proper anointing ceremonies at the Temple under the supervision of the

Temple High Priest. Instead Jesus was only anointed by Mary at a house for burial purposes.

John 12:1-8 *"Then **Mary** took about a pint of pure nard, an expensive perfume; she poured it on Jesus' feet and wiped his feet with her hair. But one of his disciples, Judas Iscariot, who was later to betray him, objected, "Why wasn't this perfume sold and the money given to the poor? It was worth a year's wages." "Leave her alone," Jesus replied.* ***"It was intended that she should save this perfume for the day of my burial.*** *You will always have the poor among you, but you will not always have me."*

Consider the fact that the Jewish Temple was controlled by wicked Priests, whose allegiance was towards Tiberias Caesar of Rome. Anyone anointed within the Temple under these circumstances would have made the ceremony meaningless. This made it impossible for Jesus to be anointed King over Israel since he was against the Temple sacrifices and doctrines of the Priests. Therefore, the Jewish anointing argument has no merit.

The false Prophecy in Jeremiah 33:17 is just one of many attempts within the book of Jeremiah that the Jews depended on false authors pretending to be their prophets concerning their future anointed ruler. Note:

In Jeremiah 33:17 it states: **"For thus saith the LORD; David shall never want a man to sit upon the throne of the house of Israel. Neither shall the priests the Levites want a man before me to offer burnt offerings, and to kindle meat offerings, and to do sacrifice continually."**

The last King to sit on the throne of Judah was Zedekiah (597-586 B.C.) who was a direct relative of the King of Babylon whose name according to the author of 2nd Kings 24:17 was actually Mattaniah. Not only were these criterias of the Jews flawed concerning the strict

Judah bloodline for their anointed ruler, but the Jews are also relying on the false predictions coming from fake Scribes pretending to be the Prophets of God. In this case the author of Jeremiah 33:17-18 is pretending to be the Prophet Jeremiah for the purpose of countering the inspired words made in Jeremiah 7:21-24.

CONCLUSION: It is not the written accounts of the Prophets or Apostles that establishes the resurrection as a believable event. Rather, it is the methodical careful attempts by authors of the New Testament to cover up the real teachings of Jesus that leads me to believe the resurrection was an actual event of history. Rome had to contend with an empty tomb and the secret religious societies controlling the Temple could not simply deny the resurrection either. Both were faced with the impossible task of explaining how a man raised his body after a crucifixion, especially when he had challenged them in the first place before the event had occurred. When attempts were made later to edit historical documents by late century copyists such as in the case of the Bible, some of the facts were lost through personal agendas. These desperate actions from the copyists of the the New Testament lends credibility to the fact, a real man with a life changing doctrine once lived. This makes the probability in favor of the resurrection taken place than not. It is my firm opinion that Jesus did raise himself after the crucifixion and the resurrection was a brilliant sign to leave that generation, rather than Jesus being anointed King in a Persian built Temple, overran by Babylonian Priests. Besides Tiberias Caesar would never have received Jesus as the king during that time era. However, the resurrection event did cause Rome to eventually convert to Christianity by 325 A.D., but substituting a counterfeit Christ for their figure head. Thereby editing out the essential teachings of Jesus. This decision to abandon the essential teachings of Jesus left Rome with nothing more than a Levitical/Babylonian religion.

 # CHAPTER 4

THE BLOOD OF Jesus vs.
THE BLOOD OF CHRIST

BABYLON'S APOSTLE PAUL

For the purpose of identifying the conflict between the two doctrines found within the New Testament, it became necessary for me to first identify and separate the teachings of the Pharisee Saul who later became known as Paul. Paul taught the blood of **(CHRIST)** as it were a bloody sacrifice for sins. Whereras, the real historical **(Jesus)** taught that his own blood and flesh had a hidden meaning known only by his faithful followers.

Evidence would suggest that Paul was never a true Apostle of Jesus and Paul's conversion story was a clever fabrication. The latter prophets such as Isaiah, Micah, Jeremiah, Amos and Hosea along with John the Baptist and Jesus would never have endorsed Paul's version of the gospel. There are far more words in the New Testament attributed to Paul than there are words attributed directly from Jesus. Here we have Paul an outsider, upon which, 13 books of the New Testament were attributed to him, without so much as a whiff of suspicion. Out of the twelve apostles chosen by Jesus not one of them endorsed Paul as a fellow apostle in any of their personal writings nor was any of these twelve Apostles given the same privilege to write about Jesus as Paul was given in the King James Bible. Paul never walked or talked with Jesus, nor was Paul ever taught by Jesus personally. Historically Paul was a bounty hunter for a secret religious society known as the Pharisees and the authors highlighted Paul as the central Apostle of the New Testament who mysteriously meets Jesus while on one of his Christian hunting excursions. Paul's history is filled with the beatings and the attempted murders of those that professed to be the true followers of Jesus and in other written historical accounts Paul refers to the actual Apostles of Jesus as miserable men, yet modern Christianity defines Paul as the greatest Apostle of all. In the book of Acts there are different authors having difficulty describing the encounter of Paul with CHRIST on the road to Damascus. The authors can't decide if the men traveling with Paul heard the voice of Christ or not. This claim (Paul being the Apostle of Jesus) led to the development of a whole new religion; a religion that wasn't taught by Jesus, but invented and twisted by Paul. This led to the divergence between **THE BLOOD OF Jesus vs. THE BLOOD OF CHRIST.**

In ACTS 9:3&7, only **Paul fell** to the ground upon seeing the light while *"**the men stood speechless.**"*

However, in ACTS 26:14 the men fell to the ground *"**And when we all were fallen to the earth.........**"*

In ACTS 22:6-9 **the men** with Paul saw the light but **did not hear the voice**.

Acts 22:9: *"And they that were with me saw indeed the light, and were afraid; "**BUT THEY HEARD NOT THE VOICE OF HIM THAT SPOKE TO ME.**"*

However in Acts 9:7: *"And the men which journeyed with Saul stood speechless, "**HEARING A VOICE, but seeing no man.**"*

138

THE BLOOD OF Jesus vs. THE BLOOD OF CHRIST

Essential to learning the hidden teachings of Jesus starts with comparing them with the carnal teachings of Paul. We can compare the teachings of these mutual exclusive doctrines side by side. "**The Blood of the New Testament**" mentioned by Jesus in Matthew 26:28 as compared to "**The Blood of Christ**" taught by Paul recorded in many of the New Testament books attributed to him. The following are excerpts from the teachings of Jesus concerning his essential doctrine: A thorough explanation of the hidden meaning behind **The Blood of the New Testament** is dealt with on page 168-172.

1. John 6:53" *I say unto you,* ***Except ye eat the flesh of the son of man, and drink his blood, ye have no life in you.*** "
2. John 6:54 ***"Whoso eateth my flesh and drinketh my blood, hath eternal life; and I will raise him in the last day."***
3. Matthew 9:13: ***"I will have MERCY, and not sacrifice."***
4. Matthew 12:7: ***"I will have MERCY, and not sacrifice."***
5. Matthew 5:7: ***"Blessed are the MERCIFUL: for they shall obtain Mercy."***
6. Matthew 6:14: ***"For if you forgive men their trespasses, your heavenly Father will also forgive you."***

Paul's teachings of **the blood of Christ** as modified from the Mosaic levitical blood of the covenant:
1. Romans 5:9: *"Much more then, being now justified* ***BY HIS BLOOD,*** *we shall be saved from wrath through him."*

THE BLOOD OF Jesus Vs. THE BLOOD OF CHRIST

2. Ephesians 2:13: *"But now in Christ Jesus ye who sometimes were afar off are made nigh **BY THE BLOOD OF CHRIST**."*
3. Ephesians 1:7: *"In whom we have **REDEMPTION THROUGH HIS BLOOD,** the forgiveness of sins, according to the riches of his grace."*
4. Colossians 1:14: *"In whom we have **REDEMPTION THROUGH HIS BLOOD,** even the forgiveness of sins."*

In no way did Jesus ever teach his Apostles to trust in his physical shed blood for their salvation. A rational question to ask oneself is this. Why would Jesus turn himself into a bloody sacrifice for others, if he had taught everyone for years that he demanded Mercy - not sacrifice? According to Jesus, God's forgiveness was essentually based on forgiving others as they transgressed against you. With this concept, the cycle of revenge and blood-shed is eliminated, and the name of the Creator is reflected. Using rational independent thinking and the writings of the Old Testament Prophets, we deduced that God declared the Mosaic blood covenant of the LORD an evil engineered plot. For how can the blood of any animal purge the conscience from sin? It can only increase the condemnation. Jesus knew he had to confront this doctrine head on. It wasn't good enough to teach against these laws of the Torah. The resurrection was the only way to show, beyond any shadow of doubt, which doctrine was inspired from God.

Paul's gospel is straight forward and simple.

1st Corinthians 15:3 ***"For I delivered unto you first of all that which I also received, how that Christ died for our sins according to the scriptures"***.

There are no Old Testament scriptures that even remotely hint to Jesus dying for anyones sins, nor does Paul quote any Old Testament scriptures to verify and substantiate this statement of his. Instead, the authors of Paul leave it up to the reader to find his elusive scriptures. Even scriptures that Christianity tries to elude to today can not convince the uninformed for very long. Eventually Christians will catch on to this occult scam. The gospel of Paul was later sanctioned as the official STATE religion of Rome in 325 A.D. And this version is still being taught in all denominations of Christianity today. Paul's teachings required no turning away from the doctrine of the Babylonians. Paul simply modified the animal blood offering doctrine as practiced by the Babylonians into a false Christ blood offering doctrine. The author of the book of Hebrews (also attributed to Paul's writings) taught the exact same doctrine and cursed anyone that called " The LORD'S blood of the covenant" an unholy thing.

Hebrews 10:29 "Of how much sorer punishment, suppose ye, shall he be thought worthy, who hath trodden under foot the Son of God, and hath counted **the blood of the covenant,** *wherewith he was sanctified,* **an unholy thing......"**
Paul never once taught the true hidden meaning behind the blood and flesh of Jesus. This is because Paul never knew Jesus personally nor the divine meaning behind the blood and flesh of Jesus. Paul's teaching's relied on the same old mystical superstition that the LORD'S anger has to be avenged by a blood offering sacrifice, thereby making mainline Christianity and their god a modified babylonian religion. In Ephesians, Paul described the crucifixion of Christ as it were a sweet smelling savor unto the LORD emphasizing the same wording found in the book of Leviticus:

Ephesians 5:2 "And walk in love, as Christ also hath loved us, and hath given himself for us an offering and a sacrifice **to God for a sweet smelling savor."** Leviticus 1:

141

9,13,17. Here Paul reveals the psychological profile of the Babylonian LORD that loved the sweet smell of burnt animals on altars. Paul describes the crucifixion of Christ as if he read it right out of the book of Leviticus. There is nothing sweet smelling about human flesh being ripped away from the bones through a scourging and then nailed to a cross. Prior to Paul's alleged conversion, men like Paul (Pharisees) turned the temple of God into a slaughter house for animals. As stated by Jesus it was originally intended to be a House of Prayer built and dedicated to God. By accepting the teachings of Paul, one in essence, is willfully endorsing the crucifixion of a human being, thereby making a believer of this doctrine an accessory to a 2000 year old murder. One in essence is believing that God is incapable of forgiving human beings without first seeing a blood offering to avenge his lust for revenge first, thereby giving God the same personality trait as that of a typical moronic revengeful priest. Jesus taught in Matthew 6:14&15 that showing mercy and forgiveness towards ones neighbor and enemy is the only way to obtain forgiveness from the Father, because this was the way the Father conducted his affairs with men. It was one thing for Jesus to overcome and expose the doctrines of the Temple priests through his resurrection. It is yet another for anyone to assume that he went to the cross to pay for anyone's sins. Christianity would even allow Jesus to be murdered today had they not believed it took place 2000 years ago. Hypothetically speaking, if Jesus came today for the first time instead of 2000 years ago, who would murder him? Remember, according to Paul's gospel in 1st Corinthians Christ must die for our sins.

1st Corinthians 15:3 *"how that Christ died for our sins according to the scriptures".*, or Hebrews 9:22 *"And almost all things are by the law purged with blood; and without shedding of blood is no remission".*

So hypothetically speaking who would murder Jesus today? If you were faced with the choice of either saving your soul by killing Jesus according to Paul's blood covenant LORD or lose your soul for Jesus sake by rejecting the blood covenant and granting Jesus a total pardon from execution, which would you choose?

So hypothetically speaking, if you chose not to murder Jesus today in order to save your soul according to the blood covenant law, why would you believe in the same blood covenant taught by Paul 2000 years ago? To believe in such a doctrine (that allows a human being to die in the behalf of another human or community) makes one an accessory to that murder. To promote such a blood covenant doctrine today is the same as raising your voice and shouting to Pilate: *"CRUCIFY HIM for we need our sins to be washed away by his blood,"* - then sit back and let the Romans carry out this twisted belief. Where is the love and integrity behind that kind of faith? By discerning the teachings and purpose of Jesus correctly, the sign of the resurrection takes away the infected doctrine out of the conscience of an awakened mind.

Within the King James New Testament, the story of the cross represents the focal point from which two doctrines sprang, one of them was true - the other a counterfeit. **Seventy percent of the King James New Testament is written in such a way as to promote Paul's gospel (the blood of Christ) verses the doctrine of the real historical Jesus (the blood of the New Testament).** This is because 13 of the written books of the New Testament are directly attributed to the writings of Paul and not the direct teachings of Jesus himself or his Apostles. Rational sense tells me that if anything has to die (animal or human) for another persons transgressions, then that doctrine is no different than the cultural religions practiced in Babylon.

SLAVERY

Paul endorsed Slavery as an acceptable Godly way of life. It was easy for him to teach this doctrine, because he never was a slave. He was born a Roman citizen with full Roman rights. He never experienced life as a down trodden rejected slave. So how could he ever relate to one? Nor does he teach how one could ever work hard enough to be free again. Rather he teaches others to accept their slavery with fear and trembling while devoting the rest of their life in slavery praising the LORD for their miserable status in life.

1. Ephesians 6:5: *"Servants, be obedient to them that are **your Masters** according to the flesh, **with fear and trembling,** in singleness of your heart, as unto Christ."*

2. Colossians 3:22: *"Servants, obey in all things **your masters** according to the flesh; not with eye-service, as menpleasers; but in singleness of heart, fearing God."*

3. 1st Timothy 6:2: *"And they that have {BELIEVING **MASTERS}**, let them not despise them, because they are brethren; but rather do them service, because they are faithful and beloved, partakers of the benefit. **These things teach and exhort.**"*

Jesus actually taught that no one but himself was to be called Master, and in the teachings of Jesus the greatest among the people was to be considered the greatest servant of all.

1. Matthew 23:10-11: ***"Neither be ye called {MASTERS}:*** *for one is your Master, even Christ. But he that is greatest among you, shall be your servant."*

2. Matthew 7:12: ***"Therefore all things whatso***

ever ye would that men should do to you, do ye even so to them: for this is the law and the prophets."

One merely needs to ask themself these two questions:

1. Would you want anyone to make a fearing and trembling slave out of you?

2. Then why would anyone believe in any doctrine that promotes slavery on others?

Paul made slavery a staple of his religion. This is because slavery was the doctrine of Babylon and Rome.

EQUALITY

Paul taught that women should be ruled by men, and that women should have a sub-ordinate non-existent status in the church. This is a doctrine no one can find Jesus ever teaching. The following statements are allegedly attributed to Paul.

1. Corinthians 11:9: "*Neither was the man created for the woman; but the woman for the man*."

2. Ephesians 5:22-24: "*Wives submit yourselves unto your own husbands, as unto the LORD, For the husband is the head of the wife, even as Christ is the head of the church: Therefore as the church is subject unto Christ, so let the wives be to their own husbands in everything*."

3. 1 Corinthians 14: 34&35: "*Let your women keep silent in the churches: for it is not permitted unto them to speak; but they are commanded to be under obedience, as also saith the law.*" *And if they will learn any thing, let them ask their husbands at home: for it is a shame for women to speak in the church*."

By silencing christian women in the churches, Paul

could limit the amount of verbal opposition raised against him. Paul didn't mind husbands submitting to their wives at home or any where else as mentioned in Ephesians 5:21, but not in the church where Paul preached. By dividing the sexes through silencing the christian women, Paul, with threats of violence, would then condemn and curse anyone that disagreed with him on issues, even if it was an angel from heaven.

Galatians 1:8 *"But though we,or **an angel from heaven**, preach any other gospel unto you than that which we have preached unto you, **let him be accursed**."*

In other words, if you disagreed with Paul and his gospel, you could expect a personal visit from Paul and his henchmen at a later date. One example is found in an ancient Essene Christian manuscript titled, **THE CLEMENTINE HOMILIES AND RECOGNITIONS.** Herein the Apostle Peter describes an incident regarding the Apostles who received a visit from Paul and his band when the Apostles were invited by the high priests at the Temple.

Paul was recorded in history as attacking the Apostles over the interpretation of the word of Jesus. Essene Nazarene Christianity was still true to the teachings of Jesus, being led by James, the brother of Jesus. Paul, an agent of the Babylonian religion tolerated by imperial Rome, then made his first appearance, leading a bloody assault on the Apostles in the Temple at Jerusalem. That vicious attack in which many Christians were murdered by Paul and his henchmen - an historical fact not found in the King James Bible - is described by the Apostle Peter in an ancient Essene Christian manuscript titled, **THE CLEMENTINE HOMILIES AND RECOGNITIONS**; we read:

"... the high priest of the Jewish Temple in Jerusalem had often sent priests to ask us that we might discourse with one another concerning Jesus: when it seemed a fit oppor-

tunity, and it pleased all of our church, we accepted the invitation and went up to the temple. It was crowded with people who had come to listen, many Jews and many of our own brethren. **First the high priest told people that they should listen patiently and quietly....** ***Then, he began exalting with many praises the rite of animal sacrifice for the remission of sins and found fault with the baptism given by our Jesus to replace animal sacrifice....*** "To him our James began to show, by abundant proof that Jesus is the Christ, and that in Him are fulfilled all the prophecies which related to His humble advent. For, James showed that two advents of Him are foretold: one in humiliation, which He has now accomplished; the other in glory, which is yet to be accomplished.... "And when James had plainly taught the people concerning these things, he added this also, that unless a man be baptized in water, in the name of the three-fold blessedness, as the True Prophet taught, he can neither receive remission of sins nor enter the kingdom of heaven: and he declared that this is the prescription of the unbegotten God.... And when James had spoken some more things about baptism, through seven successive days he persuaded all the people and even the high priest that they should hasten straightaway to receive baptism.... **"And when matters were at that point that they would all come and be baptized, Paul and his men entered the temple: and Paul cried out: 'Oh men of Israel, why are you so easily influenced by these miserable men?' He began to excite the people and raise a tumult... and drive all into confusion with shouting, and to undo what had been done by James. Paul rebuked the priests for having listened to James, and, like a madman, began to excite the priests and people to murder James and the brethren, saying 'Do not hesitate; grab them and pull them to pieces.' Paul then, seizing a strong brand from**

147

the altar, set the example of smiting. Then others also, seeing him, joined in the beating. Much blood was shed. Although James and the brethren were more numerous and more powerful they rather suffered themselves to be killed by an inferior force, than to kill others. Paul attacked James and threw him headlong from the top of the steps; and supposing him to be dead left him."

The actions of Jesus at the Temple incited the high priests to destroy him, and it was the resurrection of Jesus that will ultimately destroy the BLOOD COVENANT OF THE LORD. The different interpretations over the Sabbath, the treatment of God's creations on altars (animals) are obvious. In every case the doctrine of Jesus leads toward preserving life, whereas the central doctrine of Paul always leads to a society full of slaves, Roman masters and murderers.

The Essene's and Ebionites were edited out of the Bible completely, yet, it was from Qumram, the southern community of the Essenes, that John the Baptist most likely came from. This community did not attach themselves to the violent blood shedding cults of the Jewish Temple (also known as the Babylonian inspired Pharisees and Saducees). Another group of people identfied with Jesus of Nazareth were the Ebionites. These were the ebionim, the 'poor in spirit' referred to in the Beatitudes found in Matthew 5:3. Like Jesus the Ebionites had a respect for all life, and subsequently were non-violent and non-revengeful people by practice.

When Paul finished his work for Rome, he most likely disappeared into, what I suspect to be some "Secret society Protection Relocation Program". Paul was never to be heard from again. There is no historical records of Paul being executed by Rome or by anyone in history. **Paul just disappears.** One important fact to keep in mind is that Roman citizens, like Paul, were rarely, if ever executed. Besides, Rome had a vested interest in preserving the teachings of Paul. Paul's teachings fell in line with the old gods Rome had worshipped, being that his teachings produced a belief in blood-shed, slavery, bondage, and inequality. We are also left with silly contradictory statements made by good Paul/bad Paul throughout the New Testament such as this example:

Galatians 6:2 *"Bear ye one another's burdens, and so fulfill the law of Christ."*

Galatians 6:5 *"For every man shall bear his own burden."*

The author of 2nd Timothy chapter 4 has Paul in a Roman jail saying these parting words to his followers as he tries to make himself into an offering unto the LORD.

2 Timothy 4:6 *"For I am now ready to be offered, and the time of my departure is at hand."*

So out the back door Paul went and retired I suspect. Since Rome could not refute the resurrection and many inside the Roman government were converting over to this resurrected man, it became Rome's best interest to adopt Paul's teachings and twist the purpose of the crucifixion back under a blood-shed sacrifice, thereby making Jesus a sacrificed Roman Deity. By preserving the teachings of Paul, Rome could then redirect the Roman empire back under their old Babylonian/Roman deities. By simply turning Jesus into a final fulfillment of the old Levitical/Babylonian law, Rome preserved the Torah's Holy Virus (The LORD'S Blood of the covenant). This made Christianity more tolerable to become the official STATE religion of Rome by Constantine in 325 A.D. As long as religions accept **Exodus 24:8 "The Blood Of the Covenant"** allegedly initiated on Mount Sinai, they will always remain infected with this psychological mental disorder and remain separated from the true teachings of Jesus. This doctrine in Exodus 24:8 believes God is a God that demands punishment for all sin and he needs to satisfy that revenge, rather than changing and amending peoples evil ways through Mercy. Jesus came to destroy the bloody sacrifices laws grafted onto the Torah. The road toward the occult is paved with doctrines that shed innocent blood for the atonement of sins. These superstitous blood-offering cults serve no other purpose then to rob, kill, and destroy life under the pretense of atonement. It is odd that we derive the word human from the word humane. Yet the definition of the word humane is:

"HUMANE" - marked by compassion, sympathy, or consideration for humans or animals.

Whereas the word "inhumane" is defined as:

"INHUMANE" - Lacking and reflecting lack of pity and compassion for humans or animals.

THE DEAD SEA SCROLLS

In January of 1947 a young shepherd boy called Juna, while herding his goats, had strayed up near some caves. There the boy stumbled upon the first findings of the Dead Sea Scrolls in a cave above Khirbet Qumran, near the north end of the Dead Sea. Within a fairly short time after the discovery, the historical, paleographic, and linguistic evidence, including carbon-14 dating, established that the scrolls and the Qumran ruin were dated from the third century B.C. to 68 B.C. They were indeed ancient - dating back to the late Second Temple Period. Since their discovery nearly half a century ago, the scrolls, and the identity of the nearby settlement, have been the object of great scholarly and public interest, as well as heated debate and controversy. While other scrolls have been discovered since in caves all along the Dead Sea, the scrolls at Qumran are by far the most important (as far as Christians are concerned) because they are the only ones throughout the Dead Sea region that pre-date, or are contemporary with the time of Jesus Christ. Most scholars have identified the Qumran brotherhood with the Essenes, a Jewish sect as described by Josephus and Philo.

Although many Christians would like the information in the scrolls to be confined to the world of academia, it will increasingly impact traditional Christianity. Comparatively little was known about the Essenes, although ancient historians like Josephus and Philo wrote about them and were impressed by their lifestyle and their teachings. But until this century, it was assumed they were a monolithic group of believers, who lived in the Judean wilderness. It is thought that groups (such as the Essenes) separated from mainstream Judaism at this time because they could no longer participate in services and a way of life they considered blasphemous. Calling themselves the Sons of Zadok, the Essenes held faithful to the priestly (Zadokite) line of succession. They objected to slavery and Temple sacrifice and followed a solar calendar at odds with the Levitical lunar calendar of Judaism; this almost ensured separation, for festivals and times of worship fell on completely different days. They lived in small communities on the outskirts of villages and cities.

The Order of Nazorean Essenes is not opposed to Qumran, having been an Essene settlement at one period of its occupation, but the Order does recognize that most of the Dead Sea Scrolls found in caves near Qumran are **NOT Essene**. The more likely explanation is that the Dead Sea Scrolls were left in Qumran caves for temporary safe keeping when the Zealots were fleeing the Romans. This theory is backed up by the fact that many Dead Sea Scrolls fragments were found at Masada where the Zealots made their last stand against the Romans, and were destroyed. Had the Zealots survived Masada, they would have no doubt returned to Qumran to retrieve their scrolls. The 800 or so scrolls also indicate they were written by a multitude of scribes, far too many to have been created in house by a small sect, thus strengthening the probability that they were brought to Qumran from other locations. Internal writings within the Scrolls indicate their authors accepted Yahweh as God and the Law of Moses as binding. **We know from historians that the Nazoreans Essenes rejected the Torah and worshipped the Great Creator of Life instead of Yahweh the LORD.**

Internal writings of the Scrolls also bears out the fact the owners of the libraries were warlike Zealots, not pacifist Essenes as Pliny, Philo and Josephus all indicate. Amongst the Dead Sea Scrolls there exists the War Scroll which is anything but pacifist. We know that the Essenes disapproved of slavery; yet the Dead Sea Scrolls allowed such inhuman behavior. The Essenes were vegetarian and shunned animal sacrifices; yet the Dead Sea Scrolls allowed such slaughter. The Essenes were communal with their possessions; yet the Dead Sea Scrolls speaks of personal ownership of property, although the Community rule does seem to prescribe community of goods after the third year. This practice seems quite Nazorean but may indicate simply some Nazorean influence in Zealot circles.

The historian Pliny spoke of the Essenes as being near and above Ein Gedi.

"On the west side of the Dead Sea, but out of range of the noxious exhalations of the coast, is the solitary tribe of the Essenes, which is remarkable beyond all other tribes in the whole world, as it has no women and has renounced all sexual desire, has no money, and has only palm-trees for company. Day by day the throng of refugees is recruited to an equal number by numerous accessions of people tired of life and driven thither by the waves of fortune to adopt their manners. Thus through thousands of ages — incred-

ible to relate — a race in which no one is born lives on forever; so prolific for their advantage is other men's weariness of life! Lying below these (Essenes) was the formerly town of Engedi, second only to Jerusalem in fertility of its land (#) and in its groves of palm trees, but now like Jerusalem a heap of ashes. Next comes Masada, a fortress on a rock, itself also not far from the Dead Sea. This is the limit of Judaea." **Pliny the Elder on the Essenes,. Natural History Book 5, Chap XVIII, 73**

There were Essenes who lived a monk-like existence, isolated at Qumran, but there were also those who lived in family units in and around Jerusalem, and in other parts of Palestine. Just as the term "Christianity" encompasses a variety of beliefs and lifestyles, so does Essenism. And as the information contained in the scrolls is more widely disseminated, it becomes apparent that along with the Pharisees and Sadducees, the Essenes were an important religious influence in the time of Jesus. Like them, Jesus opposed the slaughter of animals at the Jerusalem Temple (John 2:13-16). Like them, he included women as disciples and said that for females, as well as for males, their most important function was spiritual, not biological (Luke 11:27,28). And like these Essenes, Jesus taught, and lived by the principle of nonviolence. He even went to his death refusing to overcome violence by violence, telling his disciples that those who lived by the sword would die by the sword (Matt. 26:52). How can Christianity reconcile *"the book of the wars of the LORD "* in Numbers 21:14 with Jesus.

From the beginning, there were always groups of Christians who sought to follow the teachings of Jesus. But as the centuries went by, principles of nonviolence, the equality of women, along with various other teachings, were expunged from mainstream Christianity.

Those who insisted on living out these principles, claiming that only they were the true followers of Jesus, were branded as heretics. The churches eliminated their influence by eliminating them in a variety of ways.

Another principle by which these "heretics" lived also reflected Essene teachings. They were similar to vegetarians, and their refusal to eat the flesh of animals was a logical extension of the rule of nonviolence, unlike the Christians of today, who fall into the category of the Aletnu tribes along the region of the world known as the Ring of Fire. As these people imagined that their volcanic god required a young virgin to be sacrificed for the atonement of the whole community, likewise Paul's version of Christianity is ensnared with the same psychological devise written by the authors of Paul within the alleged infallible King James Bible. Nowhere within the New Testament does John the Baptist state that "the Messiah will die for the sins of others", nor will one find Jesus making any such similar statements. There is only one New Testament sourch from which these beliefs originated and that is from the New Testament books attributed to Paul's writings. Due to the teachings of Paul, Christianity has taken on the same carnal habits practiced by their Roman Christian ancestors by consuming animals in violation of the prime commandment of Jesus and the belief that the shedding of the Saviour's blood will redeem them from the wrath of the LORD. Children today are subliminally endoctrinated into this concept that someone must die for the transgressions of the community, to appease the vengeance of their mystical LORD through occult fantasy stories such as: The Chronicles of Narnia by C.S.Lewis.

Before Christianity can proclaim the actual Gospel of Jesus and change others, they will need to renounce the beliefs that holds them captive.

1. The Blood of the Covenant. Exodus 24:8

2. Christianity will have to recognize their King James Bible is flawed based upon the above mentioned doctrine and is thereby not infallible.

To solve this problem, one has to change the infected thinking process from which human actions are first derived. To expect better results, a new understanding needs to be embraced and the old way of thinking will automatically be discarded. Albert Einstein said it best when he said these words:

"It is impossible to get out of a problem by using the same kind of thinking that took to get you into it." **Albert Einstein**

The fundamental problem of Christianity is that it has embraced a human blood-offering sacrifice as the central focus of their religion. Just like the alcoholic that embraces the bottle for comfort, Christianity embraces the Babylonian/Levitical blood covenant doctrine I call **The HOLY VIRUS.** Christianity has embraced this corrupted interpretation version for so long, that some will never accept the real purpose behind Jesus going to the cross, even if Jesus came and told them in person. To believe Jesus was sent to shed his blood for a price for all your sins is simply absurd. Finding a solution to this flawed blood-offering doctrine will require exposing this doctrine for the well engineered fraud that it is and replace it with the true historical teachings of Jesus.

MODERN BIBLES

The Bibles printed today are more flexible in their key interpretations of scriptures than the King James Bible. Jeremiah 7:22-23 for example, are just two Bible versions released in 1978 and 2004 where authors edited in their own interpretation of Jeremiah 7:22.

The New International version and the Devotional Bible reads like this:

NIV and Devotional version of Jeremiah 7:22 *"For when I brought your forefathers out of Egypt and spoke to them, I did not JUST give them commands about burnt offerings and sacrifices."*

There is no Hebrew manuscript that supports these newer Bible versions. (i.e. the addition of **"JUST "** Note this addition changes the whole meaning of the Hebrew statement into a positive statement, rather than a negative statement as compared to the original King James Version.

KJV Jeremiah 7:22 *"For I spake not unto your fathers, nor commanded them in the day I brought them out of the land of Egypt, concerning burnt offerings or sacrifices."*

The world does not appear to be lacking in different versions of the Bible. Here are just a few.

MAINSTREAM BIBLES

1. King James Bible 1611
2. American Standard Version 1901
3. Revised Standard Version 1952
4. New English Bible 1970

5. Good News Bible 1976
6. New American Standard Bible 1977
7. New International Version 1978
8. New Revised Standard Version 1990
9. The Message 1993
10. Contempory English Version 1995
11. New International Reader's Version 1996
12. English Standard Version 2001
13. Prayer Devotional Bible 2004

NON-MAINSTREAM BIBLES

1. The Amplified Bible
2. New Living Translation
3. The New Translation by James Moffatt
4. The New King James Version
5. Darby Translation Bible
6. New American Bible
7. New Century Version
8. Phillips New Testament Version
9. 21st Century King James Version
10. World Wide English (New Testament)
11. Young's Literal Translation
12. Wycliff's New Testament
13. International Children's Bible
14. The Living Bible
15. Natural Equivalent Translation

The true test of any Bible is found in the way it ultimately changes the conscience of the people. Look closely; has Christianity or any religion really changed people for the better or are religions just manipulating their bibles to satisfy their predisposed beliefs?

THE GOSPEL OF THE HOLY TWELVE

My research on the King James Bible has revealed that there are conflicts within the Old Testament and contradictions of doctrine between Jesus and Paul within the New Testament. My focus then, was directed towards searching out a version of the Gospel that had not been obviously tampered with by Rome or some zealot religious group with a hidden agenda. There is one complete uncopyrighted New Testament version that has captured my attention concerning its assertion to be the actual Gospel of the true historical Jesus and written collectively by the actual twelve Apostles. Even though it is too early for me to endorse this version as the actual words of Jesus, I can not find any psychological problems written within its pages. In fact the wisdom written within this version is filled with sound indepth explanations. **I find myself compelled to include this uncopyrighted version freely within this book, because the reader is not going to find this version in any christian book store nor will the reader find this version endorsed by any corporate institution due to its life changing doctrine**. This version, also known as the Gospel of the Perfect Life, is considered an original, unaltered New Testament version. This version needs further investigations and proper dating for authenticity. The one requirement Jesus made upon his Apostles was that the Gospel be given out freely, just as the Apostles received it freely. This would have made Jesus the author of the Gospel, while the Apostles were collectively the only authorized distributers or publishers of the Gospel.

Matthew 10:7&8 *"And as ye go, preach, saying, The kingdom of heaven is at hand. Heal the sick, cleanse the lepers, raise the dead, cast out devils: FREELY YE HAVE RECEIVED, FREELY GIVE."*

This historical version was translated from the original Aramaic language and edited by the Rev. Gideon Jasper Richard Ousley in 1892. He obtained this version from a Buddhist monastery in Tibet where it was hidden by some of the Essene community for safety. Common reason tells me this version has merit and that the true records of Jesus would have been the collective work of all twelve Apostles, rather than the botched up edited conflicting accounts now known as the four Gospels of the King James Bible. It makes better sense that the Creator would preserve the whole original Gospel for any future close examination.

The Gospel of the Holy 12 records Judas as one that always pressed to infiltrate this group and not as one of the original 12 Apostles as being taught in the King James Bible. This version also makes no mention of Paul or any of his influences. It makes better sense if one were to ask, why would an all wise Son of God select a couple of corrupt men such as Judas and Paul to become his Apostles? The correct names of all the Apostles within **the Gospel of the Holy 12** are found in Lection 17 or XVII verse 1-3.

The names of the 12 Apostles

1. **Peter**, called Cephas, for the tribe of Reuben.
2. **James**, for the tribe of Naphtali
3. **Thomas,** called Dydimus, for the tribe of Zabulon.
4. **Matthew**, called Levi for the tribe of Gad.
5. **John**, for the tribe of Ephrain.
6. **Simon**, for the tribe of Issachar.
7. **Andrew**, for the tribe of Joseph.
8. **Nathanael**, for the tribe of Simeon.
9. **Thaddeus**, for the tribe Zabulon.
10. **Jacob**, for the tribe of Benjamin.
11. **Jude**, for the tribe of Dan.
12. **Philip**, for the tribe of Asher.

Appointed along with these 12 Apostles were 12 Prophets that Jesus personally appointed to guide each

Apostle in wisdom. In fact the whole original Gospel of the Holy 12 will captivate and answer the serious questions of anyone searching for the esoteric teachings of the true historical Jesus. This Nazirene version addresses the very problem that the King James version tries to cover up. For example, in the Gospel of the Holy Twelve, Jesus addresses the issue of blood offerings. There is no room for doubt which side Jesus is on concerning the blood-offering sacrifices performed on mount Sinai and God's denial statement in Jeremiah concerning these heinous acts on mount Sinai. Note:

In Section 4 Lection 33 verse 1-4 of the Gospel of the Holy Twelve reads:

"Jesus was teaching his disciples in the outer court of the temple and one of them said unto him: Master, it is said by the priests that without shedding of blood there is no remission. Can then the blood offering of the law take away sin? ***And Jesus answered: NO BLOOD OFFERING, OF BEAST OR BIRD, OR MAN, CAN TAKE AWAY SIN, FOR HOW CAN THE CONSCIENCE BE PURGED FROM SIN BY THE SHEDDING OF INNOCENT BLOOD? NAY, IT WILL INCREASE THE CONDEMNATION."*** *"The priests indeed receive such offering as a reconciliation of the worshippers for the trespasses against the law of Moses,* ***but for the sins against the law of God there can be no remission, save by repentance and amendment.*** *Is it not written in the prophets, Put your blood sacrifices to your burnt offerings, and away with them, and cease ye from the eating of flesh, for I spoke not to your fathers nor commanded them, when I brought them out of Egypt, concerning these things?"* See also Jeremiah 7:21-22.

Also found in the Essene New Testament - The Gospel of the Holy Twelve Section 6 Lection 51 verse 15. Jesus stated this: *"As also Jeremiah bear witness when he saith, concerning blood offerings and sacrifices I the Lord God commanded none of these things in the day that ye came out of Egypt, but only this I commanded you to do, righ-teousness, walk in the ancient paths, do justice, love mercy, and walk humbly with thy God."*

The King James Bible depicts Jesus as one that killed God's creatures for survival, cursed trees, and called Gentile people "dogs" found in Matthew 14:19-20, Luke 24:42, John 21:10-12, Mark 11:14, and Matthew 15:17. With these edited-in accusations, the unknown editors of the King James New Testament left their own personality profile upon the Christ they promoted. This is indicative of authors editing out the real Jesus from history. All these accusations about Jesus never show up in the New Testament version called "The Gospel of the Holy Twelve". The evidence of history points to this: Out of respect toward all life created by his heavenly Father, Jesus would only eat and drink from food grown from the soil. In John 14:15 Jesus is quoted as saying; "**If you love me keep my commandments**". The Twelve Commandments of Jesus demands a personal involvement from the practitioner and requires no dependance on blood sacrifices. **In fact, the blood of the New Testament symbolically means the Twelve Commandments.** The Ten Commandments given by Moses never changed the nomadic tribe in Exodus 20 and the Ten Commandments do not change people today. It is essential in the search of the Creator to discern the difference between the long list of brutal blood offering sacrifices allegedly dictated by the LORD to Moses in Leviticus and Numbers as opposed to the actual Twelve Commandments given by Jesus. One set of laws leads a person down a destructive road associated with religious vindictive psychopaths, while the other set of laws direct an individual down a path full of knowledge of the Creator and respect for all his fellow creatures.

ROMANS 13
PAUL'S LEGACY

Justice according to Paul was best left up to the sword bearing Romans. In Romans13:1-7 Paul encouraged his followers to pay tribute to such men that lived and died by the sword and called these ruling sword owners *"the ministers of God"*. When a lie is perceived within Christianity to be the truth, it becomes absorbed as distorted reality, such as in the case of Paul appointing himself as an Apostle of Jesus and the Romans as the ministers of God. Jesus never taught such absurd notions as discussed by Paul in Romans 13:1-7. The truth is, Jesus never commissioned anyone under Roman jurisdiction to judge anyone at all, let alone his own followers with the use of the Roman sword.

Today judicial systems owe part of their existence to Paul and the Roman civil law. Societies today expound upon the separation of church and STATE, yet provide only one venue from which people are judged. Judicial systems provide prison chapels for the offender, yet the offender will, in many cases, pretend to be born again by converting to Paul's blood-covenant LORD. Once released, most fail to successfully integrate back into society and within two years of their release, statistically 75% are again back in prison. Most of the remaining few that never return simply find clever legal ways to continue their stealing and extorting from others. **Judicial systems can not figure out how to change the offender, because they have not first figured out how to change themselves.**

Of course the whole judicial system is far more complex than I am making it out to be, but ultimately changing the offender into a protector and keeper of his fellow man is the objective. A life changing doctrine has to be delivered first before true change can be expected to oc-

162

cur. It is only necessary to have STATE judicial systems when the offender refuses to amend his ways, at least then, the offender decides by his own conduct, which venue he or she is to be judged in. Given the fact that Christianity today depends exclusively on the STATE for their daily bread, is it any wonder why the STATE has become their cradle to grave LORD.

Whether one believes they are an Atheist or believer, within a secular State society, the STATE ultimately becomes the highest authority, thereby making the STATE both god and religion over the Atheist and believer. STATE judicial systems, by their own actions, have assured themselves a future full of repeat offenders by applying the same revenge payment for sin approach applied by the priests of the old blood covenant. With Christianity accepting Paul's version of the blood of Christ, Christianity has forfeited the teachings of Jesus, for the perception of the STATE, thereby leaving the Christians subject only to the STATE, leaving the powers of the church a mere delusion. The truth of the matter is this, men create constitutional STATE venues for the sole purpose to contract outside God's venue so they can write their own laws to exploit his fellow man, but these men depend on the perception and consent of the governed to make it all legal. **The STATE acts on Perception** and it is by **consent** that instituted governments derive their just powers.

*"governments are instituted among men deriving their just powers from the **consent** of the governed."*
The Declaration of Independence

Once the Christians decide to take away their **perception** and **consent**, the legal powers of the STATE cease to exist.

ISAIAH 11:6-9

Isaiah described how even the animals would know who Jesus was and their wild nature would disappear in sight of this particular descendant of Jesse.

Isaiah 11:1&2 *"And there shall come forth a rod out of the stem of Jesse, and a Branch shall grow out of his roots." And the spirit of God shall rest upon him, the spirit of wisdom and understanding, the spirit of counsel and might........"*

Isaiah 11:6 *"The wolf also shall dwell with the lamb, and the leopard shall lie down with the kid; and the calf and the young lion and the fatling together;........"*

Isaiah 11:7 *"And the cow and the bear shall feed;* their young ones shall lie down together: and the lion shall eat straw like the ox."

Isaiah 11:10 *"And in that day there shall be a root of Jesse, which shall stand for an ensign of the people; to it shall the Gentiles seek: and his rest shall be glorious."*

The Gospel of the Holy Twelve Lection VI:17-19 explains in greater detail how that Jesus is the root and branch of Jesse and how he personally identified himself with the animals that were treated inhumanely by mankind upon the earth found in Isaiah 11:1 & 10. However, the New Testament authors of the King James Bible completely ignore this obvious fulfillment. In fact, the New Testament authors go out of their way to discredit Jesus by making no attempt to mention the connection between Jesus and the plight of animals, not alone the obvious Jesse/Davidic connection. Why is that? Is it possible, the four gospels of the New Testament King James Bible were edited, in such a way, as to only reveal those personality traits they wanted to present?

THE TWELVE
COMMANDMENTS OF JESUS

The twelve commandments of Jesus only show up in the The Gospel of the Holy 12 found in Lection XLVI 7-22. Practicing these twelve commandments, people were born into another doctrine known only by those that were taught by Jesus personally. These 12 commandments would never fit into the typical political corporate world of today, however the King James version fits into the modern political/corporate world perfectly and is even endorsed by the politicians. One merely has to read the first three commandments of Jesus to see how it conflicts with the profits of the modern corporate world thinking. The Babylonian priests of the Jewish Temple had the same problem with the doctrine of Jesus in their era.

7. AND Jesus said unto them, Behold a new law I give unto you, which is not new but old. Even as Moses gave the Ten Commandments to Israel after the flesh, so also I give unto you the Twelve for the Kingdom of Israel after the Spirit.

8. For who are the Israel of God? Even they of every nation and tribe who work righteousness, love mercy and keep my commandments, these are the true Israel of God. And standing upon his feet, Jesus spake, saying:

9. Hear O Israel, JOVA, thy God is One; many are My seers, and My prophets. In Me all live and move, and have subsistence.

1. *10 Ye shall not take away the life of any creature for your pleasure, nor for your profit. nor yet torment it.*

2. *11. Ye shall not steal the goods of any, nor gather lands and riches to yourselves, beyond your need or use.*

3. *12. Ye shall not eat the flesh, nor drink the blood of any slaughtered creature, nor yet any thing which bringeth disorder to your health or senses.*

4. *13. Ye shall not make impure marriages, where love and health are not, nor yet corrupt yourselves, or any creature made pure by the Holy.*

5. *14. Ye shall not bear false witness against any, nor wilfully deceive any by a lie to hurt them.*

6. *15. Ye shall not do unto others, as ye would not that others should do unto you.*

7. *16. Ye shall worship One Eternal, the Father-Mother in Heaven, of Whom are all things, and reverence the holy Name.*

8. *17. Ye shall revere your fathers and your mothers on earth, whose care is for you, and all the Teachers of Righteousness.*

9. *18. Ye shall cherish and protect the weak, and those who are oppressed, and all creatures that suffer wrong.*

10. *19. Ye shall work with your hands the things that are good and seemly; so shalt ye eat the fruits Of the earth, and live long in the land.*

11. *20. Ye shall purify yourselves daily and rest the Seventh Day from labour, keeping holy the Sabbaths and the Festival of your God.*

12. *21. Ye shall do unto others as ye would that others should do unto you.*

22. And when the disciples heard these words, they smote upon their breasts, saying: Wherein we have offended. O God forgive us: and may thy wisdom, love and truth within us incline our hearts to love and keen this Holy Law.

THE BLOOD OF JESUS MATTHEW 26:28

"For this is MY BLOOD OF THE NEW TES-TAMENT, which is shed for the remission of sins."

Nowhere in the New Testament will you find Jesus even remotely saying *"My **shed blood** will pay the price for the sins of others"*. The true mystery is in the proper interpretation of the blood that Jesus spoke about.

In lection 33 verse 1- 4 (the Gospel of the Holy twelve) Jesus was asked this question.

*1 "And it came to pass as he sat at supper with his disciples one of them said unto him: **Master, how sayest thou that thou wilt give thy flesh to eat and thy blood to drink, for it is a hard saying unto many?***

*2 And Jesus answered and said: The words that I speak unto you are Spirit and they are life. **To the ignorant and the carnally minded they savor of bloodshed and death, but blessed are they who understand.***

3 Behold the corn which groweth up into ripeness and is cut down, and ground into the mill, and baked with fire into bread! OF THIS BREAD IS MY BODY MADE, which you see: and lo the grapes which grow on the vine unto the winepress, and are plucked and crushed in the winepress and yield the fruit of the vine! of this fruit of the vine and of the water is made my blood.

*4 **For the fruits of the trees and the seeds of the herbs alone do I partake, and these are changed by***

the Spirit into my flesh and my blood. OF THESE ALONE AND THEIR LIKE SHALL YE EAT WHO BELIEVE IN ME, AND ARE MY DISCIPLES, FOR OF THESE, IN THE SPIRIT COME LIFE AND HEALTH AND HEALING UNTO MAN."
So when these words were first spoken, within the context of Matthew 26:28, Jesus was simply stating, while holding up the drinking vessel full of the fruit of the vine:

"For this is MY DOCTRINE OF THE NEW TESTAMENT, which is pour out for the remission of sins."
The fruit of the vine, which made up his blood and the bread made up his body, when drank and eaten with full understanding, represented the doctrine of saving and preserving other life by eating only those foods originally intended for mankind to eat and drink, instead of consuming and sacrificing life upon occult altars as the occult Temple Priests had performed in Jerusalem. The doctrine of Jesus is a doctrine of preservation and respect for all of God's creatures, and this doctrine should not be misconstrued to be a life style of vegetarianism. There is a vast difference between following the commandments of Jesus, for the purpose of involving one's mind with the commandments of the Creator, verses the vegetarian life style which does not contain the commandments of Jesus and is strictly a different life style. Besides, the average vegetarian, animal worshipping religions and animal rights groups would put the welfare of animals over that of their fellow human beings. Jesus turned people away from their carnal meat appetites and from their superstitious blood-offering practices. Jesus called these the true followers of God and these would be the people forgiven for all their past transgressions. Jesus was not teaching that his blood would become a blood offering for sins. Rather the blood and flesh of his own body was a physical representation of the

THE BLOOD OF Jesus Vs. THE BLOOD OF CHRIST

living doctrine he taught and lived by. Those applying this doctrine would essentually relieve their conscience from all condemnation inflicted upon them by the blood covenant Temple priests. Jesus elaborated on this doctrine in John.

John 6:53 *"Then Jesus said unto them, "Verily, Verily, I say unto you,* **Except ye eat the flesh of the son of man, and drink his blood, ye have no life in you."**

John 6:54 **"Whoso eateth my flesh and drinketh my blood, hath eternal life; and I will raise him in the last day."**

Clearly these two statements are referring to the personal teachings of Jesus and not his physical blood and body. So when one turns away from all their beliefs in bloody sacrifices for the remission of sins, whether they be Saviour or animal, then water baptism acted as the cleansing ritual for this transition. Even though the purpose and sign of the resurrection was only given to one generation, it still stands as a beacon of hope to this date.

In the following words of Jesus found in the Gospel of the the Holy 12 at **the last supper** in Lection LXXV verse 10-14 he states:
10. "In the beginning, God gave to all, the fruits of the trees, and the seeds, and the herbs, for food; but those who loved themselves more than God, or their fellows, corrupted their ways, and brought diseases into their bodies, and filled the earth with lust and violence.

11. Not by shedding innocent blood, therefore, but by living a righteous life, shall ye find the peace of God. Ye call me the Christ of God and ye say well, for I am the Way, the Truth and the Life.

12. Walk ye in the Way, and ye shall find God. Seek ye the Truth, and the Truth shall make you free. Live in the Life, and ye shall see no death. All things are alive in God, and the Spirit of God filleth all things.

13. Keep ye the commandments. Love thy God with all thy heart, and love thy neighbour as thyself. On these hang all the law and the prophets. And the sum of the law is this—Do not ye unto others as ye would not that others should do unto you. Do ye unto others, as ye would that others should do unto you.

14. Blessed are they who keep this law, for God is manifested in all creatures. All creatures live in God, and God is hid in them."

The blood of the covenant was never an ordained commandment from God to Moses. Rather the animal blood covenant allegedly (initiated by Moses) was invented by carnal minded priests. Then these practices were expanded upon by Babylonian revisionists from 586 B.C. to 430 B.C. The religious Babylonian/Pharisees such as Paul applied this doctrine to the blood of Christ along with the endorsement of the Roman Emperor Constantine in 325 A.D. who at the time was also a Babylonian sun-god worshipper. The King James Bible of 1611 has escaped unbiased professional scrutiny and has kept the curious from questioning its validity. For the most part, Paul's teachings within the New Testament King James Bible contains the Gospel of deceit, soaked in a history of shed blood that mocks the Creator, and insults the real historical Jesus by preserving the bloody sacrifices that Jesus had vehemently taught against. The end result has been that any religion embracing Paul's version of the blood covenant will, by nature, take on the same psychopathic profile of those that originally engineered this doctrine, thereby psychologically predisposing other vulnerable minds toward the occult. The Old Testament does not gloss over the negative history of its people. The good, the bad, the high points and the low are all recorded. But in reading the Bible it is important to understand that the negative developments do not always receive a negative comment. The story of Jacob and Esau is a good case in point. Although Jacob cheated his brother out of his birthright, the Genesis account does not comment negatively on the fact that he deliberately lied, cheated and stole from his brother. But hundreds of years after the fact, the few good Prophets whom Jesus would quote from referred to Jacob's act of deception as something definitely negative. (See Isaiah 43:27 & 28 Hosea 12:2 & 3.) The same kind of judgement occurs regarding the sacrifice of animals. Opposition to the entrenched rituals of sacrificed animals became part of the biblical record. By the time of Isaiah, and those that followed him, called the people back from their violent animal rituals. The Creator, they said, had never asked for the slaughter of His own creatures: It was man himself that instituted these bloody sacrifices.

Ever since PAUL, Christianity has viewed, "The Cross" as the bloody sacrifice that cleanses them from all their sins, but to those that seek after the teachings of the actual historical Jesus, "The Cross" represents the crucifixion of:

THE HOLY VIRUS

CHAPTER 5

THE GOSPEL OF THE HOLY TWELVE

Translated from the original Aramaic language
and edited by the
Rev. Gideon Jasper Richard Ouseley in 1892.

INTRODUCTION

Rev. G. J. Ouseley

In 1881 an English minister, Rev. G. J. Ouseley, got hold of a hitherto unknown, not rewritten evangelical text. This uncorrupted text has century after century been secured from all falsification in a buddistic monastary in Tibet, since the day a man has hidden it there, a man of the Essene society. Ouseley translated the arameic text and gave it the name The Gospel of the Holy Twelve. It has later been translated into German.

During the last century many old fragments of the gospel have come into light. Some have been found in old libraries and other from excavations. These fragments are called Logins or Agraphas. Their great value is due to the fact that they are uncorrupted and many parts of these fragments mostly agree, word for word, with the Gospel of Ouseley, though they are completely missing in the Constantine's canonical gospels.

The Original Gospel, representing the teachings of Christ, taught compassion to all living beings, including both animals and humans. The Roman Churchmen at Nicea opposed these doctrines and eliminated them from the Gospels, which they radically changed so as to be acceptable to Constantine, who loved the red meats and flowing wine of his midnight feasts too much to accept a religion that prohibited these pleasures, which was a main reason why he so bitterly persecuted the early Christians who advocated these doctrines. For this reason the Church Fathers changed the Gospel in such a way that Love and Compassion were limited only to human beings but the animal expressions of life were excluded from receiving these benefits.

INDEX

Lection I
The Parentage And Conception
Of John The Baptist

1. THERE was in the days of Herod, the King of Judea, a certain priest named Zacharias, of the course of Abia; and his wife was of the daughters of Aaron, and her name was Elisabeth.

2. And they were both righteous before God, walking in all the commandments and ordinances of the Lord blameless. And they had no child, because that Elisabeth was barren, and they both were now well stricken in years.

3. And it came to pass, that while he executed the priest's office before God in the order of his course, according to the custom of the priest's office, his lot was to burn incense when he went into the temple IOVA. And the whole multitude of the people were praying without at the time of the offering of incense.

4. And there appeared unto him an angel of the Lord standing over the altar of incense. And when Zacharias saw, he was troubled, and fear fell upon him. But the angel said unto him, Fear not, Zacharias, for thy prayer is heard; and thy wife Elisabeth, shall bear thee a son, and thou shalt call his name John.

5. And thou shalt have joy and gladness; and many shall rejoice at his birth; for he shall be great in the sight of the Lord, and shall neither eat flesh meats, nor drink strong drink; and he shall be filled with the Holy Spirit, even from his mother's womb.

6. And many of the children of Israel shall he turn to the Lord their God; And he shall go before him in the spirit and power of Elias, to turn the hearts of the fathers to the children, and the disobedient to the wisdom of the just; to make ready a people prepared for the Lord.

7. And Zacharias said unto the angel, Whereby shall I know

this? for I am an old man, and my wife is well stricken in years. And the angel answering said unto him, I am Gabriel, that stand in the presence of God; and am sent to speak unto thee, and to announce unto thee these glad tidings.

8. And, behold, thou art dumb, and not able to speak, until the day that these things shall be performed, then shall thy tongue be loosed that thou mayest believe my words which shall be fulfilled in their season.

9. And the people waited for Zacharias, and marvelled that he tarried so long in the temple. And when he came out, he could not speak unto them; and they perceived that he had seen a vision in the temple; for he made signs unto them, and remained speechless.

10. And it came to pass, that, as soon as the days of his ministration were accomplished, he departed to his own house. And after those days, his wife Elisabeth, conceived, and hid herself five months saying, Thus hath the Lord dealt with me in the days wherein he looked on me, to take away my reproach among men.

Lection II
The Immaculate Conception
Of Iesus The Christ

1. AND in the sixth month the angel Gabriel was sent from God, unto a city of Galilee, named Nazareth, to a virgin espoused to a man whose name was Joseph, of the house of David; and the virgin's name was Mary.

2. Now Joseph was a just and rational Mind, and he was skilled in all manner of work in wood and in stone. And Mary was a tender and discerning Soul, and she wrought veils for the temple. And they were both pure before God; and of them both was Jesu-Maria who is called the Christ.

3. And the angel came in unto her and said, Hail, Mary, thou that art highly favoured, for the Mother of God is with thee: blessed art thou among women and blessed be the

fruit of thy womb.

4. And when she saw him, she was troubled at his saying, and cast in her mind what manner of salutation this should be. And the angel said unto her, Fear not, Mary, for thou hast found favour with God and, behold, thou shalt conceive in thy womb and bring forth a child, and He shall be great and shalt be called a Son of the Highest.

5. And the Lord God shall give unto him the throne of his father David: and he shall reign over the house of Jacob forever; and of his kingdom there shall be no end.

6. Then said Mary unto the angel, How shall this be, seeing I know not a man? And the angel answered and said unto her The Holy Spirit shall come upon Joseph thy Spouse, and the power of the Highest shall overshadow thee, O Mary, therefore also that holy thing which shall be born of thee shall be called the Christ, the Child of God, and his Name on earth shalt be called Jesu-Maria, for he shall save the people from their sins, whosoever shall repent and obey his Law.

7. Therefore ye shall eat no flesh, nor drink strong drink, for the child shall be consecrated unto God from its mother's womb, and neither flesh nor strong drink shall he take, nor shall razor touch his head.

8. And, behold, thy cousin Elisabeth, she hath also conceived a son in her old age: and this is the sixth month with her, who was called barren. For with God no thing shall be impossible. And Mary said, Behold the handmaid of the Lord; be it unto me according to thy word. And the angel departed from her.

9. And in the same day the angel Gabriel appeared unto Joseph in a dream and said unto him, Hail, Joseph, thou that art highly favoured, for the Fatherhood of God is with thee. Blessed art thou among men and blessed be the fruit of thy loins.

10. And as Joseph thought upon these words he was troubled, and the angel of the Lord said unto him, Fear

not, Joseph, thou Son of David, for thou hast found favour with God, and behold thou shalt beget a child, and thou shalt call his name Jesu-Maria for he shall save his people from their sins.

11. Now all this was done that it might be fulfilled which was written in the prophets saying, Behold a Maiden shall conceive and be with child and shall bring forth a son, and shall call his name Emmanuel, which being interpreted is, God Within Us.

12. Then Joseph being raised from sleep did as the angel had bidden him, and went in unto Mary, his espoused bride, and she conceived in her womb the Holy One.

13. AND Mary arose in those days and went into the hill country with haste, into a city of Judea and entered into the house of Zacharias, and saluted Elisabeth.

14. And it came to pass, that, when Elisabeth heard the salutation of Mary, the babe leaped in her womb; and Elisabeth was filled with the power of the Spirit and spake, with a clear voice and said, Blessed art thou among women and blessed is the fruit of thy womb.

15. Whence is this to me, that the mother of my Lord should come to me? For, lo, as soon as the voice of thy salutation sounded in my ears, the babe leaped for joy. And blessed is she that believed: for there shall. be a performance of those things which were told her from the Holy One.

16. And Mary said: My soul doth magnify Thee, the Eternal, and my spirit doth rejoice in God my Saviour. For thou hast regarded the low estate of thy handmaiden; for, behold, from henceforth all generations shall call me blessed.

17. For Thou that art mighty hast done to me great things; and holy is Thy Name. And Thy mercy is on them that fear Thee from generation to generation.

18. Thou hast shewed strength with Thy arm; thou hast scattered the proud in the imagination of their hearts.

19. Thou hast put down the mighty from their seats and exalted the humble and the meek. Thou hast fill the hun-

gry with good things and the rich Thou dost send empty away.

20. Thou dost help thy servant Israel, in remembrance of thy mercy: as Thou spakest to our ancestors to Abraham and to his seed for ever. And Mary abode with her about three months and returned to her own house.

21. And these are the words that Joseph spake,, saying: Blessed be the God of our fathers and our mothers in Israel: for in an acceptable time Thou hast heard me, and in the day of salvation hast Thou helped me.

22. For Thou saids't I will preserve and make thee a covenant of the people to renew the face of the earth: and to cause the desolate places to be redeemed from the hands of the spoiler.

23. That thou mayest say to the captives, Go ye forth and be free; and to them that are in darkness, Show yourselves in the light. And they shall feed in the ways of pleasantness; and they shall no more hunt nor worry the creatures which I have made to rejoice before me.

24. They shall not hunger nor thirst any more neither shall the heat smite them nor the cold destroy them. And I will make on all My mountains a way for travellers; and My high places shall be exalted.

25. Sing ye heavens and rejoice thou earth; O ye deserts break forth with song: for Thou O God dost comfort Thy people; and console them that have suffered wrong.

Lection III
The Nativity Of John The Baptist

1. NOW Elisabeth's full time came that she should be delivered; and she brought forth a son. And her neighbours and her cousins heard how the Lord had shewed great mercy upon her; and they rejoiced with her.

2. And it came to pass, that on the eighth day they came to circumcise the child; and they called him Zacharias, after

the name of his father. And his mother answered and said, Not so; but he shall be called John. And they said unto her, There is none of thy kindred that is called by thy name.

3. And they made signs to his father, how he would have him called. And he asked for a writing table, and wrote, saying, his name is John. And they all marvelled, for his mouth was opened immediately, and his tongue loosed, and he spake, and praised God.

4. And great awe came on all that dwelt round about them; and all these came on all that dwelt round about them; and all these sayings were made known abroad throughout all the hilly country of Judea. And all they that heard them laid them up in their hearts, saying, What manner of child shall this be! And the hand of Jova was with him.

5. And his father Zacharias was filled with the holy Spirit, and prophesied, saying, Blessed be thou, O God of Israel; for thou hast visited and redeemed thy people. And hast raised up an horn of salvation for us in the house of thy servant David. As thou spakest by the mouth of thy holy prophets, which have been since the world began.

6. That we should be saved from our enemies, and from the hand of all that hate us. To perform the mercy promised to our ancestors, and to remember thy holy covenant.

7. The oath which thou did'st sware to our father Abraham, that thou wouldest grant unto us, that we being delivered out of the hand of our enemies might serve thee without fear, in holiness and righteousness before thee all the days of our life.

8. And this child shalt be called the Prophet of the Highest: for he shalt go before Thy face, O God, to prepare Thy ways; to give knowledge of salvation unto Thy people by the remission of their sins.

9. Through the tender mercy of our God, whereby the dayspring from on high hath visited us; to give light to them that sit in darkness and in the shadow of death, to

guide our feet into the way of peace.

10. And the child grew, and waxed strong in spirit, and his mission was hidden till the day of his shewing forth unto Israel.

Lection IV
The Nativity Of Iesus The Christ

1. NOW the birth of Jesu-Maria the Christ was on this wise. It came to pass in those days, that there went out a decree from Caesar Augustus, that all the world should be taxed. And all the people of Syria went to be taxed, every one into his own city, and it was midwinter.

2. And Joseph with Mary also went up from Galilee, out of the city of Nazareth into Judea, unto the city of David, which is called Bethlehem (because they were of the house and lineage of David), to be taxed with Mary his espoused wife, who was great with child.

3. And so it was, that, while they were there, the days were accomplished that she should be delivered. And she brought forth her firstborn child in a Cave, and wrapped him in swaddling clothes, and laid him in a manger, which was in the cave; because there was no room for them in the inn. And behold it was filled with many lights, on either side Twelve, bright as the Sun in his glory.

4. And there were in the same cave an ox, and a horse, and an ass, and a sheep, and beneath the manger was a cat with her little ones, and there were doves also, overhead, and each had its mate after its kind, the male with the female.

5. Thus it came to pass that he was born in the midst of the animals which, through the redemption of man from ignorance and selfishness, he came to redeem from their sufferings, by the manifestation or the sons and the daughters of God.

185

6. And there were in the same country, shepherds abiding in the field, keeping watch over their flock by night. And when they came, lo, the angel of God came upon them, and the glory of the Highest shone round about them; and they were sore afraid.

7. And the angel said unto them, Fear not: for, behold, I bring you good tidings of great joy, which shall be to all people, for unto you is born this day in the city of David a saviour, which is Christ, the Holy One of God. And this shall be a sign unto you; Ye shall find the babe wrapped in swaddling clothes lying in a manger.

8. And suddenly there was with the angel a multitude of the heavenly host praising God and saying, Glory to God in the highest, and on earth peace toward men of goodwill.

9. And it came to pass, as the angels were gone away from them into heaven, the shepherds said to one another, Let us now go even unto Bethlehem, and see this thing which is come to pass, which our God hath made known unto us.

10. And they came with haste, and found Mary and Joseph in the cave, and the Babe lying in a manger. And when they had seen these things, they made known abroad the saying which was told them concerning the child.

11. And all they that heard it, wondered at those things told them by the shepherds; but Mary kept all these things, and pondered them in her heart. And the shepherds returned, glorifying and praising God for all the things that they had heard and seen.

12. AND when eight days were accomplished for the circumcising of the child, his name was called Jesu-Maria, as was spoken by the angel before he was conceived in the womb. And when the days of her purification according to the law of Moses were accomplished, they brought the child to Jerusalem, to present it unto God (as it is written in the law of Moses, every male that openeth the womb shall be called holy to the Lord).

13. And, behold, there was a man in Jerusalem, whose

name was Simeon; and the same man was just and devout, waiting for the consolation of Israel; and the Holy Spirit was upon him. And it was revealed unto him that he should not see death, before he had seen the Christ of God.

14. And he came by the Spirit into the temple; and when the parents brought in the child Jesus, to do for him after the custom of the law, he perceived the child as it were a Pillar of light. Then took he him "up in his arms, and blessed God, and said:

15. Now lettest thou thy servant depart in peace, according to thy word. For mine eyes have seen thy salvation, which thou has prepared before the face of all people; to be a light to lighten the Gentiles, and to be the glory of thy people Israel. And his parents marvelled at those things which were spoken of him.

16. And Simeon blessed them, and said unto Mary his mother, Behold, this child is set for the falling and rising again of many in Israel; and for a Sign which shall be spoken against (yea, a sword shall pierce through thy own soul also), that the thoughts of many hearts may be revealed.

17. And there was one Anna, a prophetess, the daughter of Phanuel of the tribe of Aser, of a great age, who departed not from the temple, but served God with fastings and prayers night and day.

18. And she coming in that instant gave thanks likewise unto God, and spake of him to all them that looked for redemption in Jerusalem. And when they had performed all things according to the law they returned into Galilee, to their own city Nazareth.

Lection V
The Manifestation Of Iesus To The Magi

1. Now when Jesus was born in Bethlehem of Judea, in the days of Herod the king, behold, there came certain

Magi men from the east to Jerusalem, who had purified themselves and tasted not of flesh nor of strong drink, that they might find the Christ whom they sought. And they said, Where is he that is born King of the Jews? for we in the East have seen his Star, and are come to worship him.

2. When Herod the king had heard these things he was troubled, and all Jerusalem with him. And when he had gathered all the chief priests and scribes of the people together, he demanded of them where the Christ should be born.

3. And they said unto him, Bethlehem of Judea; for thus it is written by the prophet, and thou Bethlehem, in the land of Judea, art not the least among the princes of Judah; for out of thee shall come forth a Governor, that shall rule my people Israel.

4. Then Herod, when he had privily called the Magi, enquired of them diligently what time the Star appeared. And he sent them to Bethlehem, and said, Go and search diligently for the young child; and when ye have found him, bring me word again, that I may come and worship him also.

5. When they had heard the king, they departed; and, lo, the Star which the Magi of the East saw, and the angel of the Star went before them, till it came and stood over the place where the young child was, and the Star had the appearance of six rays.

6. And as they went on their way with their camels and asses laden with gifts, and were intent on the heavens seeking the child by the Star, they forgot for a little, their weary beasts who had borne thee burden and heat of the day, and were thirsty and fainting, and the Star was hidden from their sight.

7. In vain they stood and gazed, and looked one upon the other in their trouble. Then they bethought them of their camels and asses, and hastened to undo their burdens that they might have rest.

8. Now there was near Bethlehem a well by the way, And as they stooped down to draw water for their beasts, lo, the Star which they had lost appeared to them, being reflected in the stillness of the water.

9. And when they saw it they rejoiced with exceeding great joy.

10. And they praised God who had shewn his mercy unto them even as they shewed mercy unto their thirsty beasts.

11. And when they were come into the house, they saw the young child with Mary his mother, and fell down, and worshipped him: and when they had opened their treasures, they presented unto him gifts; gold, and frankincense, and myrrh.

12. And being warned of God in a dream that they should not return to Herod, they departed into their own country another way. And they kindled a fire according to their custom and worshipped God in the Flame.

13. And when they were departed, behold the angel of God appeared to Joseph in a dream, saying, Arise, and take the young child and his mother, and flee into Egypt, and there remain until I bring thee word, for Herod will seek to destroy him.

14. AND when he arose, he took the young child and his mother by night, and departed into Egypt, and was there for about seven years until the death of Herod, that it might be fulfilled which was spoken of God by the prophet, saying, Out of Egypt have I called my son.

15. Elizabeth too when she heard it, took her infant son and went up into a mountain and hid him. And Herod sent his officers to Zacharias in the temple and said to him, Where is thy child? And he answered I am a minister of God and am continually in the temple. I know not where he is.

16. And he sent again, saying, Tell me truly where is thy son, Dost thou not know thy life is in my hand? And Zacharias answered, The Lord is witness if thou shed my

blood, my spirit will God receive, for thou sheddest the blood of the innocent.

17. And they slew Zacharias in the Temple between the holy place and the altar; and the people knew it, for a voice was heard, Zacharias is slain, and his blood shall not be washed out until the avenger shall come. And after a time the priests cast lots, and the lot fell upon Simeon, and he filled his place.

18. Then Herod, when he saw that he was mocked of the wise men, was exceedingly wroth, and sent forth, and slew all the children that were in Bethlehem, and in all the coasts thereof, from two years old and under, according to the time which he had diligently enquired of the wise men.

19. Then was fulfilled that which was spoken by Jeremy the prophet, saying, In Rama was there a voice heard, lamentation, and weeping, and great mourning, Rachel weeping for her children, and would not be comforted, because they are not.

20. BUT when Herod was dead, behold, an angel of God appeared in a dream to Joseph in Egypt. Saying, Arise, and take the young child and his mother, and return into the land of Israel: for they are dead which sought the young child's life.

21. And he arose, and took the young child and his mother and came into the land of Israel. And they came and dwelt in a city called Nazareth; and he was called the Nazarene.

Lection VI
The Childhood And Youth Of
Iesus the Christ
He Delivereth A LionFrom The Hunters

1. NOW, Joseph and Mary, his parents, went up to Jerusalem every year at the Feast of the Passover and they observed the feast after the manner of their brethren, who

abstained from bloodshed and the eating of flesh and from strong drink. And when he was twelve years old, he went to Jerusalem with them after the custom of the feast.

2. And when they had fulfilled the days, as they returned, the child Jesus tarried behind in Jerusalem; and his parents knew not of it. But they, supposing him to have been in the company, went a day's Journey and they sought him among their kinsfolk and acquaintance. And when they found him not, turned back to Jerusalem, seeking him.

3. And it came to pass, that after three days they found him in the temple, sitting in the midst of the doctors, both hearing them, and asking them questions. And all that heard him were astonished at his understanding and answers.

4. And when they saw him, they were amazed; and his mother said unto him, Son, why hast thou thus dealt with us? Behold, thy father and I have sought thee sorrowing. And he said unto them, How is it that ye sought me? Wist ye not that I must be in my Parents' House. And they understood not the saying which he spake unto them. But his mother kept all these sayings in her heart.

5. And a certain prophet seeing him, said unto him, Behold the Love and the Wisdom of God are one in thee, therefore in the age to come shalt thou be called Jesu-Maria, for by the Christ shall God save mankind, which now is verily as the bitterness of the sea, but it shall yet be turned into sweetness, but to this generation the Bride shall not be manifest, nor yet to the age to come.

6. And he went down with them, and came to Nazareth, and was subject unto them. And he made wheels, and yokes, and tables also, with great skill. And Jesus increased in stature, and in favour with God and man.

7. AND on a certain day the child Jesus came to a place where a snare was set for birds, and there were some boys there. And Jesus said to them, who hath set this snare for

the innocent creatures of God? Behold in a snare shall they in like manner be caught. And he beheld twelve sparrows as it were dead.

8. And he moved his hands over them, and said to them, Go, fly away, and while ye live remember me. And they arose and fled away making a noise. And the Jews, seeing this, were astonished and told it unto the priests.

9. And other wonders did the child, and flowers were seen to spring up beneath his feet, where there had been naught but barren ground before. And his companions stood in awe of him.

10. A certain day after this, the child Jesus was playing with his companions, younger than himself and they gathered round him, and chose him as their king. And as he sat they twined an olive branch with flowers and they made it into a crown, and they placed it on his heads and a reed in his hand for a sceptre.

11. And they made obeisance to him, saying, Hail, King of Israel! And he said unto them, Hold your peace, ye know not what ye say. Tell it not unto any. Such words are not for you to proclaim, but for them to whom it shall be given.

12. And they marvelled, and one passing by heard it, and he said, Yea, truly, ye have chosen well, for he is a comely child and of great nobility.

13. AND in the eighteenth year of his age, Jesus was espoused unto Miriam, a virgin of the tribe of Judah with whom he lived seven years, and she died, for God took her, that he might go on to the higher things which he had to do, and to suffer for the sons and daughters of men.

14. And Jesus, after that he had finished his study of the law, went down again into Egypt that he might learn of the wisdom of the Egyptians, even as Moses did. And going into the desert, he meditated and fasted and prayed, and obtained the power of the Holy Name, by which he wrought many miracles.

15. And for seven years he conversed with God face to face,

and he learned the language of birds and of beasts, and the healing powers of trees, and of herbs, and of flowers, and the hidden secrets of precious stones, and he learned the motions of the Sun and the Moon and the stars, and the powers of the letters, and mysteries of the Square and the Circle and the Transmutation of things, and of forms, and of numbers, and of signs. From thence he returned to Nazareth to visit his parents, and he taught there and in Jerusalem as an accepted Rabbi, even in the temple, none hindering him.

16. AND after a time he went into Assyria and India and into Persia and into the land of the Chaldeans. And he visited their temples and conversed with their priests, and their wise men for many years, doing many wonderful works, healing the sick as he passed through their countries.

17. And the beasts of the field had respect unto him and the birds of the air were in no fear of him, for he made them not afraid, yea even the wild beasts of the desert perceived the power of God in him, and did him service bearing him from place to place.

18. For the Spirit of Divine Humanity filling him, filled all things around him, and made all things subject unto him, and thus shall yet be fulfilled the words of the prophets, The lion shall lie down with the calf, and the leopard with the kid, and the wolf with the lamb, and the bear with the ass, and the with the dove. And a child shall lead them.

19. And none shall hurt or destroy in my holy mountain, for the earth shall be full of the knowledge of the Holy One even as the waters cover the bed of the sea. And in that day I will make again a covenant with the beasts of the earth and the fowls of the air, and the fishes of the sea and with all created things. And will break the bow and the sword and all the instruments of warfare will I banish from the earth, and will make them to lie down in safety, and to live without fear.

20. And I will betroth thee unto me for ever in righteous-

ness and in peace and in loving kindness, and thou shalt know thy God, and the earth shalt bring forth the corn the wine and the oil, and I will say unto them which were not my people, Thou art my people; and they shall say unto me, Thou art our God.

21. And on a certain day as he was passing by a mountain side nigh unto the desert, there met him a lion and many men were pursuing him with stones and javelins to slay him.

22. But Jesus rebuked them, saying, Why hunt ye these creatures of God, which are more noble than you? By the cruelties of many generations they were made the enemies of man who should have been his friends.

23. If the power of God is shown in them, so also is shown his long suffering and compassion. Cease ye to persecute this creature who desireth not to harm you, see ye not how he fleeth from you, and is terrified by your violence?

24. And the lion came and lay at the feet of Jesus, and shewed love to him; and the people were astonish , and said, Lo, this man loveth all creatures and hath power to command even these beasts from the desert, and they obey him.

Lection VII
The Preaching Of John The Baptist

1. NOW in the fifteenth year of the reign of Tiberius Caesar, Pontius Pilate being governor of Judea, and Herod being tetrarch of Galilee (Caiaphas being the high priest, and Annas chief of the Sanhedrim) the word of God came unto John the son of Zacharias, in the wilderness.

2. And he came into all the country about Jordan, preaching the baptism of repentance for the remission of sins. As it is written in the prophets, Behold I send my messenger before thy face, who shall prepare thy way before thee; the voice of one crying in the wilderness, Prepare ye the way of

the Holy One, make straight the paths of the Anointed.
3. Every valley shall be filled, and every mountain and hill shall be brought low; and the crooked shall be made straight, and the rough ways shall be made smooth. And all flesh shall see the salvation of God.
4. And the same John had his raiment of camel's hair, and a girdle of the same about his loins, and his meat was the fruit of the locust tree and wild honey. Then went out to him Jerusalem, and all Judea, and all the region round about Jordan, and were baptized of him in the Jordan confessing their sins.
5. And he said to the multitude that came forth to be baptized of him, O generation of disobedient ones, who hath warned you to flee from the wrath to come? Bring forth therefore fruits worthy of repentance and begin not to say within yourselves, We have Abraham to our father.
6. For I say unto you, that God is able of these stones to raise up children unto Abraham. And now also the axe is laid unto the root of the trees: every tree therefore which bringeth not forth good fruit is hewn down, and cast into the fire.
7. And the wealthier people asked him, saying, What shall we do then? He answereth and saith unto them, He that hath two coats, let him impart to him that hath none; and he that hath food let him do likewise.
8. Then came also certain taxgatherers to be baptised and said unto him, Master, what shall we do? And he said unto them, Exact no more than that which is appointed you, and be merciful after your power.
9. And the soldiers likewise demanded of him, saying, And what shall we do? And he said unto them, Do violence to no man, neither accuse any falsely; and be content with sufficient wages.
10. And to all he spake, saying, Keep yourselves from blood and things strangled and from dead bodies of birds and beasts, and from all deeds of cruelty, and from all that is

gotten of wrong; Think ye the blood of beasts and birds will wash away sin! I tell you Nay, Speak the Truth. Be just, Be merciful to one another and to all creatures that live, and walk humbly with your God.

11. And as the people were in expectation, and all men mused in their hearts of John, whether he were the Christ or not, John answered; saying unto them all, I indeed baptize you with water; but One mightier than I cometh, the latchet of whose shoes I am not worthy to unloose.

12. He shall also baptize you with water and with fire. Whose fan is in his hand, and he will thoroughly purge his floor, and will gather the wheat into his garner; but the chaff he will burn with fire unquenchable. And many other things in his exortation preached he unto the people.

Lection VIII
The Baptism of Jesu Maria The Christ

1. AND it was in the midst of the summer, the tenth month. Then cometh Jesus from Galilee to Jordan unto John, to be baptized of him. But John forbade him, saying, I have need to be baptized of thee, and comest thou to me? And Jesus answering said unto him, Suffer it to be so now, for thus it becometh us to fulfil all righteousness. Then he suffered him.

2. And Jesus, when he was baptized, went up straightway out of the water; and, lo, the heavens were opened unto him, and a bright cloud stood over him, and from behind the cloud Twelve Rays of light, and thence in the form of a Dove, the Spirit of God descending and lighting upon him. And, lo, a voice from heaven saying, This is my beloved Son, in whom I am well pleased; this day have I begotten thee.

3. And John bare witness of him ,saying, This was he of whom I spake, He that cometh after me is preferred before

me, for he was before me. And of his fulness have all we received, and grace for grace. For the law was in part given by Moses, but grace and truth cometh in fulness by Jesus Christ.

4. No man hath seen God at any time. The only begotten which cometh from the bosom of the Eternal in the same is God revealed. And this is the record of John, when the Jews sent priests and Levites from Jerusalem to ask him, Who art I thou ? And he deified not, but confessed I am not the Christ.

5. And they asked him, What then? Art thou Elias? And he saith, I am not, Art thou that prophet of whom Moses spake? And he answered, No. Then said they unto him, Who art thou ? that we may give an answer to them that sent us. What sayest thou of thyself? And he said, I am the voice of one crying in the wilderness, Make straight the way of the Holy One, as said the Prophet Esaias.

6. And they which were sent were of the Pharisees, and they asked him and said unto him, Why baptizest thou then, if thou be not that Christ, nor Elias, neither that prophet of whom Moses spake?

7. John answered them, saying, I baptize with water; but there standeth One among you, whom ye know not, He shall baptize with water and with fire. He it is who coming after me is preferred before me, whose shoe's latchet I am not worthy to unloose.

8. These things were done in Bethabara, beyond Jordan, where John was baptizing. And Jesus began at this time to be thirty years of age, being after the flesh indeed the Son of Joseph and Mary; but after the Spirit. the Christ, the Son of God, the Father and Mother Eternal, as was declared by the Spirit of holiness with power.

9. AND Joseph was the son of Jacob and Elisheba, and Mary was the daughter of Eli (called Joachim) and Anna, who were the children of David and Bathsheba, of Judah and Shela, of Jacob and Leah, of Isaac and Rebecca, of

Abraham and Sarah, of Seth and Maat, of Adam and Eve, who were the children of God.

Lection IX
The Four Temptations

1. THEN was Jesus led up of the spirit into the wilderness to be tempted of the Devil. And the wild beasts of the desert were around him, and became subject unto him. And when he had fasted forty days and forty nights he was afterwards an hungered.

2. And when the tempter came to him, he said, If thou be the Son of God, command that these stones be made bread, for it is written, I will feed thee with the finest of wheat and with honey, out of the rock will I satisfy thee.

3. But he answered and said, It is written, Man shall not live by bread alone, but by every word that proceeded out of the mouth of God.

4. Then the Devil placeth before him a woman, of exceeding beauty and comeliness and of subtle wit, and a ready understanding withal, and he said unto him. Take her as thou wilt, for her desire is unto thee, and thou shalt have love and happiness and comfort all thy life, and see thy children's children, yea is it not written, It is not good for man that he should be alone?

5. And Jesu-Maria said, Get thee behind me, for it is written, Be not led away by the beauty of woman, yea, all flesh is as grass and the flower of the field; the grass withereth and the flower fadeth away, but the Word of the Eternal endureth for ever. My work is to teach and to heal the children of men, and he that is born of God keepeth his seed within him.

6. And the Devil taketh him up into the holy city, and setteth him on a pinnacle of the Temple. And saith unto him, If thou be the Son of God, cast thyself down; for it is

written, He shall give his angels charge concerning thee; and in their hands they shall bear thee up lest at any time thou dash thy foot against a stone.

7. And Jesus said unto him, It is written again, Thou shalt not tempt the Lord thy God.

8. Then the Devil took him up into an exceeding high mountain in the midst of a great plain and, round about, twelve cities and their peoples, and shown from thence he shown unto him all the kingdoms of the world in a moment of time. And the Devil said unto him, All this power will I give thee, and the glory of them: for that is delivered unto me; and to whomsoever I will, I give it: for it is written, thou shalt have dominion from sea to sea, so thou shalt judge thy people with righteousness and thy poor with mercy, and. make a full end of oppression. If thou therefore wilt worship me, all shall be thine.

9. And Jesu-Maria answered and said unto him, get thee behind me, Satan; for it is written, Thou shalt worship thy God, and Him only shalt thou serve. Without the power of God, the end of evil cannot come.

10. Then the Devil having ended all the temptations leaveth him and departed for a season. And behold, angels of God came and ministered unto him.

Lection X
Joseph And Mary Make A Feast Unto Iesus
Andrew And Peter Find Iesus

1. AND when he had returned from the wilderness, the same day, his parents made him a feast, and they gave unto him the gifts which the Magi had presented to him in his infancy. And Mary said, These things have we kept for thee even to this day, and she gave unto him the gold and the frankincense and the myrrh. And he took of the frankincense, but of the gold he gave unto his parents for the

poor, and of the myrrh he gave unto Mary who is called Magdalene.

2. Now this Mary was of the city of Magdala in Galilee. And she was a great sinner, and had seduced many by her beauty and comeliness. And the same came unto Jesus by night and confessed her sins, and he put forth his hand and healed her, and cast out of her seven demons, and he said unto her, Go in peace, thy sins are forgiven thee. And she arose and left all and followed him, and ministered unto him of her substance, during the days of his ministry in Israel.

3. THE next day John saw Jesus coming unto him, and said, Behold the Lamb of God, which by righteousness taketh away the sin of the world. This is he of whom I said, He was before me; and I knew him not; but that he should be made manifest to Israel; therefore am I come baptizing with water.

4. And John bare record, saying, I saw the Spirit descending from heaven like a Dove, and it abode upon him. And I knew him not, but he that sent me to baptize with water, the same said unto me, Upon whom thou shalt see the Spirit descending, and remaining on him, the same is he which baptized with water and with fire, even the Spirit. And I saw, and bare record that this was the Son of God.

5. THE day after, John stood by the Jordan and two of his disciples. And looking upon Jesus as he walked, he saith, Behold the Christ, the Lamb of God! And the two disciples heard him speak, and they followed Jesus.

6. Then Jesus turned and saw them following and saith unto them, What seek ye? They said unto him, Rabbi (which is, being interpreted, Master), where dwellest thou? He saith unto them, Come and see. They came and saw where he dwelt, and abode with him that day: for it was about the tenth hour.

7. One of the two which heard John speak and followed him was Andrew, Simon Peter's brother. He first findeth

his own brother Simon and said unto him, We have found the Messias, which is, being interpreted the Christ. And he brought him to Jesus And when Jesus beheld him, he said, Thou art Simon Bar Jona: thou shalt be called Kephas (which is, by interpretation, a rock).

8. THE day following, Jesus goeth forth into Galilee, and findeth Philip, and saith unto him, Follow me. Now Philip was of Bethsaida, the city of Andrew and Peter. Philip findeth Nathanael, who is called Bar Tholmai, and saith unto him, We have found him, Of whom Moses in the law and the Prophets did write, Jesus of Nazareth, the son of Joseph and Mary, And Nathanael said unto him, Can there any good thing come out of Nazareth ? Philip said unto him, Come and see.

9. Jesus saw Nathanael coming to him and saith of him, Behold an Israelite indeed, in whom is no guile! Nathanael saith unto him, Whence knowest thou me? Jesus answered and said unto him, Before that Philip called thee, when thou wast under the Fig tree, I saw thee. Nathanael answered and saith unto him, Rabbi, thou art the Son of God. thou art the King of Israel. Yea, under the Fig tree did I find thee. 10. Jesus answered and said unto him, Nathanael Bar Tholmai, because I said unto thee, I saw thee under the Fig tree, believest thou ? thou shalt see greater things than these. And he saith unto him, Verily, verily, I say unto you, hereafter ye shall see heaven open, and the angels of God ascending and descending upon the Son of man.

Lection XI
The Anointing By Mary Magdalene

1. AND one of the Pharisees desired him that he would eat with him. And he went into the Pharisee's house and sat down to eat.

2. And behold a certain woman of Magdala, who was reputed to be a sinner, was in the city, and when she knew that Jesus sat at meat in the Pharisee's house, she brought an Alabaster box of ointment, and stood at his feet behind him, weeping, and washed His feet with tears, and did wipe them with the hairs of her head and kissed his feet, and anointed them with ointment.

3. Now when the Pharisee which had bidden him saw it, he thought within himself, saying, This man, if he were a prophet, would have known who and what manner of woman this is that toucheth him: for she is a sinner.

4. And Jesus answering said unto him, Simon, I have somewhat to say unto thee. And he saith, Master, say on.

5. There was a certain creditor which had two debtors: the one owed five hundred pence and the other fifty. And when they had nothing to pay, he frankly forgave them both. Tell me, therefore, which of them will love him most.

6. Simon answered and said, I suppose that he to whom he forgave most. And he said unto him, Thou hast rightly judged.

7. And he said unto Simon, Seest thou this woman? I entered into thine house, thou gavest me no water for my feet; but she hath washed my feet with tears and wiped them with the hairs of her head. Thou gavest me no kiss: but this woman since the time I came in hath not ceased to kiss my feet. My head with oil thou didst not anoint: but this woman hath anointed my feet with ointment.

8. Wherefore I say unto thee, man but also beast and birds of the air, yea, even the fishes of the sea; but to whom little is forgiven, the same loveth little. Her sins, which are many, are forgiven, for she loved much, not only man but also beast and birds of the air, yea, even the fishes of the sea; but to whom little is forgiven, the same loveth little.

9. And he said unto her, Thy sins are forgiven, and they who sat at the table began to say within themselves, who is this that forgiveth sins also?

10. Though he had said not, I forgive thee, but Thy sins are forgiven thee, for he discerned true faith and penitence in her heart. And Jesus needed not that any should testify of any man, for he himself knew what was in man.

Lection XII
The Marriage In Cana
The Healing Of The Nobleman's Son

1. AND the next day there was a marriage in Cana of Galilee; and the mother of Jesus was there: And both Jesus and Mary Magdalene were there, and his disciples came to the marriage.

2. And when they wanted wine the mother of Jesus saith unto him, They have no wine. Jesus saith unto her, Woman, what is that to thee and to me ? mine hour is not yet come. His mother saith unto the servants, Whatsoever he saith unto you, do it.

3. And there were set there six waterpots of stone, after the manner of the purifying of the Jews, containing two or three firkins apiece. And Jesus saith unto them, Fill the waterpots with water. And they filled them up to the brim. And he said unto them, Draw out now, and bear unto the governor of the feast. And they bare it.

4. When the ruler of the feast had tasted the water that was made wine to them, and knew not whence it was; the governor of the feast called the bridegroom, and saith unto him. Every man at the beginning doth set forth good wine and when men have well drunk, then that which is worse; but thou hast kept the good wine until now.

5. This beginning of miracles did Jesus in Cana of Galilee, and manifested forth his glory; and many disciples believed on him.

6. After this he went down to Capernaum, he, and his

mother, with Mary Magdalene, and his brethren, and his disciples: and they continued there for many.

7. And there arose a question between some of John's disciples and the Jews about purifying. And they came unto John, and said unto him, Rabbi, he that was with thee beyond Jordan, to whom thou bearest wittness, behold, the same baptizeth, and all do come to him.

8. John answered and said, A man can receive nothing, except it be given him from heaven. Ye yourselves bear me witness, that I said, I am not the Christ, but that I am sent before him.

9. He that hath the bride is the bridegroom; but the friend of the bridegroom, which standeth and heareth him, rejoiceth greatly because of the bridegroom's voice; this my joy therefore is fulfilled. He must increase; but I must decrease. He that is of the earth is earthly, and speaketh of the earth: he that cometh from heaven is above all.

10. AND certain of the Pharisees came and questioned Jesus, and said unto him, how sayest thou that God will condemn the world ? And Jesus answered, saying, God so loveth the world, that the only begotten Son is given, and cometh into the world, that whosoever believeth in him may not perish, but have everlasting life. God sendeth not the Son into the world to condemn the world; but that the world through him may be saved.

11. They who believe on him are not condemned: but they that believe not are condemned already, because they have not believed in the name of the only begotten of God. And this is the condemnation, that the light is come into the world, and men love darkness rather than light, because their deeds are evil .

12. For all they that do evil hate the light, neither come they to the light, lest their deeds may be condemned. But they that do righteousness come to the light, that their deeds may be made manifest, that they are wrought in God.

13. AND there was a certain nobleman, whose son was sick at Capernaum. When he heard that Jesus was come into Galilee, he went unto him, and besought him that he would come down, and heal his son; for he was at the point of death.

14. Then said Jesus unto him, Except ye see signs and wonders, ye will not believe. The nobleman saith unto him, Sir, come down ere my child die.

15. Jesus saith unto him, Go thy way; thy son liveth. And the man believed the word that Jesus had spoken unto him, and he went his way. And as, he was now going down, his servants met him, and told him, saying, Thy son liveth.

16. Then enquired he of them the hour when he began to amend. And they said unto him, Yesterday of the seventh hour the fever left him. So the father knew that it was at the same hour, in the which Jesus said unto him, Thy son liveth. And himself believed, and his whole house.

Lection XIII
The First Sermon In The Synagogue Of Nazareth

1. AND Jesus came to Nazareth, where he had been brought up: and, as his custom was, he went into the synagogue on the sabbath day, and stood up for to read. And there was delivered unto him the roll of the prophet Esaias.

2. And when he had opened the roll, he found the place where it was written. The Spirit of the Lord Is upon me, because he hath anointed me to preach the gospel to the poor; he hath sent me to heal the brokenhearted, to preach deliverance to the captives and recovering of sight to the blind, to set at liberty them that are bound. To preach the acceptable year of the Lord.

3. And he closed the roll, and gave it again to the minister, and sat down, And the eyes of all them that were in the

synagogue were fastened on him. And he began saying unto them. This day is this scripture fulfilled in your ears. And all bare him witness, and wondered at the gracious words which proceeded out of his mouth. And they said, Is not this Joseph's son ?

4. And some brought unto him a blind man to test his power, and said, Rabbi, here is a son of Abraham blind from birth. Heal him as thou hast healed Gentiles in Egypt. And he, looking upon him, perceived his unbelief and the unbelief of those that brought him, and their desire to ensnare him. And he could do no mighty work in that place because of their unbelief.

5. And they said unto him, Whatsoever we have heard done in Egypt, do also here in thy own country. And he said, Verily I say unto you, No prophet is accepted in his own home or in his own country, neither doth a physician work cures upon them that know him.

6. And I tell you of a truth, many widows were in Israel in the days of Elias, when the heaven was shut up three years and six months, when great famine was throughout all the land. But unto none of them was Elias sent, save unto Sarepta, a city of Sidon, unto a woman that was a widow.

7. And many lepers were in Israel in the time of Eliseus the prophet; and none of them was cleansed, saving Naaman the Syrian.

8. And all they in the synagogue, when they heard these things, were filled with wrath. And rose up, and thrust him out of the city, and led him unto the brow of the hill whereon their city was built, that they might cast him down headlong. But he, passing through the midst of them, went his way and escaped them.

Lection XIV
The Calling Of Andrew And Peter
The Teaching of Cruelty In Animals
The Two Rich Men

1. NOW Herod the tetrarch, being reproved by John the Baptist for Herodias his brother Philip's wife, and for all the evils which he had done, added yet this above all, that he shut up John in prison.

2. And Jesus began to preach, and to say, Repent; for the kingdom of heaven is at hand. And as he was walking by the sea of Galilee, he saw Simon called Peter, and Andrew his brother, casting a net in the sea; for they were fishers. And he saith unto them, Follow me, and I will make you fishers of men. And they straightway forsook their nets, and followed him.

3. And going on from thence, he saw other two brethren, James the son of Zebedee, and John his brother, in a ship with Zebedee their father, mending their nets; and he called them. And they immediately left their nets, and the ship, and their father, and followed him.

4. And Jesus went about all Galilee, teaching in, their synagogues, and preaching the gospel of the kingdom, and healing all manner of sickness and all manner of disease among the people. And the fame of his miracles went throughout all Syria, and they brought unto him many sick people that were taken with divers diseases and torments, and those which were lunatick, and those that had the palsy, and he healed them.

5. And there followed him great multitudes of people from Galilee, and from Decapolis, and from Jerusalem, and from Judea, and from beyond Jordan.

6. AND as Jesus was going with some of his disciples he met with a certain man who trained dogs to hunt other creatures. And he said to the man, Why doest thou thus? and the man said, By this I live and what profit is there to

any in these creatures? these creatures are weak, but the dogs they are strong. And Jesus said, Thou lackest wisdom and love. Lo, every creature which God hath made hath its end, and purpose, and who can say what good is there in it? or what profit to thyself, or mankind?

7. And, for thy living, behold the fields yielding their increase, and the fruit-bearing trees and the herbs; what needest thou more than these which honest work of thy hands will not give to thee? Woe to the strong who misuse their strength, Woe to the hunters for they shall be hunted.

8. And the man marvelled, and left off training the dogs to hunt, and taught them to save life rather than destroy, And he learned of the doctrines of Jesus and became his disciple.

9. AND behold there came to him two rich men, and one said, Good Master. But he said, Call me not good, for One alone is the All good, and that is God.

10. And the other said to him, Master, what good thing shall I do and live? Jesus said, Perform the Law and the prophets. He answered, I have performed them. Jesus answered, Go, sell all thou hast and divide with the poor, and follow me. But this saying pleased him not.

11. And the Lord said unto him, How sayest thou that thou hast performed the Law and the prophets? Behold many of thy brethren are clad with filthy rags, dying from hunger and thy house is full of much goods, and there goeth from it nought unto them.

12. And he said unto Simon, It is hard for the rich to enter the kingdom of heaven, for the rich care for themselves, and despise them that have not.

Lection XV
Healing Of The Leper And
The Man With Palsy
The Deaf Man Who Denied
That Others Could Hear

1. AND it came to pass, when he was in a certain city, behold a man full of leprosy, who, seeing Jesus, fell toward the earth, and besought him, saying, Lord if thou wilt, thou canst make me clean. And he put forth his hand, and touched him, saying, Blessed be thou who believest; I will, be thou clean. And immediately the leprosy departed from him.

2. And he charged him saying, Tell no man: but go, and shew thyself to the priest, and offer for thy cleansing, according as Moses commanded, for a testimony unto them. But so much the more went there a fame abroad of him; and great multitudes came together to hear, and to be healed by him of their infirmities. And he withdrew himself into the wilderness, and prayed.

3. AND it came to pass on a certain day, as he was teaching, that there were Pharisees and doctors of the law sitting by, to see them which were come out of every town, of Galilee, and Judea, and Jerusalem, and the power of God was present to heal them.

4. AND, behold, they brought in a bed a man who was taken with a palsy: and they sought means to bring him in, and to lay him before him. And when they could not find by what way they might bring him in because of the multitude, they went upon the housetop, and let him down through the tiling with his couch into the midst before Jesus. And when he saw their faith, he said unto him, Man, thy sins are forgiven thee.

5. And the scribes and the pharisees began to reason, saying, Who is this which speaketh blasphemies? Who can

forgive sins, but God alone? But when Jesus perceived their thoughts, he answering said unto them, What reason ye in your hearts? Can even God forgive sins, if man repent not? Who said, I forgive thee thy sins? Said I not rather, Thy sins are forgiven thee?

6. Whether is easier to say. Thy sins be forgiven thee; or to say, Rise up and walk? But that ye may know that the Son of Man hath power upon earth to discern, and declare the forgiveness of sins (he said unto the sick of the palsy), I say unto thee, Arise, and take up thy couch, and go to thine house.

7. And immediately he arose up before them, and took up that whereon he lay, and departed to his own house, glorifying God. And they were all amazed, and they glorified God, and were filled with the Spirit of reverence, saying, We have seen strange things to day.

8. AND as Jesus was going into a certain village there met him a man who was deaf from his birth. And he believed not in the sound of the rushing wind, or the thunder, or the cries of the beasts, or the birds which complained of their hunger or their hurt, nor that others heard them.

9. And Jesus breathed into his ears, and they were opened, and he heard. And he rejoiced with exceeding joy in the sounds he before denied. And he said, Now hear all things.

10. But Jesus said unto him. How sayest thou, I hear all things? Canst thou hear the sighing of the prisoner, or the language of the birds or the beasts when they commune with each other, or the voice of angels and spirits? Think how much thou canst not hear, and be humble in thy lack of knowledge.

Lection XVI
Calling of Matthew
Parable of The The New Wine
In The Old Bottles

1. AND after these things he went forth, and saw a tax gatherer, named Levi, sitting at the receipt of custom: and he said unto him, Follow me. And he left all, rose up, and followed him.

2. And Levi made him a great feast in his own house: and there was a great company of taxgatherers and of others that sat down with them. But the Scribes and Pharisees murmured against his disciples, saying, Why do ye eat and drink with publicans and sinners ?

3. And Jesus answering said unto them, They that are whole need not a physician; but they that are sick. I came not to call the righteous, but sinners to repentance.

4. And they said unto him, Why do the disciples of John fast often, and make prayers, and likewise the disciples of the Pharisees; but thine do eat and drink ?

5. And he said unto them, Wherewith shall I liken the men of this generation, and to what are they like? They are like unto children, sitting in the market place and calling one to another and saying, We have piped unto you, and ye have not danced, we have mourned to you and ye have not lamented.

6. For John the Baptist came neither eating nor drinking, and ye say, He hath a devil, The Son of Man cometh eating and drinking the fruits of the earth, and the milk of the flock, and the fruit of the vine, and ye say, Behold a glutton and wine bibber, a friend of publicans and sinners.

7. Can ye make the children of the bridechamber fast, while the bridegroom is with them? But the days will come, when the bridegroom shall be taken away from them, and then shall they fast in those days.

8. AND he spake also this parable unto them, saying, No

man putteth a piece of new cloth upon an old garment; for then the new agreeth not with the old, and the garment is made worse.

9. And no one putteth new wine into old bottles; else the new wine will burst the bottles, and be spilled, and the bottles shall perish. But new wine must be put into new bottles, and both are preserved.

10. None also having drunk old wine, straightway desire new: for they say, The old is better. But the time cometh when the new shall wax old, and then the new shall be desired by them. For as one changeth old garments for new ones, so do they also change the body of death for the body of life, and that which is past for that which is coming.

Lection XVII
Iesus Sendeth Forth The Twelve
And Their Fellows

1. AND Jesus went up into a mountain to pray. And when he had called unto him his twelve disciples, he gave them power against unclean spirits to cast them out and to heal all manner of sickness and all manner of disease. Now the names of the twelve apostles are these who stood for the twelve tribes of Israel:

2. Peter, called Cephas, for the tribe of Reuben James, for the tribe of Naphtali; Thomas, called Dydimus, for the tribe of Zabulon; Matthew, called Levi for the tribe of Gad; John, for the tribe of Ephraim Simon, for the tribe of Issachar.

3. Andrew, for the tribe of Joseph; Nathanael, for the tribe of Simeon; Thaddeus, for the tribe of Zabulon; Jacob, for the tribe of Benjamin; Jude, for the tribe of Dan; Philip, for the tribe of Asher. And Judas Iscariot, a Levite, who betrayed him, was also among them (but was not of them). And Matthia and Barsabbas were also present with them.

4. Then he called in like manner twelve others to be Prophets, men of light to be with the Apostle and shew unto them the hidden things of God. And their names were Hermes, Aristobulus, Selenius, Nereus, Apollos, and Barsabbas; Andronicus, Lucius, Apelles, Zachaeus, Urbanus, and Clementos. And then he called twelve who should be Evangelists, and twelve who should be Pastors. A fourfold twelve did he call that he might send them forth to the twelve tribes of Israel, unto each, four.

5. And they stood around the Master, clad in white linen raiment, called to be a holy priesthood unto God for the service of the twelve tribes whereunto they should be sent.

6. These fourfold Twelve Jesus sent forth and charged them, saying, I will that ye be my Twelve Apostle with your companions, for a testimony into Israel. Go ye into the cities of Israel and to the lost sheep of the House of Israel. And as ye go, preach, saying, The kingdom of heaven is at hand. As I have baptized you in wader, so baptize ye them who believe.

7. Anoint and heal the sick, cleanse the lepers, raise the dead, cast out devils, freely ye have received, freely give. Provide neither gold, nor silver, nor brass in your purses. Nor scrip for your journey, neither two coats, neither shoes, nor yet staves; for the workman is worthy of his food; and eat that which is set before you, but of that which is gotten by taking of life, touch not, for it is not lawful to you.

8. And into whatsoever city or town ye shall enter, enquire who in it is worthy; and there abide till ye go thence. And when ye come into an house, salute it. And if the house be worthy, let your peace come upon it: but if it be not worthy, let your peace return to you.

9. Be ye wise as serpents and harmless as doves. Be ye innocent and undefiled. The Son of Man is: not come to destroy but to save, neither to take life, but to give life, to body and soul.

10. And fear not them which kill the body but are not able

to kill the soul; but rather fear him who is able to destroy both soul and body in Gehenna.

11. Are not two sparrows sold for a farthing? and one of them shall not fall on the ground without permission of the All Holy. Yea, the very hairs of your head are all numbered. Fear yet not therefore, if God careth for the sparrow, shall he not care for you!

12. It is enough for disciples that they be as their master, and the servants as their lord. If they have called the master of the house Beelzebub, how much more shall they call them of his household? Fear them not therefore, for there is nothing covered, that shall not be revealed; or hid, that shall not be known.

13. What I tell you in darkness, that speak ye in light when the time cometh: and what ye hear in the ear, that preach ye upon the housetops. Whosoever therefore shall confess the truth before men, them will I confess also before my Parent Who is in heaven. But whosoever shall deny the truth before men, them will I also deny before my Parent Who is in heaven.

14. Verily I am come to send peace upon earth, but when I speak, behold a sword followeth. I am come to unite, but, behold, a man shall be at variance with his father, and the daughter with her mother, and the daughter-in-law with her mother-in-law. And a man's foes shall be they of his own household. For the unjust cannot mate with them that are just.

15. They who take not their cross and follow after me are not worthy of me. He that findeth his life shall lose it; and he that loseth his life for my sake, shall find it.

Lection XVIII
He Sendeth Forth Of The Two and Seventy

1. AFTER these things the Lord appointed two and seventy

also, and sent them two and two before his face into every city and place of the tribes whither he himself would come.

2. Therefore said he unto them, The harvest truly is great, but the labourers are few, pray ye therefore the Lord of the harvest that he would send forth labourers into the harvest.

3. Go your ways, behold I send you forth as lambs among wolves. Carry neither purse, nor scrip, nor shoes, and salute no man by the way.

4. And into whatsoever house ye enter, first say, Peace be to this house. And if the spirit of peace be there your peace shall rest upon it, if not it shall turn to you again.

5. And into whatsoever city ye enter, and they receive you, eat such things as are set before you without taking of life. And heal the sick that are therein, and say unto them, The kingdom of God is come nigh unto you.

6. And in the same house remain, eating and drinking such things as they give without shedding of blood, for the labourer is worthy of his hire. Go not from house to house.

7. But into whatsoever city ye enter and they receive you not, go your ways out into the streets of the same and say, Even the very dust of your city, which cleaveth on us, we do wipe off against you, notwithstanding be ye sure of this, that the kingdom of God is come nigh unto you.

8. Woe unto thee, Chorazin! woe unto thee, Bethsaida! for if the mighty works had been done in Tyre and Sidon, which have been done in you, they had a great while ago repented, sitting in sackcloth and ashes. But it shall be more tolerable for them in the judgement than for you.

9. And thou, Capernaum, which art exalted to heaven shalt be thrust down to hades. They that hear you, hear also me; and they that despise you, despise also me; and they that despise me, despise Him that sent me. But let all be persuaded in their own minds.

10. AND again Jesus said unto them: Be merciful, so shall ye obtain mercy. Forgive others, so shall ye be forgiven.

With what measure ye mete, with the same shall it be meted unto you again.

11. As ye do unto others, so shall it be done you. As ye give, so shall it be given unto you. As ye judge others, so shall ye be judged. As ye serve others, so. shall ye be served.

12. For God is just, and rewardeth every one according to their works. That which they sow they shall also reap.

Lection XIX
Iesus Teacheth How to Pray
Error Even In Prophets

1. As Jesus was praying in a certain place on a mountain, some of his disciples came unto him, and one of then said, Lord teach us how to pray. And Jesus said unto them, When thou prayest enter into thy secret chamber, and when thou hast closed the door, pray to Abba Amma Who is above and within thee, and thy Father-Mother Who seest all that is secret shall answer thee openly.

2. But when ye are gathered together, and pray in common, use not vain repetitions, for your heavenly Parent knoweth what things ye have need of before ye ask them. After this manner therefore pray ye:—

3. Our Father-Mother Who art above and within: Hallowed be Thy Name in twofold Trinity. In Wisdom, Love and Equity Thy Kingdom come to all. Thy will be done, As in Heaven so in Earth. Give us day by day to partake of Thy holy Bread, and the fruit of the living Vine. As Thou dost forgive us our trespasses, so may we forgive others who trespass against us. Shew upon us Thy goodness, that to others we may shew the same. In the hour of temptation, deliver us from evil.

4. For Thine are the Kingdom, the Power and the Glory; From the Ages of ages, Now and to the Ages of ages. Amun.

5. And wheresoever there are seven gathered together in My Name there am I in the midst of them; yea, if only there

be three or two; and where there is but one who prayeth in secret, I am with that one.

6. Raise the Stone, and there thou shall find me. Cleave the wood, and there am I. For in the fire and in the water even as in every living form, God is manifest as it's Life and it's Substance.

7. AND the Lord said, If thy brother hath sinned in word seven times a day, and seven times a day hath made amendment, receive him. Simon said to him, Seven times a day ?

8. The Lord answered and said to him, I tell thee also unto seventy times seven, for even in the Prophets, after they were anointed by the Spirits utterance of sin was found.

9. Be ye therefore considerate, be tender, be ye pitiful, be ye kind, not to your own kind alone, but to every creature which is within your care, for ye are to them as gods, to whom they look in their need. Be ye slow to anger for many sin in anger which they repented or when their anger was past.

10. AND there was a man whose hand was withered and he came to Jesus and said, Lord, I was a mason seeking sustenance by my hands, I beseech thee restore to me my health that I may not beg for food with shame. And Jesus healed him, saying There is a house made without hands, seek that thou mayest dwell therein.

Lection XX
The Return Of The Two and Seventy

1. AND after a season the two and seventy returned again with joy, saying, Lord, even the demons are subject unto us through thy name.

2. And he said unto them, I beheld Satan as lightning fall from heaven.

3. Behold I give unto you power to tread on serpents and scorpions, and over all the power of the enemy; and noth-

ing shall by any means hurt you. Notwithstanding in this, rejoice not, that the spirits are subject unto you; but rather rejoice, because your names are written in Heaven.

4. In that hour Jesus rejoiced in spirit, and said I thank thee, Holy Parent of heaven and earth, that thou hast hid these things from the wise and prudent, and hast revealed them unto babes: even so, All Holy, for so it seemed good in thy sight.

5. All things are delivered to me of the All-Parent: and no man knoweth the Son who is the Daughter, but the All Parent; nor who the All-Parent is, but the Son even the Daughter, and they to whom the Son and the Daughter will reveal it.

6. And he turned him unto his disciples, and said privately, Blessed are the eyes which see the things that ye see. For I tell you, that many prophets and kings have desired to see those things which ye see, and have not seen them; and to hear those things which ye hear, and have not heard them.

7. Blessed are ye of the inner circle who hear my word and to whom mysteries are revealed, who give to no innocent creature the pain of prison or of death, but seek the good of all, for to such is everlasting life.

8. Blessed are ye who abstain from all things gotten by bloodshed and death, and fulfill all righteousness: Blessed are ye, for ye shall attain to Beatitude.

Lection XXI
Iesus Rebuketh Cruelty To A Horse
Condemneth the Service of Mammon
Blesseth Infants

1. AND it came to pass that the Lord departed from the City and went over the mountains with this disciples. And they came to a mountain whose ways were steep and there

they found a man with a beast of burden.

2. But the horse had fallen down, for it was over laden, and he struck it till the blood flowed. And Jesus went to him and said: "Son of cruelty, why strikest thou thy beast? Seest thou not that it is too weak for its burden, and knowest thou not that it suffereth ?"

3. But the man answered and said: "What hast thou to do therewith ? I may strike it as much as it pleaseth me, for it is mine own, and I bought it with a goodly sum of money. Ask them who are with thee, for they are of mine acquaintance and know thereof."

4. And some of the disciples answered and said: Yea, Lord, it is as he saith, We have seen when he bought it. And the Lord said again "See ye not then how it bleedeth, and hear ye not also how it waileth and lamenteth ?" But they answered and said: "Nay, Lord, we hear not that it waileth and lamenteth?"

5. And the Lord was sorrowful, and said: "Woe unto you because of the dulness of your hearts, ye hear not how it lamenteth and crieth unto the heavenly Creator for mercy, but thrice woe unto him against whom it crieth and waileth in its pain."

6. And he went forward and touched it, and the horse stood up, and its wounds were healed. But to the man he said: "Go now thy way and strike it henceforth no more, if thou also desireth to find mercy."

7. AND seeing the people come unto him, Jesus, said unto his disciples, Because of the sick I am sick; because of the hungry I am hungry; because of the thirsty I am athirst.

8. He also said, I am come to end the sacrifices and feasts of blood, and if ye cease not offering and eating of flesh and blood, the wrath of God shall not cease from you, even as it came to your fathers in the wilderness, who lusted for flesh, and they eat to their content, and were filled with rottenness, and the plague consumed them.

9. And I say unto you, Though ye be gathered together in

my bosom, if ye keep not my commandments I will cast you forth. For if ye keep not the lesser mysteries, who shall give you the greater.

10. He that is faithful in that which is least is faithful also in much: and he that is unjust in the least is unjust also in much.

11. If therefore ye have not been faithful in the mammon of unrighteousness, who will commit to your trust the true riches? And if ye have not been faithful in that which is another man's, who shall give you that which is your own ?

12. No servant can serve two masters: for either he will hate the one, and love the other; or else he will hold to the one and despise the other. Ye cannot serve God and mammon. And the Pharisees also, who were covetous, heard all these things, and they derided him.

13. And he said unto them, Ye are they which justify yourselves before men; but God knoweth your hearts: for that which is highly esteemed among men is abomination in the sight of God.

14. The law and the prophets were until John; since that time the kingdom of God is preached, and every man presseth into it. But it is easier for heaven and earth to pass away, than one title of the law to fail.

15. Then there came some women to him and brought their infants unto him, to whom they yet gave suck at their breasts, that he should bless them; and some said, Why trouble ye the master?

16. But Jesus rebuked them, and said, Of such will come forth those who shall yet confess me before men. And he took them up in his arms and blessed them.

Lection XXII
The Restoration Of Iairus Daughter

1. AND behold there cometh one of the rulers of the synagogue, Iairus by name; and when he saw him, he fell at his

feet, and he besought him greatly, saying, My little daughter lieth at the point of death; I pray thee, come and lay thy hands on her, that she may be healed, and she shall live. And Jesus went with him, and much people followed him and thronged him.

2. AND a certain woman, which had an issue of blood twelve years, and had suffered many things of many physicians, and had spent all that she had, and was nothing bettered, but rather grew worse.

3. When she had heard of Jesus, she came in the press behind and touched his garments For she said, If I may touch but his garment, I shall be whole. find straightway the fountain of her blood was dried up; and she felt in her body that she was healed of that plague.

4. And Jesus, immediately knowing in himself that virtue had gone out of him, turned him about in the press and said, Who touched my vesture? And his disciples said unto him, Thou seest the multitude thronging thee and sayeth thou, Who touched me?

5. And he looked round about to see her that had done this thing. But the woman, fearing and trembling, knowing what was done in her, came and fell down before him and told him all the truth. And he said unto her, Daughter, thy faith hath made thee whole; go in peace and be whole of thy plague.

6. WHILE he yet spake, there came from the ruler of the synagogue's house certain which said, Thy daughter is dead: why troublest thou the Master any further ?

7. As soon as Jesus heard the word that was spoken, he saith unto the ruler of the synagogue, Be not afraid, only believe. And he suffered no man to follow him save Peter and James and John the brother of James.

8. And he cometh to the house of the ruler of the synagogue, and seeth the tumult and the minstrels, and them that lamented and wailed greatly.

9. And when he was come in he said unto him, Why make ye this ado and weep? the damsel is not dead but sleepeth. And they laughed him to scorn, for they thought she was dead, and believed him not. But when he had put them all out, he taketh two of his disciples with him, and entered in where the damsel was lying.

10. And he took the damsel by the hand and said unto her, Talitha cumi; which is, being interpreted, Damsel, I say unto thee arise.

11. And straightway the damsel arose and walked. And she was of the age of twelve years. And they were astonished with a great astonishment.

12. And he charged them straightly that no man should make it known, and commanded that something should be given to her to eat.

Lection XXIII
Iesus And The Samaritan Woman

1. THEN cometh Jesus to a city of Samaria, which is called Sychar, near to the parcel of ground that Jacob gave to his son Joseph.

2. Now Jacob's well was there. Jesus therefore, being wearied with his journey, sat alone on the edge of the well, and it was about the sixth hour.

3. And there cometh a woman of Samaria to draw water; Jesus saith unto her, Give me to drink. (For his disciples were gone away unto the city to buy food).

4. Then saith the woman of Samaria unto him, How is it that thou being a Jew, asketh drink of me, who am a woman of Samaria? (for the Jews have no dealings with the Samaritans.)

5. Jesus answered and said unto her, If thou knewest the gift of God and who it is that saith to thee, Give me drink, thou wouldest have asked of God, who would have given thee living water.

6. The woman saith unto him, Sir, thou hast nothing to draw with, and the well is deep, from whence hast thou that living water. Art thou greater than our father Jacob, who gave us the well and drank thereof, himself and his children and his camels and oxen and sheep.

7. Jesus answered and said unto her, Whosoever drinketh of this water shall thirst again, but whosoever drinketh of the water that I shall give him shall never thirst; but the water that I shall give him shall be in him a well of water springing up into everlasting life.

8. The woman saith unto him, Sir, give me this water, that I thirst not, neither come hither to draw. Jesus saith unto her, Go, call thy husband and come hither. The woman answered and said, I have no husband.

9. Jesus looking upon her, answered and said unto her, Thou hast well said, I have no husband. For thou hast had five husbands and he whom thou now hast is not called thy husband, in that saidst thou truly.

10. The woman saith unto him, Sir, I perceive that thou art a prophet. Our fathers worshipped in this mountain and ye say that in Jerusalem is the place where men ought to worship.

11. Jesus saith unto her, Woman, believe me, the hour cometh, when ye shall neither in this mountain nor yet at Jerusalem worship God. Ye worship ye know not what; we know what we worship; for salvation is of Israel.

12. But the hour cometh and now is, when the true wor-shippers shall worship the All-Parent in spirit and in truth; for such worshippers the All-Holy seeketh. God is a Spirit and they that worship, must worship in spirit and in truth.

13. The woman saith unto him, I know that Messiah cometh who is called the Christ: when he is come he will tell us all things. Jesus saith unto her, I am he Who speaketh unto thee.

14. And upon this came his disciples and marvelled that he talked with the woman, yet no man said, What seekest

thou ? or, Why talkest thou with her?

15. The woman then left her waterpot, and went her way into the city and saith unto the men, Come, see a man which told me all things that ever I did: is not this the Christ?

16. Then they went out of the city and came untohim, and many of the Samaritans believed on him, and they besought him that he would tarry with them; and he abode there two days.

Lection XXIV
Iesus Denounces Cruelty
He Healeth the Sick

1. As Jesus passed through a certain village he saw a crowd of idlers of the baser sort, and they were tormenting a cat which they had found and shamefully treating it. And Jesus commanded them to desist and began to reason with them, but they would have none of his words, and reviled him.

2. Then he made a whip of knotted cords and drove them away, saying, This earth which my Father-Mother made for joy and gladness, ye have made into the lowest hell with your deeds of violence and cruelty; And they fled before his face.

3. But one more vile than the rest returned and defied him. And Jesus put forth his hand, and the young man's arm weathered, and great fear came upon all; and one said, He is a sorcerer.

4. And the next day the mother of the young man came unto Jesus, praying that he would restore the withered arm. And Jesus spake unto them of the law of love and the unity of all life in the one family of God. And he also said, As ye do in this life to your fellow creatures, so shall it be done to you in the life to come.

5. And the young man believed and confessed his sins, and Jesus stretched forth his hand, and his withered arm

became whole even as the other, And the people glorified God who had given such power unto man.

6. AND when Jesus departed thence, two blind men followed him, crying and saying, Thou son of David, have mercy on us. And when he was come into the house the blind men came to him, and Jesus saith unto them, Believe ye that I am able to do this?

7. They said unto him, Yea, Lord. Then touched he their eyes, saying, According to your faith be it unto you. And their eyes were opened, and Jesus straitly charged them, saying, See that ye tell no man, But they, when they were departed, spread abroad his fame in all that country.

8. As they went forth, behold, they brought to him a dumb man possessed with a demon. And when the demon was cast out the dumb spake, and the multitude marvelled° saying, It was never so seen in Israel. But the Pharisees said, He casteth out demons through the prince of the demons.

9. AND Jesus went about all the cities and villages, teaching in their synagogues and preaching the gospel of the kingdom and healing every sickness and every disease among the people.

10. But when he saw the multitudes he was moved with compassion on them, because they fainted and were scattered abroad, as sheep having no shepherd.

11. Then said he unto his disciples, The harvest truly is plentiful, but the labourers are few; pray ye therefore the Lord of the harvest, that he will send forth labourers into his harvest.

12. AND his disciples brought him two small baskets with bread and fruit, and a pitcher of water. And Jesus set the bread and the fruit before them and also the water. And they did eat and drink and were filled.

13. And they marvelled, for each had enough and to spare, and there were four thousand. And they departed blessing God for what they had heard and seen.

Lection XXV
The Sermon On The Mount (Part I)

1. JESUS seeing the multitudes, went up into a mountain: and when he was seated, the twelve came unto him, and he lifted up his eyes on his disciples and said:

2. Blessed in spirit are the poor, for theirs is the kingdom of heaven. Blessed are they that mourn: for they shall be comforted. Blessed are the meek; for they shall inherit the earth. Blessed are they who do hunger and thirst after righteousness: for they shall be filled.

3. Blessed are the merciful: for they shall obtain mercy. Blessed are the pure in heart: for they shall see God. Blessed are the peacemakers: for they shall be called the children of God. Blessed are they which are persecuted for righteousness sake: for theirs is the kingdom of God.

4. Yea, blessed are ye, when men shall hate you' and when they shall separate you from their company, and shall reproach you, and cast out your name as evil, for the Son of man's sake. Rejoice ye in that day, and leap for joy: for, behold, your reward is great in heaven; for in the like manner did their fathers unto the prophets.

5. Woe unto you that are rich! for ye have received in this life your consolation. Woe unto you that are full! for ye shall hunger. Woe unto you that laugh now! for ye shall mourn and weep. Woe unto you when all men shall speak well of you' for so did their fathers to the false prophets.

6. Ye are the salt of the earth, for every sacrifice must be salted with salt, but if the salt have lost its savour, wherewith shall it be salted? it is thenceforth good for nothing, but to be cast out, and to be trodden under foot.

7. Ye are the light of the world. A city that is built on a hill cannot be hid. Neither do men light a candle, and put it under a bushel, but on a candlestick; and it giveth light unto all that are in the house. Let your light so shine before men, that they may see your good works, and glorify

your Parent who is in heaven.

8. Think not that I am come to destroy the law, or the prophets: I am not come to destroy, but to fulfil. For verily I say unto you, Till heaven and earth pass, one jot or one tittle shall in no way pass from the law or the prophets till all be fulfilled. But behold One greater than Moses is here. and he will give you the higher law, even the perfect Law, and this Law shall ye obey.

9. Whosoever therefore shall break one of these commandments which he shall give, and shall teach men so, they shall be called the least in the kingdom; but whosoever shall do, and teach them, the same shall be called great in the kingdom of Heaven.

10. Verily they who believe and obey shall save their souls, and they who obey not shall lose them. For I say unto you, That except your righteousness shall, exceed the righteousness of the scribes and Pharisees ye shall not enter the kingdom of Heaven.

11. Therefore if thou bring thy gift to the altar and there rememberest that thy brother hath aught against thee, leave there thy gift before the altar, and go thy way; first be reconciled to thy brother, and then come and offer thy gift.

12. Agree with thine adversary quickly, while thou art in the way with him; lest at any time thy adversary deliver thee to the Judge, and the judge deliver thee to the officer, and thou be cast into prison. Verily I say unto thee. Thou shalt by no means come out thence till thou hast paid the uttermost farthing.

13. Ye have heard that it hath been said, Thou shalt love thy neighbour and hate thine enemy. But I say unto you which hear, Love your enemies, do good to them which hate you.

14. Bless them that curse you, and pray for them which despitefully use you. That ye may be the children of your Parent Who maketh the sun to rise on the evil and the good, and sendeth rain on the Just and on the unjust.

15. For if ye love them which love you what thank have ye? for sinners also love those that love them. And if ye do good to them which do good to you, what thank have ye? for sinners even do the same. And if ye salute your brethren only, what do ye more than others? do not even so the taxgatherers?

16. And if a desire be unto thee as thy life, and it turn thee from the truth, cast it out from thee, for it is better to enter life possessing truth, than losing it, to be cast into outer darkness.

17. And if that seem desirable to thee which costs another pain or sorrow, cast it out of thine heart; so shalt thou attain to peace. Better it is to endure sorrow, than to inflict it, on those who are weaker.

18. Be ye therefore perfect, even as your Parent Who is in heaven is perfect.

Lection XXVI
The Sermon On The Mount (Part II)

1. TAKE heed that ye do not your alms before men, to be seen of them: otherwise ye have no reward of your Parent who is in heaven. Therefore when thou doest thine alms, do not sound a trumpet before thee, as the hypocrites do in the synagogues and in the streets, that they may have glory of men. Verily I say unto you, they have their reward.

2. But when thou givest alms, let not thy left hand know what thy right hand doeth, and take heed that thine alms may be in secret; and the Secret One which seest in secret shall approve then openly.

3. And when thou prayest, thou shalt not be as the hypocrites are: for they love to pray standing in the synagogues and on the corners of the streets that they may be seen of men. Verily I say unto you, They have their reward.

4. But thou, when thou prayest enter into thy chamber and when thou hast shut thy door pray to thy Father-

Mother who is in secret; and the secret One that seeth in secret shall approve thee openly.

5. And when ye pray in common, use not vain petitions, as the heathen do: for they think that they shall be heard for their much speaking. Be not ye therefore like unto them: for your heavenly Parent knoweth what things ye have need of, before ye ask After this manner therefore pray ye, when ye are gathered together:

6. Our Parent Who art in heaven: Hallowed be Thy Name. Thy kingdom come. Thy will be done; in earth as it is in heaven. Give us day by day our daily bread, and the fruit of the living Vine. As Thou forgivest us our trespasses, so may we forgive the trespasses of others. Leave us not in temptation. Deliver us from evil: For Thine are the kingdom and the power and the glory, for ever and ever, Amun.

7. For if ye forgive men their trespasses, your heavenly Parent will also forgive you: but if ye forgive not men their trespasses, neither will your Parent in heaven forgive you your trespasses.

8. Moreover when ye fast, be not, as the hypocrites, of a sad countenance; for they disfigure their faces, that they may appear unto men to fast. Verily I say unto you, they have their reward.

9. And I say unto you, Except ye fast from the world and its evil ways, ye shall in no wise find the Kingdom; and except ye keep the Sabbath and cease your haste to gather riches, ye shall not see the Father-Mother in heaven. But thou, when thou fastest, anoint thine head and wash thy face, that thou appear not unto men to fast, and the Holy One who seeth in secret will approve thee openly.

10. Likewise also do ye, when ye mourn for the dead and are sad, for your loss in their gain. Be not as those who mourn before men and make loud lamentation and rend their garments, that they may be seen of men to mourn. For all souls are in the hands of God, and they who have done good, do rest with your ancestors in the bosom of the Eternal.

11. Pray ye rather for their rest and advancement, and consider that they are in the land of rest, which the Eternal hath prepared for them, and have the just reward of their deeds, and murmur not as those without hope.

12. Lay not up for yourselves treasures upon earth, where moth and rust doth corrupt, and where thieves break through and steal; but lay up for yourselves treasures in heaven, where neither moth not rust doth corrupt and where thieves do not break through nor steal. For where your treasure is, there will your heart be also.

13. The lamps of the body are the eyes: if therefore thy sight be clear, thy whole body shall be full of light. But if thine eyes be dim or lacking, thy whole body shall be full of darkness. If therefore the light that is in thee be darkness, how great is that darkness!

14. No man can serve two masters; for either he will hate the one and love the other; or else he will hold the one and despise the other. Ye cannot serve God and mammon.

15. Therefore I say unto you, Be not over anxious for your life what ye shall eat, or what ye shall drink; nor yet for your body, what ye shall put on. Is not the life more than meat and the body than raiment? And what shall it profit a man if he gain the whole world and lose his life ?

16. Behold the fowls of the air; for they sow not, neither do they reap, nor gather into barns; yet your heavenly Parent feedeth them. Are ye not much better cared for than they? Which of you by taking thought can add one cubit unto his stature? And why spend all your thought for raiment ? Consider the lilies of the field, how they grow; they toil not, neither do they spin. And yet I say unto you, Solomon in all his glory was not arrayed like one of these.

17. Wherefore shall not God who clothes the grass of the field, which to day is, and tomorrow is cast into the oven, much more clothe you, O ye of little faith?

18. Therefore be not over anxious, saying, What shall we eat? or, What shall we drink? or, Wherewithal shall we be

clothed? (all Which things do the Gentiles seek). For your heavenly Parent knoweth that ye have need of all these things. But seek ye first the kingdom of God and its righteousness and all these things shall be added unto you. Meet not in advance the evils of the morrow; sufficient unto the day is the evil thereof.

Lection XXVII
The Sermon On The Mount (Part III)

1. JUDGE not, that ye be not judged. For with what judgement ye judge, ye shall be judged: and with what measure ye mete, it shall be measured to you again; and as ye do unto others, so shall it be done unto you.
2. And why beholdest thou the mote that is in thy brother's eye, but considerest not the beam that is in thine own eye? Or how wilt thou say to thy brother, Let me pull the mote out of thine eye; and behold a beam is in thine own eye? Thou hypocrite, first cast the beam out of thine own eye; and then shall thou see clearly to cast the mote out of thy brother's eye.
3. Give not that which is holy unto the dogs' neither cast ye your pearls before swine; lest they trample them under their feet and turn again and rend you.
4. Ask and it shall be given you; seek, and ye shall find; knock, and it shall be opened unto you: for everyone that asketh receiveth, and he that seeketh findeth, and to them that knock it shall be opened.
5. What man is there of you who, if his child ask bread, will give it a stone? Or, if it ask a fish, will give it a serpent? If ye then, being evil, know how to give good gifts unto your children, how much more shall your Parent Who is in heaven give good things to them that ask?
6. Therefore all things whatsoever ye would that men should do to you, do ye even so to them. And what ye would not that men should do unto you, do ye not so unto them; for

this is the Law and the prophets.

7. Enter ye in at the strait gate, for strait is the way and narrow the gate that leadeth unto life, and few there be that find it. But wide is the gate and broad is the way that leadeth to destruction, and many there be who go in thereat.

8. Beware of false prophets, which come to you in sheep's clothing, but inwardly are ravening wolves. Ye shall know them by their fruits. Do men gather grapes of thorns, or figs of thistles?

9. Even so, every good tree bringeth forth good fruit, but a corrupt tree bringeth forth evil fruit. Every tree that bringeth not forth good fruit is only fit to be hewn down and cast into the fire. Wherefore by their fruits ye shall know the good from the evil.

10. Not every one that saith unto me, Lord, Lord, shall enter into the kingdom of heaven; but he that doeth the will of my Father-Mother Who is in heaven. Many will say to me in that day, Lord, Lord, have we not prophesied in thy Name? and in thy Name have cast out devils? and in thy Name done many wonderful works? And then will I say unto them, I never knew you: depart from me, ye that work iniquity.

11. Therefore whosoever heareth these sayings of mine, and doeth them, I will liken him unto a wise man who built his house foursquare upon a rock. And the rain descended, and the floods came, and the winds blew upon that house; and it fell not, for it was founded upon a rock.

12. And everyone that heareth these sayings of mine, and doeth them not, shall be likened unto a foolish man, who built his house upon the sand, and the rain descended, and the floods came and the winds blew and beat upon that house, and it fell, and great was the fall of it. But a city which is built foursquare, enclosed in a circle or on the top of a hill, and established on a rock, can neither fall nor be hidden.

13. And it came to pass, when Jesus had ended these sayings, the people were astonished at his doctrine. For he taught them as one appealing to the reason and the heart, and not as the scribes who taught rather by authority.

Lection XXVIII
Iesus Releases The Rabbits And Pigeons

1. IT came to pass one day as Jesus had finished his discourse, in a place near Tiberias where there are seven wells, a certain young man brought live rabbits and pigeons, that he might have to eat with his disciples.
2. And Jesus looked on the young man with love and said to him, Thou hast a good heart and God shall give thee light, but knowest thou not that God in the beginning gave to man the fruits of the earth for food, and did not make him lower than the ape, or the ox, or the horse, or the sheep, that he should kill and eat the flesh and blood of his fellow creatures.
3. Ye believe that Moses indeed commanded such creatures to be slain and offered in sacrifice and eaten, and so do ye in the Temple, but behold a greater than Moses is herein and he cometh to put away the bloody sacrifices of the law, and the feasts on them, and to restore to you the pure oblation and unbloody sacrifice as in the beginning, even the grains and fruits of the earth.
4. Of that which ye offer unto God in purity shall ye eat, but of that kind which ye offer not in purity shall ye not eat, for the hour cometh when your sacrifices and feasts of blood shall cease, and ye shall worship God with a holy worship and a pure Oblation.
5. Let these creatures therefore go free, that they may rejoice in God and bring no guilt to man. And the young man set them free, and Jesus break their cages and their bonds.
6. But lo, they feared lest they should again be taken cap-

233

tive, and they went not away from him, but he spake unto them and dismissed them, and they obeyed his word, and departed in gladness.

7. AT that time as they sat by the well, which was in the midst of the six Jesus stood up and cried out, If any are thirsty, let them come unto me and drink, for I will give to them of the waters of life.

8. They who believe in me, out of their hearts shall flow rivers of water, and that which is given unto them shall they speak with power, and their doctrine shall be living water.

9. (This he spake of the Spirit, which they that believed on him should receive, for the fulness of the Spirit was not yet given because that Jesus was not yet glorified).

10. Whosoever drinketh of the water that I shall give shall never thirst, but the water which cometh from God shall be in them a well of water, springing up unto everlasting life.

11. AND at that time John sent two of his disciples, saying, Art thou he that should come, or look we for another? and in that same hour he cured many of their infirmities and plagues, and of evil spirits, and unto many blind, he gave sight.

12. Then Jesus answering said unto them, Go your way, and tell John what things ye have seen and heard; how that the blind see, the lame walk, the lepers are cleansed, the deaf hear, the dead are raised, to the poor the gospel is preached. And blessed is he, whosoever shall not be offended in me.

13. And when the messengers of John were departed, he began to speak unto the people concerning John, What went ye out into the wilderness for to see? A reed shaken with the wind, or a man clothed in soft raiment? Behold, they which are georgeously apparelled, and live delicately, are in kings' courts.

14. But what went ye out for to see? A prophet Yea, I say

unto you, and the greatest of prophets.

15. This is he, of whom it is written, Behold, I send my messenger before thy face, which shall prepare thy way before thee. For I say unto you, Among those that are born of women, there is not a greater prophet than John the Baptist.

16. And all the people that heard him, and the taxgatherers, justified God, being baptized with the baptism of John. But the Pharisees and lawyers rejected the counsel of God against themselves, being not baptized of him.

Lection XXIX
He Feedeth Five Thousand With Six Loaves And Seven Clusters Of Grapes Healing Of The Sick Iesus Walketh On The Water

1. AND the Feast of the Passover drew nigh, and the Apostles and their fellows gathered themselves together unto Jesus and told him all things, both what they had done and what they had taught. And he said unto them, Come ye yourselves apart into a desert place and rest a while: for there were many coming and going, and they had no leisure so much as to eat.

2. And they departed into a desert place by ship privately. And the people saw them departing, and many knew him, and ran afoot thither out of all cities, and outwent them, and came together unto him.

3. And Jesus, when he came forth, saw much people and was moved with compassion towards them, because they were as sheep having not a shepherd.

4. And the day was far spent, and his disciples came unto him and said, This is a desert place, and now the time is far passed. Send them away, that they may go into the

country round about into the villages, and buy themselves bread, for they have nothing to eat.

5. He answered and said unto them, Give ye them to eat. And they say unto him, Shall we go and buy two hundred pennyworth of bread, and give them to eat ?

6. He saith unto them, How many loaves have ye? go and see. And when they knew, they said, Six loaves and seven clusters of grapes. And he commanded them to make all sit down by companies of fifty upon the grass. And they sat down in ranks by hundreds and by fifties.

7. And when he had taken the six loaves and the seven clusters of grapes, he looked up to heaven, and blessed and brake the loaves, and the grapes also and gave them to his disciples to set before them and they divided them among them all.

8. And they did all eat and were filled. And they took up twelve baskets full of the fragments that were left. And they that did eat of the loaves and of the fruit were about five thousand men, women and children, and he taught them many things.

9. And when the people had seen and heard, they were filled with gladness and said, Truly this is that Prophet that should come into the world. And when he perceived that they would take him by force to make him a king, he straightway constrained his disciples to get into the ship, and to go to the other side before him unto Bethsaida, while he sent away the people.

10. And when he had sent them away he departed into a mountain to pray. And when even was come, he was there alone, but the ship was now in the midst of the sea, tossed with waves, for the wind was contrary.

11. The third watch of the night Jesus went unto them, walking on the sea. And when the disciples saw him walking on the sea, they were troubled, saying, It is a spirit; and they cried out for fear. But straightway Jesus spake unto them, saying. Be of good cheer; it is I; be not afraid.

12. And Peter answered him and said, Lord, if it be thou, bid me come unto thee on the water. And he said, Come. And when Peter was come down out of the ship, he walked on the water, to go to Jesus. But when he saw the wind boisterous, he was afraid, and beginning to sink, he cried, saying, Lord, save me.

13. And immediately Jesus stretched forth his hand, and caught him, and said unto him, O thou of little faith, wherefore didst thou doubt? For did I not call thee ?

14. And he went up unto them into the ship, and the wind ceased, and they were sore amazed in themselves beyond measure and wondered. For they considered not the miracle of the loaves and the fruit, for their heart was hardened. 15. And when they were come into the ship there was a great calm. Then they that were in the ship came and worshipped him, saying, Of a truth thou art a Son of God.

16. And when they had passed over, they came unto the land of Gennesaret and drew to the shore And when they were come out of the ship straightway they knew him. And ran through that whole region round about, and began to carry about in beds, those that were sick, where they heard he was.

17. And withersoever he entered, into villages, or cities, or country, they laid the sick in the streets, and besought him that they might touch if it were but the border of his garment, and as many as touched him were made whole.

18. After these things Jesus came with his disciples into Judea, and there he tarried and baptized many who came unto him and received his doctrine.

Lection XXX

The Bread Of Life And The Living Vine

1. The day following, the people which stood on the other

side of the sea, saw that there had been no other boat there, save the one whereinto his disciples had entered and that Jesus went not with his disciples into the boat, but that his disciples were gone alone. And when the people therefore saw that Jesus was not there, neither his disciples, they also took ship and came to Capernaum, seeking for Jesus.

2. And when they had found him on the other side of the sea, they said unto him, Rabbi, how camest thou hither? Jesus answered them and said, Verily, verily, I say unto you, ye seek me, not because ye saw the miracles, but because ye did eat of the loaves and the fruit, and were filled. Labour not for the meat which perisheth, but for that meat which endureth unto everlasting life, which the Son of Man, Who is also the Child of God, shall give unto you, for him hath God the All Parent sealed.

3. Then said they unto him, What shall we do that we may work the works of God? Jesus answered and said unto them, This is the work of God, that ye believe the truth, in me who am, and who giveth unto you, the Truth and the Life.

4. They said therefore unto him, What sign shewest thou then that we may see and believe thee? What dost thou work? Our fathers did eat manna in the desert; as it is written, He gave them bread from heaven to eat.

5. Then Jesus said unto them, Verily, verily, I say unto you, Moses gave you not the true bread from heaven, but my Parent giveth you the true bread from heaven and the fruit of the living vine. For the food of God is that which cometh down from heaven, and giveth life unto the world.

6. Then said they unto him, Lord, evermore give us this bread, and this fruit. And Jesus said unto them, I am the true Bread, I am the living Vine, they that come to me shall never hunger; and they that believe on me shall never thirst. And verily I say unto you, Except ye eat the flesh and drink the blood of God, ye have no life in you. But ye

have seen me and believe not.

7. All that my Parent hath given to me shall come to me and they that come to me I will in no wise cast out. For I came down from heaven, not to do mine own will, but the will of God who sent me. And this is the will of God who hath sent me, that of all which are given unto me I should lose none, but should raise them up again at the last day.

8. The Jews then murmured at him, because he said I am the bread which cometh down from heaven. And they said, Is not this Jesus, the son of Joseph and Mary whose parentage we know? how is it then that he saith, I came down fromheaven?

9. Jesus therefore answered and said unto them, Murmur ye not among yourselves. None can come to me except holy Love and Wisdom draw them, and these shall rise at the last day. It is written in the prophets, They shall be all taught of God. Every man therefore that hath heard and hath learned of the Truth, cometh unto me.

10. Not that anyone hath seen the Holiest at any time, save they which are of the Holiest, they alone, see the Holiest. Verily, verily, I say unto you, They who believe the Truth, have everlasting life.

Lection XXXI
The Bread of Life And The Living Vine
Iesus Teacheth The Thoughtless Driver

1. AGAIN Jesus said, I am the true Bread and the living Vine. Your fathers did eat manna in the wilderness and are dead. This is the food of God which cometh down from heaven, that whosoever eat thereof shall not die. I am the living food which came down from heaven, if any eat of this food they shall live for ever; and the bread that I will give is My truth and the wine which I will give is my life.

2. And the Jews strove amongst themselves, saying, How can this man give us himself for food? Then Jesus said,

Think ye that I speak of the eating of flesh, which ye ignorantly do in the Temple of God?

3. Verily my body is the substance of God, and this is meat indeed, and my blood is the life of God and this is drink indeed. Not as your ancestors, who craved for flesh, and God gave them flesh in his wrath, and they ate of corruption till it stank in their nostrils, and their carcases fell by the thousand in the wilderness by reason of the plague.

4. Of such it is written, They shall wander nine and forty years in the wilderness till they are purified from their lusts, ere they enter into the land of rest, yea, seven times seven years shall they wander because they have not known My ways, neither obeyed My laws.

5. But They who eat this flesh and drink this blood dwell in me and I in them. As the Father-Mother of life hath sent me, and by Whom I live, so they that eat of me who am the truth and the life, even they shall live by me.

6. This is that living bread which coming down from heaven giveth life to the world. Not as your ancestors did eat manna and are dead. They that eat of this bread and this fruit, shall live for ever. These things said he in the synagogue, as he taught in Capernaum. Many therefore of his disciples, when they heard this, said, This is an hard saying, who can receive it?

7. When Jesus knew in himself that his disciples murmured at it, he said unto them, Doth this offend you? What and if ye shall see the Son and Daughter of man ascend to where they were before? It is the spirit that quickeneth, the flesh and blood profiteth nothing. The words that I speak unto you, they are spirit and they are life.

8. But there are some of you that believe not, For Jesus knew from the beginning who they were who should believe not, and who should betray him. Therefore said he unto them. No one can come unto me, except it were given from above.

9. From that time many of his disciples went back and

walked no more with him. Then said Jesus unto the twelve, Will ye also go away ?

10. Then Simon Peter answered him, Lord to whom shall we go? thou hast the words of eternal life. And we believe and we are sure that thou art that Christ, a Son of the living God.

11. Jesus answered them, Have not I chosen you Twelve, and one also who is a traitor ? He spake of Judas Iscariot son of Simon the Levite, for he it was that should betray him.

12. AND Jesus was travelling to Jerusalem, and there came a camel heavy laden with wood, and the camel could not drag it up the hill whither he went for the weight thereof, and the driver beat him and cruelly ill-treated him, but he could make him go no further.

13. And Jesus seeing this, said unto him, Wherefore beatest thou thy brother? And the man answered, I wot not that he is my brother, is he not a beast of burden and made to serve me?

14. And Jesus said, Hath not the same God made of the same substance the camel and thy children who serve thee, and have ye not one breath of life which ye have both received from God?

15. And the man marvelled much at this saying, and he ceased from beating the camel, and took off some of the burden and the camel walked up the hill as Jesus went before him, and stopped no more till he ended his journey.

16. And the camel knew Jesus, having felt of the love of God in him. And the man inquired further of the doctrine, and Jesus taught him gladly and he became his disciple.

Lection XXXII
God The Food And Drink Of All

1. AND it came to pass as he sat at supper with his dis-

ciples one of them said unto him: Master, how sayest thou that thou wilt give thy flesh to eat and thy blood to drink, for it is a hard saying unto many?

2. And Jesus answered and said: The words which I spake unto you are Spirit and they are Life. To the ignorant and the carnally minded they savour of bloodshed and death, but blessed are they who understand.

3. Behold the corn which groweth up into ripeness and is cut down, and ground in the mill, and baked with fire into bread! of this bread is my body made, which ye see: and lo the grapes which grow on the vine unto ripeness, and are plucked and crushed in the winepress and yield the fruit of the vine! of this fruit of the vine and of water is made my blood.

4. For of the fruits of the trees and the seeds of the herbs alone do I partake, and these are changed by the Spirit into my flesh and my blood. Of these alone and their like shall ye eat who believe in me, and are my disciples, for of these, in the Spirit come life and health and healing unto man.

5. Verily shall my Presence be with you in the Substance and Life of God, manifested in this body, and this blood; and of these shall ye all eat and drink who believe in me.

6. For in all places I shall be lifted up for the life of the world, as it is written in the prophets; From the rising up of the sun unto the going down of the same, in every place a pure Oblation with incense shall be offered unto my Name.

7. As in the natural so in the spiritual. My doctrine and my life shall be meat and drink unto you, — the Bread of Life and the Wine of Salvation.

8. As the corn and the grapes are transmuted into flesh and blood, so must your natural minds be changed into spiritual. Seek ye the Transmutation of the natural into the Spiritual.

9. Verily I say unto you, in the beginning, all creatures of

God did find their sustenance in the herbs and the fruits of the earth alone, till the ignorance and the selfishness of man turned many of them from the use which God had given them to that which was contrary to their original use, but even these shall yet return to their natural food, as it is written in the prophets, and their words shall not fail.

10. Verily God ever giveth of the Eternal Life and Substance to renew the forms of the universe. It is therefore of the flesh and blood, even the Substance and Life of the Eternal, that ye are partakers unto life, and my words are spirit and they are life.

11. And if ye keep My commandments and live the life of the righteous, happy shall ye be in this life, and in that which is to come. Marvel not therefore that I said unto you, Except ye eat of the flesh and drink the blood of God, ye have no life in you.

12. And the disciples answered saying: Lord, evermore give us to eat of this bread, and to drink of this cup, for thy words are meat and drink indeed;. By thy Life and by thy Substance may we live forever.

Lection XXXIII
By The Shedding Of Blood Of Others Is No Remission Of Sins

1. JESUS was teaching his disciples in the outer court of the Temple and one of them said unto him: Master, it is said by the priests that without shedding of blood there is no remission. Can then the blood offering of the law take away sin?

2. And Jesus answered: No blood offering, of beast or bird, or man, can take away sin, for how can the conscience be purged from sin by the shedding of innocent blood? Nay, it will increase the condemnation.

3. The priests indeed receive such offering as a reconcilia-

tion of the worshippers for the trespasses against the law of Moses, but for sins against the Law of God there can be no remission, save by repentance and amendment.

4. Is it not written in the prophets, Put your blood sacrifices to your burnt offerings, and away with them, and cease ye from the eating of flesh, for I spake not to your fathers nor commanded them, when I brought them out of Egypt, concerning these things? But this thing I commanded saying:

5. Obey my voice and walk in the ways that I have commanded you, and ye shall be my people, and it shall be well with you. But they hearkened not, nor inclined their ear.

6. And what doth the Eternal command you but to do justice, love mercy and walk humbly with your God? Is it not written that in the beginning God ordained the fruits of the trees and the seeds and the herbs to be food for all flesh?

7. But they have made the House of Prayer a den of thieves, and for the pure Oblation with Incense, they have polluted my altars with blood, and eaten of the flesh of the slain.

8. But I say unto you: Shed no innocent blood nor eat ye flesh. Walk uprightly, love mercy, and do justly, and your days shall be long in the land.

9. The corn that groweth from the earth with the other grain, is it not transmuted by the Spirit into my flesh? The grapes of the vineyard, with the other fruits are they not transmuted by the Spirit into my blood? Let these, with your bodies and souls be your Memorial to the Eternal.

10. In these is the presence of God manifest as the Substance and as the Life of the world. Of these shall ye eat and drink for the remission of sins, and for eternal life, to all who obey my words.

11. Now there is at Jerusalem by the sheep market, a pool which is called Bethesda, having five porches. In these lay a great multitude of impotent folk, of blind, halt, withered,

waiting for the moving of the waters.

12. For at a certain season, an angel went down into the pool and troubled the waters; whosoever went first into the waters was made whole of whatever disease he had. And a man impotent from his birth was there.

13. And Jesus said unto him. Bring not the waters healing? He said unto him. Yea, Lord, but I have no man when the water is troubled to put me in, and while I am trying to come another steppeth down before me. And Jesus said to him, Arise, take up thy bed and walk. And immediately he rose and walked. And on the same day was the Sabbath.

14. The Jews therefore said to him, It is the Sabbath it is not lawful for thee to carry thy bed. And he that was healed wist not that it was Jesus. And Jesus had conveyed himself away, a multitude being in that place.

Lection XXXIV
Love Of Iesus For All Creatures His Care For A Cat

1. WHEN Jesus knew how the Pharisees had murmured and complained because he made and baptized more disciples than John, he left Judea, and departed unto Galilee.   2. AND Jesus came to a certain Tree and abode beneath it many days. And there came Mary Magdalene and other women and ministered unto him of their substance, and he taught daily all that came unto him.

3. And the birds gathered around him, and welcomed him with their song, and other living creatures came unto his feet, and he fed them, and they ate out of his hands.

4. And when he departed he blessed the women who shewed love unto him, and turning to the fig tree, he blessed it also, saying. Thou hast given me shelter and shade from the burning heat, and withal thou hast given me food also.

5. Blessed be thou, increase and be fruitful, and let all who come to thee, find rest and shade and food, and let

the birds of the air rejoice in thy branches.

6. And behold the tree grew and flourished exceedingly, and its branches took root downward, and sent shoots upward, and it spread mightily, so that no tree was like unto it for its size and beauty, and the abundance and goodness of its fruit.

7. AND as Jesus entered into a certain village he saw a young cat which had none to care for her, and she was hungry and cried unto him, and he took her up, and put her inside his garment, and she lay in his bosom.

8. And when he came into the village he set food and drink before the cat, and she ate and drank, and shewed thanks unto him. And he gave her unto one of his disciples, who was a widow, whose name was Lorenza, and she took care of her.

9. And some of the people said, This man careth for all creatures, are they his brothers and sisters that he should love them ? And he said unto them, Verily these are your fellow creatures of the great Household of God, yea, they are your brethren and sisters, having the same breath of life in the Eternal.

10. And whosoever careth for one of the least of these, and giveth it to eat and drink in its need, the same doeth it unto me, and whoso willingly suffereth one of these to be in want, and defendeth it not when evilly entreated, suffereth the evil as done unto me; for as ye have done in this life, so shall it be done unto you in the life to come.

Lection XXXV
The Good Law   -   The Good Samaritan
Mary And Martha On Divine Wisdom

1. AND behold a certain lawyer stood up and tempted him, saying, Master, what shall I do to gain eternal life? He said unto him, What is written in the law ? how readest thou?

2. And he answering, said, Thou shalt not do unto others,

as thou wouldst not that they should do unto thee. Thou shalt love thy God with all thy heart and all thy soul and all thy mind. Thou shalt do unto others, as thou wouldst not that they should do unto thee.

3. And he said unto him, Thou hast answered right, this do and thou shalt live; on these three commandments hang all the law and the prophets, for who loveth God, loveth his Neighbour also.

4. But he, willing to justify himself, said unto Jesus, And who is my neighbour? And Jesus answering said, A certain man went down from Jesusalem to Jericho, and fell among, thieves, which stripped him of his raiment and wounded him and departed leaving him half dead.

5. And by chance there came down a certain priest that way, and when he saw him he passed by on the one side. And likewise a Levite also came and looked on him, and passed by on the other side.

6. But a certain Samaritan, as he journeyed, came where he was, and when he saw him he had compassion on him. And went to him and bound up his wounds, pouring in oil and wine, and set him on his own beast, and brought him to an inn and took care of him.

7. And on the morrow when he departed he took out two pence, and gave them to the host, and said, Take care of him and whatsoever thou spendest more, when I come again, I will repay thee.

8. Which now of these three, thinkest thou, was neighbour unto him that fell among thieves? And he said. He that shewed mercy on him. Then said Jesus unto him, Go, and do thou likewise.

9. Now it came to pass, as they went, that he entered into a certain village, and a woman named Martha received him into her house. And she had a sister called Mary, who also sat at Jesus, feet, and heard his word.

10. But Martha was cumbered about much serving and came to him saying, Lord, dost thou not care that my sister

hath left me to serve alone? bid her therefore that she may help me.

11. And Jesus answered and said unto her, Martha, Martha, thou art careful and troubled about many things, but one thing is needful, and Mary hath chosen that good part, which shall not be taken away from her.

12. AGAIN, as Jesus sat at supper with his disciples in a certain city, he said unto them, As a Table set upon twelve pillars, so am I in the midst of you.

13. Verily I say unto you, Wisdom buildeth her house and heweth out her twelve pillars. She doth prepare her bread and her oil, and mingle her wine. She doth furnish her table.

14. And she standeth upon the high places of the city, and crieth to the sons and the daughters of men! Whosoever will, let them turn in hither, let them eat of my bread and take of my oil, and drink of my wine.

15. Forsake the foolish and live, and go in the way of understanding. The veneration of God is the beginning of wisdom, and the knowledge of the holy One is understanding. By me shall your days be multiplied, and the years of your life shall he increased.

Lection XXXVI
The Woman Taken In Adultery
The Pharisee and the Publican

1. ON a certain day, early in the morning, Jesus came again into the temple, and all the people came unto him, and he sat down and taught them.

2. And the scribes and Pharisees brought unto him a woman taken in adultery, and when they had set her in the midst, they said unto him, Master, this woman was taken in adultery, in the very acts. Now Moses in the law commanded us that such should be stoned, but what sayest thou?

3. This they said, tempting him, that they might have to

accuse him. But Jesus stooped down, and with his finger wrote on the ground, as though he heard them not.

4. So when they continued asking him, he lifted up himself, and said unto them, He that is without sin among you, let him cast the first stone at her.

5. And again he stooped down and wrote on the ground. And they which heard it, being convicted by their own conscience, went out one by one, beginning at the eldest, even unto the last; and Jesus was left alone, and the woman standing in the midst.

6. When Jesus had lifted up himself, and saw none but the woman, he said unto her, Woman, where are those thine accusers? hath no man condemned thee? She said unto him, No man, Lord. And Jesus said unto her, Neither do I condemn thee. From henceforth sin no more; go in peace.

7. AND he spake this parable unto certain which trusted in themselves that they were righteous, and despised others: Two men went up into the Temple to pray; the one a rich Pharisee, learned in the law, and the other a taxgatherer, who was a sinner.

8. The Pharisee stood and prayed thus with himself; God, I thank thee, that I am not as other men are, extortioners, unjust, adulterers, or even as this taxgatherer. I fast twice in the week, 1 give tithes of all that I possess.

9. And the taxgatherer, standing afar off, would not lift up so much as his eyes unto heaven, but smote upon his breath, saying, God be merciful to me a sinner.

10. I tell you, this man went down to his house justified rather than the other; for every one that exalteth himself shall be abased; and he that humbleth himself shall be exalted.

Lection XXXVII
The Regeneration Of The Soul

1. JESUS sat in the porch of the Temple, and some came to learn his doctrine, and one said unto him, Master, what teachest thou concerning life?

2. And he said unto them, Blessed are they who suffer many experiences, for they shall be made perfect through suffering: they shall be as the angels of God in Heaven and shall die no more, neither shall they be born any more, for death and birth have no more dominion over them.

3. They who have suffered and overcome shall be made Pillars in the Temple of my God, and they shall go out no more. Verily I say unto you, except ye be born again of water and of fire, ye cannot see the kingdom of God.

4. And a certain Rabbi (Nicodemus) came unto him by night for fear of the Jews, and said unto him. How can a man be born again when he is old? can he enter a second time into his mother's womb and be born again?

5. Jesus answered, Verily I say unto you except a man be born again of flesh and of spirit, he cannot enter into the kingdom of God. The wind bloweth where it listeth, and ye hear the sound thereof, but cannot tell whence it cometh or whither it goeth.

6. The light shineth from the East even unto the West; out of the darkness, the Sun ariseth and goeth down into darkness again; so is it with man, from the ages unto the ages.

7. When it cometh from the darkness, it is that he hath lived before, and when it goeth down again into darkness, it is that he may rest for a little, and thereafter again exist.

8. So through many changes must ye be made perfect, as it is written in the book of Job, I am a wanderer, changing place after place and house after house, until I come unto the City and Mansion which is eternal.

9. And Nicodemus said unto him, How can these things be? And Jesus answered and said unto him, Art thou a

teacher in Israel, and understandeth not these things? Verily we speak that which we do know, and bear witness to that which we have seen, and ye receive not our witness. 10. If I have told you of earthly things and ye believe not, how shall ye believe if I tell you of Heavenly things? No man hath ascended into Heaven, but he that descended out of Heaven, even the Son-Daughter of man which is in Heaven.

Lection XXXVIII
Iesus Condemneth
The Ill Treatment Of Animals

1. AND some of his disciples came and told him of a certain Egyptian, a son of Belial, who taught that it was lawful to torment animals, if their sufferings brought any profit to men.

2. And Jesus said unto them, Verily I say unto you, they who partake of benefits which are gotten by wronging one of God's creatures, cannot be righteous: nor can they touch holy things, or teach the mysteries of the kingdom, whose hands are stained With blood, or whose mouths are defiled with flesh.

3. God giveth the grains and the fruits of the earth for food: and for righteous man truly there is no other lawful sustenance for the body.

4. The robber who breaketh into the house made by man is guilty, but they who break into the house made by God, even of the least of these are the greater sinners. Wherefore I say unto all who desire to be my disciples, keep your hands from bloodshed and let no flesh meat enter your mouths, for God is just and bountiful, who ordaineth that man shall live by the fruits and seeds of the earth alone.

5. But if any animal suffer greatly, and if its life be a misery unto it, or if it be dangerous to you, release it from its life quickly, and with as little pain as you can, Send it forth

in love and mercy, but torment it not, and God the Father-Mother will shew mercy unto you, as ye have shown mercy unto those given into your hands.

6. And whatsoever ye do unto the Cast of these my children, ye do it unto me. For I am in them and they are in me, Yea, I am in all creatures and all creatures are in me. In all their joys I rejoice, in all their afflictions I am afflicted. Wherefore I say unto you: Be ye kind one to another, and to all the creatures of God.

7. AND it came to pass the day after, that he came into a city called Nain; and many of his disciples went with him, and much people.

8. Now when he came nigh to the gate of the city, behold there was a dead man carried out the only son of his mother, and she was a widow: and much people of the city was with her.

9. And when the Lord saw her, he had compassion on her, and said unto her, Weep not, thy son sleepeth. And he came and touched the bier: and they that bare him stood still. And he said, Young man, I say unto thee, Arise.

10. And he that was esteemed dead sat up, and began to speak. And he delivered him to his mother. And there came an awe upon all: and they glorified God, saying, A great prophet is risen up among us; and God hath visited his people.

Lection XXXIX
The Kingdom Of Heaven
(Seven Parables)

1. AGAIN Jesus was sitting under the Fig tree, and his disciples gathered round him, and, round them came a multitude of people to hear him, and said unto them, Whereunto shall I liken the Kingdom of Heaven ?

2. AND he spake this parable, saying. The kingdom of Heaven is like to a certain seed, small among seeds, which

a man taketh and soweth in his field, but when it is grown it becometh a great tree which sendeth forth its branches all around, which again, shooting downward into the earth take root and grow upward, till the field is covered by the tree, so that the birds of the air come and lodge in the branches thereof and the creatures of the earth find shelter beneath it.

3. ANOTHER parable put he forth unto them, saying, The kingdom of Heaven is like unto a great treasure hid in a field, the which when a man findeth he hideth it, and for joy thereof goeth and selleth all that he hath and buyeth that field, knowing how great will be the wealth therefrom.

4. AGAIN is the kingdom of Heaven like to one pearl of great price, which is found by a merchant seeking goodly pearls, and the merchant finding it, selleth all that he hath and buyeth it knowing how many more times it is worth than that which he gave for it.

5. AGAIN, the Kingdom of Heaven is like unto a woman who taketh of the incorruptible leaven and hideth it in three measures of meal, till the whole is leavened, and being baked by fire, becometh one loaf. Or, again, to one who taketh a measure of pure wine, and poureth it into two or four measures of water, till the whole being mingled becometh the fruit of the vine.

6. AGAIN, the Kingdom of Heaven is like unto a City built foursquare on the top of a high hill, and established on a rock, and strong in its surrounding wall, and its towers and its gates, which lie to the north, and to the south, and to the east, and to the west. Such a city falleth not, neither can it be hidden, and its gates are open unto all, who, having the keys, will enter therein.

7. AND he spake another parable, saying: The Kingdom of Heaven is like unto good seed that man sowed in his field, but in the night, while men slept, his enemy came and sowed tares also among the wheat, and went his way. But when the blade sprung up and brought forth fruit in the

ear, there appeared the tares also.

8. And the servants of the householder came unto him and said, Sir, didst thou not sow good seed in thy field, whence then hath it tares? And he said unto them, An enemy hath done this.

9. And the servants said unto him, Wilt thou then that we go and gather them up ? But he said, Nay, lest haply while ye gather up the tares, ye root up the good wheat with them. 10. Let both grow together until the harvest, and in the time of the harvest I will say to the reapers, Gather up first the tares and bind them in bundles to burn them and enrich the soil, but gather the wheat into my barn. 11. AND again he spake, saying, The kingdom of Heaven is like unto the sowing of seed. Behold a sower went forth to sow, and as he sowed, some seeds fell by the wayside, and the fowls of the air came and devoured them.

12. And others fell upon rocky places without much earth, and straightway they sprang up because they had no deepness of earth, and when the sun was risen they were scorched, and because they had no root they whithered away.

13. And others fell among thorns, and the thorns grew up and choked them. And others fell upon good ground, ready prepared, and yielded fruit, some a hundredfold, some sixty, some thirty. They who have ears to hear let them hear.

Lection XL
Iesus Expounds His Inner Teaching To The Twelve

1. AND the disciples came and said unto him, Why speakest thou unto the multitude in parables? He answer and said unto them, Because it is given unto you to know the mysteries of the kingdom of Heaven, but to them it is not given.

2. For whosoever hath to him shall be given and he shall

have more abundance; but whosoever hath not, from him shall be taken away even that which he seemeth to have. 3. Therefore speak I to them in parables because they seeing see not, and hearing they hear not, neither do they understand.

4. For in them is fulfilled the prophecy of Esaias, which saith, Hearing ye shall hear and shall not understand and seeing ye shall see and shall not perceive; for this people's heart is waxed gross, and their ears are dull of hearing and their eyes they have closed, lest at any time they should see with their eyes, and hear with their ears, and should understand with their heart, and should be converted and I should heal them.

5. But blessed are your eyes for they see, and your ears for they hear, and your hearts for they understand. For verily I say unto you, That many prophets and righteous men have desired to see those things which ye See, and have not seen them, and hear those things which ye hear, and have not heard them.

6. Then Jesus sent the multitude away and his disciples came unto him, saying, Declare unto us the parable of the field; and he answered and said unto them, He that soweth the good seed Is the Son of man; the field is the world, the good seed are the children of the kingdom, but the tares are the children of the wicked one. The enemy that sowed them is the devil, the harvest is the end of the world, and the reapers are the angels.

7. As therefore the tares are gathered and burned in the fire so shall it be in the end of this world. The Son of man shall send forth his angels, and they shall gather out of his kingdom all things that offend, and them which do iniquity, and shall cast them into a furnace of fire, and they who will not be purified shall be utterly consumed. Then shall the righteous shine forth as the Sun in the kingdom of Heaven. 8. Hear ye also the parable of the sower. The seed that fell by the wayside is like as when any hear the

word of the kingdom, and understand it not, then cometh the wicked one and catcheth away that which was sown in their heart. These are they which received seed by the wayside.

9. And they that received the seed into stony places, the same are they that hear the Word and anon with joy receive it. Yet have they not root in themselves but endure only a while, for when tribulation or persecution ariseth because of the Word, by and by they are offended.

10. They also that received seed among the thorns are they that hear the Word, and the cares of this world and the deceitfulness of riches choke the Word, and they become unfruitful.

11. But they that receive the seed into the good ground, are they that hear the Word and understand it, who also bear fruit and bring forth, some thirty, some sixty, some a hundred fold.

12. These things I declare unto you of the inner circle; but to those of the outer in parables. Let them hear who have ears to hear.

Lection XLI
Iesus Setteth Free The Caged Birds
The Blind Man Who Denied That Others Saw

1. AND as Jesus was going to Jericho there met him a man with a cage full of birds which he had caught and some young doves. And he saw how they were in misery having lost their liberty, and moreover being tormented with hunger and thirst.

2. And he said unto the man, What doest thou with these? And the man answered, I go to make my living by selling these birds which I have taken.

3. And Jesus said, What thinkest thou, if another, stronger than thou or with greater craft, were to catch thee and

bind thee, or thy wife, or thy children, and cast thee into a prison, in order to sell thee into captivity for his own profit, and to make a living?

4. Are not these thy fellow creatures, only weaker than thou? And doth not the same God our Father-Mother care for them as for thee? Let these thy little brethren and sisters go forth into freedom and see that thou do this thing no more, but provide honestly for thy living.

5. And the man marvelled at these words and at his authority, and he let the birds go free. So when the birds came forth they flew unto Jesus and stood on his shoulder and sang unto him.

6. And the man inquired further of his doctrine, and he went his way, and learnt the craft of making baskets, and by this craft he earned his bread, and afterwards he brake his cages and his traps, and became a disciple of Jesus.

7. AND Jesus beheld a man working on the Sabbath, and he said unto him, Man, if thou knowest not the law in the spirit; but if thou knowest not, thou art accursed and a transgresor of the law.

8. And again Jesus said unto his disciples, what shall be done unto these servants who, knowing their Lord's will, prepare not themselves for his coming, neither do according to his will?

9. Verily I say unto you, They that know their Master's will, and do it not, shall be beaten with many stripes. But they who not knowing their Master's will, do it not, shall be beaten with but few stripes. To whomsoever much is given, of them is much required. And to whom little is given from them is required but little.

10. AND there was a certain man who was blind from his birth. And he denied that there were such things as Sun, Moon, and Stars, or that colour existed. And they tried in vain to persuade him that other people saw them; and they led him to Jesus, and he anointed his eyes and made him

to see.

11. And he greatly rejoiced with wonder and fear, and confessed that before he was blind. And now after this, he said, I see all, I know everything, I am god.

12. And Jesus again said unto him, How canst thou know all? Thou canst not see through the walls of thine house, nor read the thoughts of thy fellow men, nor understand the language of birds, or of beasts. Thou canst not even recall the events of thy former life, conception, or birth.

13. Remember with humility how much remains unknown to thee, yea, unseen, and doing so, thou mayest see more clearly.

Lection XLII
Iesus Teacheth Concerning Marriage
The Blessing of Children

1. And it came to pass that when Jesus had finished these sayings, he departed from Galilee and came into the coasts of Judea beyond Jordan; and great multitudes followed him and he healed them there.

2. The Pharisees also came unto him, tempting him and saying unto him, Is it lawful for a man to put away a wife for every cause?

3. And he answered and said unto them, In some nations, one man hath many wives, and putteth away whom he will for a just cause; and in some, a woman hath many husbands, and putteth away whom she will for a just cause; and in others, one man is joined to one woman, in mutual love, and this is the first and the better way.

4. For have ye not read that God who made them at the beginning, made them male and female, and said, For this cause shall a man or a woman leave father and mother, and shall cleave to his wife or her husband, and they twain shall be one flesh.

258

5. Wherefore they are no more twain, but one flesh. What therefore God have joined together, let not man put asunder.

6. They said unto him, Why did Moses then command to give a writting of divorcement? He saith unto them, Moses because of the hardness of your hearts suffered you to put away your wives, even as he permitted you to eat flesh, for many causes, but from the beginning it was not so.

7. And I say unto you, Whosoever shall put away a wife, except it be for a just cause, and shall marry another in her place, committeth adultery. His disciples say unto him, If the case of the man be so with his wife it is not good to marry.

8. But he said unto them All cannot receive this saying, save they to whom it is given. For there are some, celibates who were so born from their mother's womb, and there are some, which were made celibates of men, and there be some, who have made themselves celibates for the kingdom of Heaven's sake. He that is able to receive it, let him receive it.

9. THEN there came unto him little children that he should put his hands on them and bless them, and the disciples rebuked them.

10. But Jesus said, Suffer little children to come unto me and forbid them not, for of such is the kingdom of Heaven. And he laid his hands on them and blessed them.

11. AND as he entered into a certain village, there met him ten men that were lepers, which stood afar off. And they lifted up their voices, and said, Jesus Master, have mercy on us.

12. And when he saw them, he said unto them Go, shew yourselves unto the priests. And it came to pass, that, as they went, they were cleansed. And one of them, when he saw that he was healed, turned back, and with a loud voice glorified God and fell down on his face at his feet, giving

him thanks: and he was a Samaritan.

13. And Jesus answering said, Were there not ten cleansed? but where are the nine? There are not found that returned to give glory to God, save this stranger. And he said unto him, Arise, go thy way: thy faith hath made thee whole.

Lection XLIII
Iesus Teacheth Concerning
The Riches Of This World
And the Washing Of Hands
And Eating Of Uncleaned Meats

1. AND, behold, one came and said unto him. Good Master, what good thing shall I do, that I may have eternal life? And he said unto him, Why callest thou me good? there is none good but one, that is, God; but if thou wilt enter into life, keep the commandments. He saith unto him, which be they?

2. Jesus said, What teacheth Moses? Thou shalt not kill, thou shalt not commit adultery, thou shalt not steal, thou shalt not bear false witness, honor thy father and thy mother and thou shalt love thy neighbour as thyself. The young man saith unto him, All these things have I kept from my youth up; what lack I yet?

3. Jesus said unto him, If thou wilt be perfect go and sell that thou hast in abundance, and give to those who have not, and thou shalt have treasure in heaven; and come and follow me.

4. But when the young man heard that saying, he went away sorrowful, for he had great possessions, yea, more than satisfied his needs.

5. Then said Jesus unto his disciple, Verily I say unto you, that the rich man shall hardly enter into the kingdom of Heaven. And again I say unto you, It is easier for a camel to go through the 'gate of the needle's eye" than for a rich

person to enter into the kingdom of God.

6. When his disciples heard it, they were exeedingly amazed, saying, Who then can be saved? But Jesus beheld them, and said unto them, For the carnal mind this is impossible, but with the spiritual mind all things are possible.

7. And I say unto you, Make not to yourselves friends of the Mammon of unrighteousness that when ye fail they may receive you into their earthly habitations; but rather of the true riches, even the Wisdom of God, that so ye may be received into everlasting mansions which fade not away.

8. Then Peter, said unto him, Behold we have forsaken all and followed thee. And Jesus said unto them, Verily I say unto you, that ye which have followed me, in the regeneration, when the Son of man shall sit in the throne of his glory, ye also shall sit upon twelve thrones, judging the twelve tribes of Israel, but the things of this world it is not mine to give.

9. And everyone that hath forsaken riches, houses, friends, for the kingdom of Heaven's sake and its righteousness, shall receive a hundred fold in the age to come and shall inherit everlasting life. But many that are first shall be last, and many that are last shall be first.

10. AND there came unto him certain of the Scribes and Pharisees who had seen one of his disciples eat with unwashen hands.

11. And they found fault, for the Jews eat not except they have first washen their hands and many other things observe they, in the washing of Cups and of vessels and of tables.

12. And they said, Why, walk not all thy disciples after the tradition of the elders, for we saw one who did eat with unwashed hands?

13. And Jesus said, Well hath Moses commanded you to be clean, and to keep your bodies clean, and your vessels clean, but ye have added things which ofttimes cannot be

261

observed by every one at all times and in all places.

14. Hearken unto me therefore, not only unclean things entering into the body of man defile the man, but much more do evil thoughts and unclean, which pour from the heart of man, defile the inner man and defile others also. Therefore take heed to your thoughts and cleanse your hearts and let your food be pure.

15. These things ought ye to do, and not to leave the others undone. Whoso breaketh the law of purification of necessity, are blameless, for they do it not of their own will, neither despising the law which is just and good. For cleanliness in all things is great gain.

16. Be ye not followers of evil fashions of the world even in appearance; for many are led into evil by the outward seeming, and the likeness of evil.

Lection XLIV
The Confession of the Twelve
Christ the True Rock

1. AGAIN Jesus sat near the sea, in a circle of twelve palm trees, where he oft resorted, and the Twelve and their fellows came unto him, and they sat under the shade of the trees, and the holy One' taught them sitting in their midst.

2. And Jesus said unto them, Ye have heard what men in the world say concerning me, but whom do ye say that I am? Peter rose up with Andrew his brother and said, Thou art the Christ, the Son of the living God, who descendeth from heaven and dwelleth in the hearts of them who believe and obey unto righteousness. And the rest rose up and said, each after his own manner, These words are true, so we believe.

3. And Jesus answered them saying, Blessed are ye my twelve who believe, for flesh and blood hath not revealed this unto you, but the spirit of God which dwelleth in you.

I indeed am the way, the Truth and the Life; and the Truth understandeth all things.

4. All truth is in God, and I bear witness unto the truth. I am the true Rock, and on this Rock do I build my Church, and the gates of Hades shall not prevail against it, and out of this Rock shall flow rivers of living water to give life to the peoples of the earth.

5. Ye are my chosen twelve. In me, the Head and and Corner stone, are the twelve foundations of my house builded on the rock, and on you in me shall my Church be built, and in truth and righteousness shall my Church be established.

6. And ye shall sit on twelve thrones and send forth light and truth to all the twelve tribes of Israel after the Spirit, and I will be with you, even unto the end of the world.

7. But there shall arise after you, men of perverse minds who shall through ignorance or through craft, suppress many things which I have spoken unto you, and lay to me things which I never taught, sowing tares among the good wheat which I have given you to sow in the world.

8. Then shall the truth of God endure the contradiction of sinners, for thus it hath been, and thus it will be. But the time cometh when the things which they have hidden shall be revealed and made known, and the truth shall make free those which were bound.

9. One is your Master, all ye are brethren, and one is not greater than another in the place which I have given unto you, for ye have one Master, even Christ, who is over you and with you and in you, and there is no inequality among my twelve, or their fellows.

10. All are equally near unto me. Strive ye not therefore for the first place, for ye are all first, because ye are the foundation stones and pillars of the Church, built on the truth which is in me and in you, and the truth and the law shall ye establish for all, as shall be given unto you.

11. Verily when ye and your fellows agree together touching anything in my Name, I am in the midst of you and

with you.

12. Woe is the time when the spirit of the world entereth into the Church, and my doctrines and precepts are made void through the corruption of men and of women. Woe is the world when the Light is hidden. Woe is the world when these things shall be.

13. AT that time Jesus lifted his voice and said, I thank thee, O most righteous Parent, Creator of Heaven and Earth, that though these things are hidden from the wise and the prudent, they are nevertheless revealed unto babes.

14. No one knoweth thee, save the Son, who is the Daughter of man. None do know the Daughter or the Son save they to whom the Christ is revealed, who is the Two in One.

15. Come unto me all ye that labour and are heavy laden, and I will give you rest. Take my yoke upon you and learn of me, for I am meek and lowly in heart, and ye shall find rest unto your souls. For my yoke is equal and it is easy, my burden is light and presseth not unequally.

Lection XLV
Seeking For Signs
The Unclean Spirit

1. THEN certain of the Scribes and of the Pharisees answered saying, Master we would see a sign from thee. But he answered and said unto them, An evil and adulterous generation seeketh after a sign and there shall no sign be given to it, but the sign of the prophet Jonas.

2. Yea, as Jonas was three days and three nights in the whale's belly, so shall the Son of Man be three days and three nights in the heart of the earth, and after he shall rise again .

3. The men of Nineveh shall rise in judgment with this generation and shall condemn it, because they repented

at the preaching of Jonas, and behold a greater than Jonas is here.

4. The Queen of the South shall rise up in the judgment with this generation, and shall condemn it; for she came from the uttermost parts of the earth to hear the wisdom of Solomon, and behold, a greater than Solomon is here.

5. AGAIN he said: When the unclean spirit is gone out of any, he walketh through dry places seeking rest, and finding none it saith, I will return into my house from whence I came out. And when he is come he findeth it empty, swept and garnished, for they asked not the Good Spirit to dwell within them, and be their eternal Guest.

6. Then he goeth and taketh with him seven other spirits more wicked than himself, and they enter in and dwell there, and the last state of all such is worse than the first. Even so shall it be also unto this wicked generation, which refuseth entrance to the Spirit of God.

7. For I say unto you, whosoever blasphemeth the Son of Man, it shall be forgiven them; but whoso blasphemeth the Holy Spirit it shall not be forgiven them either in this age, or in the next, for they resist the Light of God, by the false traditions of men.

8. WHILE, he yet talked to the people, behold his parents and his brethren and his sisters stood without, desiring to speak with him. Then one said unto him, Behold thy father and thy mother, and thy brethren and thy sisters stand without, desiring to speak with thee.

9. But he answered and said unto him that told him; Who is my father and who is my mother? and who are my brethren and my sisters?

10. And he stretched forth his hand towards his disciples and said, Behold my father and my mother, my brethren and sisters, and my children! For whosoever shall do the will Of my Parent Who is in Heaven the same is my father and my mother, my brother and my sister, my son and my daughter.

11. AND there were some Pharisees, who were covetous and proud of their riches, and he said unto them, Take heed unto yourselves, and beware of covetousness, for a man's life consisteth not in the abundance of things which he possesseth.

12. And he spake a parable unto them, saying, The ground of a certain rich man brought forth plentifully; and he thought within himself, saying, What shall I do, because I have no room where to bestow my fruits?

13. And he said, This will I do; I will pull down my barns, and build greater; and there will I bestow all my fruits and my goods.

14. And I will say to my soul, thou hast much goods laid up for many years, take thine ease, drink and be merry.

15. But God said unto him, Thou fool, this night thy life shall be required of thee; then whose shall those things be, which thou hast provided?

16. So are they that lay up treasures for themselves, and are not rich in good works to them that need, and are in want.

Lection XLVI
The Transfiguration on the Mount
The Giving of the Law

1. AFTER six days, when the Feast of Tabernacles was nigh at hand, Jesus taketh the twelve and bringeth them up into a high mountain apart, and as he was praying the fashion of his countenance was changed, and he was transfigured before them, and his face did shine as the sun, and his raiment was white as the light.

2. And, behold, there appeared unto them Moses and Elias talking with him and spake of the Law, and of his decease which he should accomplish at Jerusalem.

3. And Moses spake, saying, This is he of whom I foretold,

saying, A prophet from the midst of thy brethren, like unto me shall the Eternal send unto you, and that which the Eternal speaketh unto him, shall he speak unto you, and unto him shall ye hearken, and whoso will not obey shall bring upon themselves their own destruction.

4. Then Peter said unto Jesus, Lord, it is good for us to be here; if thou wilt let us make here three tabernacles; one for thee, and one for Moses, and one for Elias.

5. While he yet spake, behold a bright cloud overshadowed them, and twelve rays as of the sun issued from behind the cloud, and a voice came out of the cloud, which said, This is my beloved Son, in whom I am well pleased; hear ye him.

6. And when the disciples heard it, they fell on their faces and were sore amazed, and Jesus came and touched them and said, Arise and be not afraid. And when they had lifted up their eyes, they saw no man, save Jesus only. And the six glories were seen upon him.

7. AND Jesus said unto them, Behold a new law I give unto you, which is not new but old. Even as Moses gave the Ten Commandments to Israel after the flesh, so also I give unto you the Twelve for the Kingdom of Israel after the Spirit.

8. For who are the Israel of God? Even they of every nation and tribe who work righteousness, love mercy and keep my commandments, these are the true Israel of God. And standing upon his feet, Jesus spake, saying:

9. Hear O Israel, JOVA, thy God is One; many are My seers, and My prophets. In Me all live and move, and have subsistence.

14. Ye shall not take away the life of any creature for your pleasure, nor for your profit. nor yet torment it.

11. Ye shall not steal the goods of any, nor gather lands and riches to yourselves, beyond your need or use.

12. Ye shall not eat the flesh, nor drink the blood of any slaughtered creature, nor yet any thing which bringeth disorder to your health or senses.

13. Ye shall not make impure marriages, where love and health are not, nor yet corrupt yourselves, or any creature made pure by the Holy.

14. Ye shall not bear false witness against any, nor wilfully deceive any by a lie to hurt them.

15. Ye shall not do unto others, as ye would not that others should do unto you.

16. Ye shall worship One Eternal, the Father-Mother in Heaven, of Whom are all things, and reverence the holy Name.

17. Ye shall revere your fathers and your mothers on earth, whose care is for you, and all the Teachers of Righteousness.

18. Ye shall cherish and protect the weak, and those who are oppressed, and all creatures that suffer wrong.

19. Ye shall work with your hands the things that are good and seemly; so shalt ye eat the fruits Of the earth, and live long in the land.

20. Ye shall purify yourselves daily and rest the Seventh Day from labour, keeping holy the Sabbaths and the Festival of your God.

21. Ye shall do unto others as ye would that others should do unto you.

22. And when the disciples heard these words, they smote upon their breasts, saying: Wherein we have offended. O God forgive us: and may thy wisdom, love and truth within us incline our hearts to love and keen this Holy Law.

23. And Jesus said unto them, My yoke is equal and my burden light, if ye will to bear it, to you it will be easy. Lay no other burden on those that enter into the kingdom, but only these necessary things.

24. This is the new Law unto the Israel of God, and the Law is within, for it is the Law of Love, and it is not new but old. Take heed that ye add nothing to this law, neither take anything from it. Verily I say unto you, they who believe and obey this law shall be saved, and they who know and

obey it not, shall be lost.

25. But as in Adam all die so in Christ shall all be made alive. And the disobedient shall be purged through many fires; and they who persist shall descend and shall perish eternally.

26. And as they came down from the mountain, Jesus charged them, saying, Tell the vision to no man, until the Son of man be risen again from the dead.

27. His disciples asked him, saying, Why then say the scribes that Elias must first come? And Jesus answered and said unto them, Elias truly shall first come and restore all things.   28. But I say unto you, that Elias is come already, and they knew him not, but have done unto him whatsoever they listed. Likewise shall also the Son of man suffer of them. Then the disciples understood that he spake unto them of John the Baptist.

Lection XLVII
The Spirit Giveth Life
The Rich Man and the Beggar

1. AND when they were come down from the Mount one of his disciples asked him, Master, if a man keep not all these commandments shall he enter into Life? And he said, the Law is good in the letter without the spirit is dead, but the spirit maketh the letter alive.

2. Take ye heed that ye obey from the heart, and in the spirit of love, all the Commandments which I have given unto you.

3. It hath been written, Thou shalt not kill, but I say unto you, if any hate and desire to slay, they are guilty of the law, yea, if they cause hurt or torture to any Innocent Creature they are guilty, But if they kill to put an end to suffering which cannot be healed, they are not guilty, if they do it quickly and in love.

4. It hath been said, Thou shalt not steal, but I say unto you, if any, not content with that which they have, desire and seek after that which is another's or if they withhold that which is just from the worker, they have stolen in their heart already, and their guilt is greater than that of one who stealeth a loaf in necessity, to satisfy his hunger.
5. Again ye have been told, Thou shalt not commit adultery, but I say unto you, if man or woman join together in marriage with unhealthy bodies, and beget unhealthy offspring, they are guilty, even though they have not taken their neighbour's spouse: and if any have not taken a woman who belongeth to another, but desire in their heart and seek after her, they have committed adultery already in spirit.
6. And again I say unto you, if any desire and seek to possess the body of any creature for food, or for pleasure, or for profit, they defile themselves thereby.
7. Yea, and if a man telleth the truth to his neighbour in such wise as to lead him into evil, even thought it be true in the letter, he is guilty.
8. Walk ye in the spirit, and thus shall ye fulfil the law and be meet for the kingdom. Let the Law be within your own hearts rather than on tables of memorial; which things nevertheless ye ought to do and not to leave the other undone for the Law which I have given unto you is holy, just and good, and blessed are all they who obey and walk therein.
9. God is Spirit, and they who worship God must worship in spirit and in truth, at all times, and in all places.
10. AND he spake this parable unto them who were rich, saying, There was a certain rich man, which was clothed in purple, and fine linen, and fared sumptuously every day.
11. And there was a certain beggar named Lazarus, which was laid at his gate, full of sores. And desiring to be fed with the crumbs which fell from the rich man's table; moreover the dogs came and licked his sores.

12. And it came to pass, that the beggar died, and was carried by the angels into Abraham's bosom; the rich man also died, and was buried with great pomp. And in Hades he lift up his eyes, being in torments, and seeth Abraham afar off, and Lazarus in his bosom.

13. And he cried and said, Father Abraham, have mercy on me, and send Lazarus, that he may dip the tip of his finger in water, and cool my tongue, for I am tormented in this place.

14. But Abraham said, Son, remember that thou in thy lifetime receivedst thy good things, and likewise Lazarus evil things: but now he is comforted, and thou art tormented. And thus are the changes of life for the perfecting of souls. And beside all this, between us and you there is a great gulf fixed, so that they which would pass from hence to you cannot; neither can they pass to us, that would come from thence, till their time be accomplished.

15. Then he said, I pray thee therefore, father, that thou wouldest send him to my Father's house; for I have five brethren, that he may testify unto them, lest they also came into this place of torment.

16. Abraham saith unto him, They have Moses and the prophets; let them hear them. And he said, Nay, father Abraham; but if one went unto them from the dead, they will repent.

17. And Abraham said unto him, if they hear not Moses and the prophets, neither will they be persuaded, though one rose from the dead.

Lection XLVIII
Iesus Feedeth One Thousand With Five Melons
Healeth the Withered Hand On The Sabbath Day
Rebuketh Hypocrisy

1. AND it came to pass as Jesus had been teaching the multitudes, and they were hungry and faint by reason of the heat of the day, that there passed by that way a woman on a camel laden with melons and other fruits.

2. And Jesus lifted up his voice and cried, O ye that thirst, seek ye the living water which cometh from Heaven, for this is the water of life, which whoso drinketh thirsteth not again.

3. And he took of the fruit, five melons and divided them among the people, and they eat, and their thirst was quenched, and he said unto them, If God maketh the sun to shine, and the water to fill out these fruits of the earth, shall not the Same be the Sun of your souls, and fill you with the water of life?

4. Seek ye the truth and let your souls be satisfied. The truth of God is that water which cometh from heaven, without money and without price, and they who drink shall be satisfied. And those whom he fed were one thousand men, women and children—and none of them went home ahungered or athirst; and many that had fever were healed.

5. At that time Jesus went on the Sabbath day through the cornfields, and his disciples were an hungered, and began to pluck the ears of corn, and to eat.

6. But when the Pharisees saw it, they said unto him, Behold, thy disciples do that which is not lawful to do upon the Sabbath day.

7. And he said unto them, Have ye not read what David did, when he was an hungered and they that were with

him; how he entered into the house of God and did eat the shewbread, which was not lawful for him to eat, neither for them which were with him, but only for the priests?

8. Or have yet not read in the law, how that on the Sabbath days the priests in the Temple do work on the Sabbath and are blameless? But I say unto you, That in this place is One greater than the Temple.

9. But if ye had known what this meaneth, I will have mercy and not sacrifice, ye would not have condemned the guiltless. For the Son of man is Lord even of the Sabbath.

10. AND when he was departed thence, he went into their synagogue. And, behold, there was a man which had his hand withered. And they asked him, saying, is it lawful to heal on the Sabbath days? that they might accuse him.

11. And he said unto them, What man shall there be among you that shall have but one sheep, and if it fall into a pit on the Sabbath day will he not lay hold on it and lift it out? And if ye give help to a sheep, shall ye not also to a man that needeth?

12. Wherefore it is lawful to do well on the Sabbath day. Then saith he to the man, Stretch forth thine hand. And he stretched it forth, and it was restored whole, like as the other.

13. Then the Pharisees went out and held a council against him, how they might destroy him. But when Jesus knew it, he withdrew himself from thence; and great multitudes followed him, and he healed their sick and infirm, and charged them that they should not make it known.

14. So it was fulfilled, which was spoken by Esaias the prophet, saying, Behold my servant, whom I have chosen; my beloved, in whom my soul is well pleased; I will put my spirit upon him and he shall shew judgment to the Gentiles.

15. He shall not strive nor cry, neither shall any man hear his voice in the streets. A bruised reed shall he not break, and smoking flax shall he not quench till he send forth

judgment unto victory. And in his Name shall the Gentiles trust.

Lection XLIX
The True Temple of God

1. AND the Feast of the Passover was at hand. And it came to pass that some of the disciples being masons, were set to repair one of the chambers Of the Temple. And Jesus was passing by, and they said unto him, Master, Sees't thou these great buildings and what manner of stones are here, and how beautiful is the work of our ancestors?

2. And Jesus said, Yea, it is beautiful and well wrought are the stones, but the time cometh when not one stone shall be left on another, for the enemy shall overthrow both the city and the Temple.

3. But the true Temple is the body of man in which God dwelleth by the Spirit, and when this Temple is destroyed, in three days, God raiseth up a more glorious temple, which the eye of the natural man perceiveth not.

4. Know ye not that ye are the temples of the holy spirit? and whoso destroyeth one of these temples the same shall be himself destroyed.

5. AND some or the scribes, hearing him, sought to entangle him in his talk and said, If thou wouldst put away the sacrifices of sheep and oxen and birds, to what purpose was this Temple built for God by Solomon, which has been now forty and six years in restoring?

6. And Jesus answered and said, It is written in the prophets, My house shall be called a house of prayer for all nations, for the sacrifice of praise and thanksgiving. But ye have made it a house of slaughter and filled it with abominations.

7. Again it is written, From the rising of the sun unto the setting of the same, my Name shall be great among the

Gentiles, and incense with a pure Offering shall be offered unto me. But ye have made it a desolation with your offerings of blood and used the sweet incense only to cover the ill savour thereof. I am come not to destroy the law but to fulfil it.

8. Know ye not what is written? Obedience is better than sacrifice and to hearken than the fat of rams. I, the Lord, am weary of your burnt offerings, and vain oblations, your hands are full of blood.

9. And is it not written, what is the true sacrifice? Wash you and make you clean and put away the evil from before mine eyes, cease to do evil, learn to do well. Do justice for the fatherless and the widow and all that are oppressed. So doing ye shall fulfil the law.

10. The day cometh when all that which is in the outer court, which pertaineth to blood offerings, shall be taken away and pure worshippers shall worship the Eternal in purity and in truth.

11. And they said, Who art thou that seekest to do away with the sacrifices, and despiseth the seed of Abraham? From the Greeks and the Egyptians hast thou learnt this blasphemy?

12. And Jesus said, Before Abraham was, I Am. And they refused to listen and some said, he is inspired by a demon, and others said, he is mad; and they went their way and told these things to the priests and elders. And they were wrath, saying, He hath spoken blasphemy.

Lection L
Christ the Light of the World

1. THEN spake Jesus again unto them, saying, I am the Light of the world: he that followeth me shall not walk in darkness, but shall have the light of life.

2. The Pharisees therefore said unto him, Thou bearest record of thyself thy record is not true.

3. Jesus answered and said unto them, Though I bear record of myself, yet my record is true: for I know whence I came, and whither I go: but ye cannot tell whence I come, and whither I go.

4. Ye judge after the flesh; I judge no man. And yet if I judge, my judgment is true: for I am not alone, but I come from the Father-Mother who sent me.

5. It is also written in your law, that the testimony of two men is true. I am one that bear witness of myself, John bore witness of me, and he is a prophet, and the Spirit of truth that sent me bareth witness of me.

6. Then said they unto him, Where is thy Father and thy Mother? Jesus answered, Ye neither know me, nor my Parent: if ye had known me, ye should have known my Father and my Mother also.

7. And one said, shew us the Father, shew us the Mother, and we will believe thee. And he answered saying, if thou hast seen thy brother and felt his love, thou hast seen the Father, if thou hast seen thy sister and felt her love thou hast seen the Mother.

8. Far and near, the All Holy knoweth Their own, yea, in each of you, the Fatherhood and the Motherhood may be seen, for the Father and the Mother are One in God.

9. These words spake Jesus in the treasury, as he taught in the temple. And no man laid hands on him; for his hour was not yet come. Then said Jesus again unto them, I go my way, and ye shall seek me, and shall die in your sins; whither I go, ye cannot come.

10. Then said the Jews, Will he kill himself? because he said, Whither I go, ye cannot come. And he said unto them, Ye are from beneath; I am from above; ye are of this world; I am not of this world.

11. I said therefore unto you, that ye shall die in your sins; for if ye believe not that I Am of God, ye shall die in your sins.

12. Then said they unto him, Who art thou? And Jesus said unto them, Even the Same that I said unto you from the beginning.

13. I have many things to say which shall judge you: but the Holy One that sent me is true; and I speak to the world those things which I have heard from above.

14. Then said Jesus unto them, When ye have lifted up the Son of man, then shall ye know that I am sent of God, and that I do nothing of myself; but as the All Holy hath taught me, I speak these things. Who sent me is with me: the All Holy hath not left me alone; for I do always those things that please the Eternal.

15. As he spake these words, many believed on him, for they said, He is a Prophet sent from God. Him let us hear.

Lection LI
The Truth Maketh Free

1. THEN said Jesus to those Jews which believed on him, If ye continue in my word, then are ye my disciples indeed; And ye shall know the truth, and the truth shall make you free.

2. They answered him, We be Abraham's seed, and were never in bondage to any man: how sayest thou, Ye shall be made free? Jesus answered them Verily, verily, I say unto you, Whosoever committeth sin is the servant of sin. And the servant abideth not in the house for ever: but the Son even the Daughter abideth ever.

3. If the Son therefore shall make you free, ye shall be free indeed. I know that ye are Abraham's seed after the flesh; but ye seek to kill me, because my word hath no place in you.

4. I speak that which I have seen with my Parent and ye do that which ye have seen with your parent. They answered and said unto him, Abraham is our father. Jesus said unto them, If ye were Abraham's children, ye would do the works

of Abraham.

5. But now ye seek to kill me, a man that hath told you the truth, which I have heard of God: this did not Abraham. YE do the deeds of your father. Then said they to him, We be not born of fornication; we have one Father, even God.

6. Jesus said unto them, If God were your Parent, ye would love me: for I proceeded forth and came from God; neither came I of myself, but the All Holy sent me. Why do ye not understand my speech? even because ye cannot hear my word.

7. Ye are of your father the devil, and the lusts of your father ye will do. He was a murderer from the beginning, and abode not in the truth, because there is no truth in him.

8. When he speaketh a lie, he speaketh of his own; for he is a liar, and the father of it. And because I tell you the truth, ye believe me not.

9. As Moses lifted up the Serpent in the wilderness, so must the Son and Daughter of man be lifted up, that whosoever gazeth, believing should not perish, but have everlasting life.

10. Which of you convicteth me of sin ? And if I say, the truth, why do ye not believe me? He that is of God heareth God's words: ye therefore hear them not, because ye are not of God.

11. Then answered the Jews, and said unto him, Say we not well that thou art a Samaritan, and hath a demon ? Jesus answered, I have not a demon; but I honour the All Holy, and ye do dishonour me. And I seek not mine own glory, but the glory of God. But there is One who judgeth.

12. And certain of the Elders and Scribes from the Temple came unto him saying, Why do thy disciples teach men that it is unlawful to eat the flesh of beasts though they be offered in sacrifice as by Moses ordained.

13. For it is written, God said to Noah, The fear and the dread of you shall be upon every beast of the field, and

every bird of the air, and every fish of the sea, into your hand they are delivered.

14. And Jesus said unto them, Ye hypocrites, well did Esaias speak of you, and your forefathers, sayings This people draweth nigh unto Me, with their mouths, and honour me with their lips, but their heart is far from me, for in vain do they worship Me teaching and believing, and teaching for divine doctrines, the commandments of men in my name but to satisfy their own lusts.

15. As also Jeremiah bear witness when he saith, concerning blood offerings and sacrifices I the Lord God commanded none of these things in the day that ye came out of Egypt, but only this I commanded you to do, righteousness, walk in the ancient paths, do justice, love mercy, and walk humbly with thy God.

16. But ye did not hearken to Me, Who in the beginning gave you all manner of seed, and fruit of the trees and seed having been for the food and healing of man and beast. And they said, Thou speakest against the law.

17. And he said against Moses indeed I do not speak nor against the law, but against them who corrupted his law, which he permitted for the hardness of your hearts.

18. But, behold, a greater than Moses is here! and they were wrath and took up stones to cast at him. And Jesus passed through their midst and was hidden from their violence.

Lection LII
The Pre-Existence Of Christ

1. ANOTHER time Jesus said, Verily, verily, I say unto you, If a man keep my saying, he shall never see death. Then said the Jews unto him, Now we know that thou hast a demon.

2. Abraham is dead, and the prophets; and thou sayest, If a man keep my saying, he shall never taste of death. Art

thou greater than our father Abraham, which is dead ? and the Prophets are dead: whom makest thou thyself ?

3. Jesus answered, If I honour myself, my honour is nothing: it is my Father that honoureth me; of whom ye say, that he is your God: Yet ye have not known him; but I know him: and if I should say I know him not I shall be a liar like unto you; but I know the All Holy and am known of the Eternal.

4. Your father Abraham rejoiced to see my day; and he saw it, and was glad. Then said the Jews unto him, Thou art not yet forty five years old, and hast thou seen Abraham?

5. Jesus said unto them, Verily, verily, I say unto you, Before Abraham was, I AM.

6. And he said unto them, The All Holy hath sent you many prophets, but ye rose against them that were contrary to your lusts, reviling some and slaying others.

7. Then took they up stones to cast at him: but Jesus was hidden, and went out of the temple, through the midst of them, and so again passed unseen by them.

8. Again when his disciples were with him in a place apart, one of them asked him concerning the kingdom, and he said unto them:

9. As it is above, so it is below. As it is within, so it is without. As on the right hand, so on the left. As it is before, so it is behind. As with the great so with the small. As with the male, so with the female. When these things shall be seen, then ye shall see the kingdom of God.

10. For in me there is neither Male nor Female, but both are One in the All perfect. The woman is not without the man, nor is the man without the woman.

11. Wisdom is not without love, nor is love without wisdom. The head is not without the heart, nor is the heart without the head, in the Christ who atoneth all things. For God hath made all things by number, by weight, and by measure, corresponding, the one with the other.

12. These things are for them that understand, to believe.

If they understand not, they are not for them. For to believe is to understand, and to believe not, is not to understand.

Lection LIII
Iesus Healeth The Blind On The Sabbath
Iesus At The Pool Of Siloam

1. AND at another time as Jesus passed by, he saw a man which was blind from his birth. And his disciples asked him saying, Master, who did sin, this man, or his parents, that he was born blind?

2. Jesus answered, To what purport is it, whether this man sinned, or his parents, so that the works of God are made manifest in him? I must work the works of my Parent who sent me, while it is day; the night cometh, when no man can work. As long as I am in the world, I am the Light of the world.

3. When he had thus spoken, he spat on the ground, and mingled clay with the spittle, and he anointed the eyes of the blind man with the clay And said unto him, Go, wash in the pool of Siloam (this meaneth by interpretation, Sent.) He went his way therefore, and washed, and came seeing.

4. The neighbours therefore, and they which before had seen him that he was blind, said, Is not this he that sat and begged? Some said, This is he: others said, He is like him: but he said, I am he.

5. Therefore said they unto him, How were thine eyes opened? He answered and said, A man that is called Jesus made clay, and anointed mine eyes, and said unto me, Go to the pool of Siloam, and wash: and I went and washed, and I received sight.

6. Then said they unto him, Where is he? He said, I know not where he is, that made me whole.

7. Then came to Him certain of the Sadducces, who deny that there is a resurrection, and they asked him saying,

Master, Moses wrote unto us, if any man's brother die having a wife and leaving no children, that his brother should take his wife and raise up seed to his brother.

8. Now there were six brethren, and the first took a wife and he died childless: And the second took her to wife and he died childless: And the third, even unto the sixth, and they died also leaving no children Last of all the woman died also.

9. Now in the resurrection, whose of them is she, for the six had her to wife.

10 And Jesus answered them saying, whether a woman with six husbands, or a man with six wives, the case is the same. For the children of this world marry and are given in marriage.

11. But they, which being worthy, attain to the resurrection from the dead, neither marry, nor are given in marriage, neither can they die any more, for they are equal to the angels and are the children of God, being the children of the resurrection.

12. Now that the dead are raised even Moses shewed at the bush, when he called the Lord, the God Abraham, Isaac and Jacob, for he is not the God of the dead, but of the living, for all live unto Him.

Lection LIV
The Examination of the Blind Man
A Living Type of the House of God

1. THEN they brought to the Pharisees him that aforetime was blind. And it was the Sabbath day when Jesus made the clay, and opened his eyes.

2. Then again the Pharisees also asked him how he had received his sight. He said unto them, He put clay upon mine eyes, and I washed, and do see.

3. Therefore said some of the Pharisees, This man is not of God, because he keepeth not the Sabbath day. Others said,

how can a man that is a sinner do such miracles? And there was a division among them.

4. They say unto the blind man again, What sayest thou of him, that he hath opened thine eyes? He said, He is a prophet.

5. But the Jews did not believe concerning him, that he had been blind, and received his sight, until they called the parents of him that had received his sight.

6. And they asked them, saying, Is this your son, who ye say was born blind? how then doth he now see? His parents answered them and said, We know that this is our son, and that he was born blind; but by what means he now seeth we know not; nor who hath opened his eyes; he is of age; ask him, he shall speak for himself.

7. These words spake his parents, because they feared the Jews; for the Jews had agreed already, that if any man did confess that he was the Christ he should be put out of the synagogue. Therefore said his parents, He is of age? ask him.

8. Then again called they the man that was blind, and said unto him, Give God the praise: we know that this man is a sinner. He answered and said, Whether he be a sinner or no, I know not; one thing I know, that, whereas I was blind, now I see.

9. Then said they to him again, What did he to thee? how opened he thine eyes? He answered them, I have told you already, and ye did not hear: wherefore would ye hear it again? will ye also be his disciples?

10. Then they reviled him, and said, Thou art his disciple; but we are Moses' disciples. We know that God spake unto Moses: as for this fellow, we know not from whence he is.

11. The man answered and said unto them, Why herein is a marvellous thing, that ye know not from whence he is, and yet he hath opened mine eyes. Now we know that God heareth not sinners;

12. But if any man be a worshipper of God, and doeth his

will, him he heareth. Since the world began was it not heard that any man opened the eyes of one that was born blind. If this man were not of God, he could do nothing.

13. They answered and said unto him, Thou wast altogether born in sins, and dost thou teach us? And they cast him out.

14. Jesus heard that they had cast him out; and when he had found him, he said unto him, Dost thou believe on the Son of God ? He answered and said, Who is he, Lord, that I might believe on him.

15. And Jesus said unto him, Thou hast both seen him, and it is he that talketh with thee. And he said, Lord, I believe. And he worshipped him.

16. And Jesus said, For judgment I am come into this world, that they which see not might see; and that they which see might be made blind. And some of the Pharisees which were with him heard these words, and said unto him, Are we blind also?

17. AND Jesus, when he came to a certain place where seven palm trees grew, gathered his disciples around him, and to each he gave a number and a name which he only knew who received it. And he said unto them, Stand ye as pillars in the House of God, and shew forth the order according to your numbers which ye have received.

18. And they stood around him, and they made a body four square, and they counted the number, and could not. And they said unto him, Lord we cannot. And Jesus said, Let him who is greatest among you be even as the least, and the symbol of that which is first be as the symbol of that which is last.

19. And they did so, and in every way was there equality, and yet each bore a different number and the one side was as the other and the upper was as the lower, and the inner as the outer. And the Lord said, It is enough. Such is the House of the wise Master Builder. Foursquare it is, and perfect. Many are the Chambers, but the House is One.

20. Again consider the Body of man, which is a Temple of the Spirit. For the body is one, united to its head, which with it is one body. And it has many members, yet, all are one body and the one Spirit ruleth and worketh in all; so also in the kingdom.

21. And the head doth not say to the bosom, I have no need of thee, nor the right hand to the left, I have no need of thee, nor the left foot to the right, I have no need of thee; neither the eyes to the ears, we have no need of you, nor the mouth to the nose, I have no need for thee. For God hath set in the one body every member as is fitting.

22. If the whole were the head, where were the breasts? If the whole were the belly, where were the feet? yea, those members which some affirm are less honourable, upon them hath God bestowed the more honour.

23. And those parts which some call uncomely, upon them hath been bestowed more abundant comeliness, that they may care one for the other; so, if one member suffers, all members suffer with it, and if one member is honoured all members rejoice.

24. Now ye are my Body; and each one of you is a member in particular, and to each one of you do I give the fitting place, and one Head over all, and one Heart the centre of all, that there be no lack nor schism, that so with your bodies, your souls and your spirits ye may glorify the All Parent through the Divine Spirit which worketh in all and through all.

Lection LV
Christ The Good Shepherd
One With The Father

1. AT that time there passed by the way a shepherd leading his flock to the fold; and Jesus took up one of the young lambs in his arms and talked to it lovingly and pressed it to his bosom. And he spake to his disciples saying:

285

2. I am the good shepherd and know my sheep and am known of mine. As the Parent of all knoweth me, even so know I my sheep, and lay down my life for the sheep. And other sheep I have, which are not of this fold; them also must I bring, and they shall hear my voice, and there shall be one flock and one shepherd.

3. I lay down my life, that I may take it again. No man taketh it from me, but I lay it down of myself. I have power to lay my body down and I have power to take it up again.

4. I am the good shepherd; the good shepherd feedeth his flock, he gathereth his lambs in his arms and carrieth them in his bosom and gently leadeth those that are with young, yea the good shepherd giveth his life for the sheep.

5. But he that is an hireling, and not the shepherd, whose own the sheep are not, seeth the wolf coming and leaveth the sheep and fleeth, and the wolf catcheth them and scattereth the sheep. The hireling fleeth because he is an hireling and careth not for the sheep.

6. I am the door: by me all who enter shall be safe, and shall go in and out and find pasture. The evil one cometh not but for to steal and to kill and destroy; I am come that they might have life, and that they might have it more abundantly.

7. He that entereth in by the door, is the shepherd of the sheep, to whom the porter openeth, and the sheep hear his voice, and he calleth his sheep by name, and leadeth them out, and he knoweth the number.

8. And when he putteth forth his sheep he goeth before them and the sheep follow him for they know his voice. And a stranger will they not follow, but will flee from him, for they know not the voice of strangers.

9. This parable spake Jesus unto them, but they understood not what things they were which he spake unto them. Then said Jesus unto them again, My sheep hear my voice, and I know them, and they follow me and I give unto them eternal life and they shall never perish, neither shall any

man pluck them out of my hand.

10. My Parent who gave them me, is greater than all and no man is able to pluck them out of my Parent's hand. I and my Parent are One.

11. Then the Jews took up stones again to stone him. Jesus answered them, Many good works have I shewed you from my Parent, for which of those works do ye stone me?

12. The Jews answered him, saying, For a good work we stone thee not, but for blasphemy, because that thou being a man maketh thyself equal with God. Jesus answered them, Said I that I was equal to God? nay, but I am one with God. Is it not written in the Scripture, I said, Ye are gods?

13. If he called them gods, unto whom the word of God came, and the Scripture cannot be broken, say ye of him, whom the Parent of all hath sanctified and sent into the world. Thou blasphemest; because I said I am the Son of God, and therefore One with the All Parent?

14. If I do not the works of my Parent believe me not, but if I do, though ye believe not me, believe the works, that ye may know and believe that the Spirit of the great Parent is in me, and I in my Parent.

15. Therefore they sought again to take him, but he escaped out of their hands and went away again beyond Jordan, into the place where John at first baptized and there he abode.

16. And many resorted unto him, and said, John, indeed did not miracle, He is the Prophet that should come. And many believed on him.

Lection LVI
The Raising of Lazarus
From His Sleep In The Tomb

1. Now a certain man was sick, named Lazarus of Bethany, the town of Mary and her sister Martha. (It was that Mary

who anointed the Lord with ointment and wiped his feet with her hair, whose brother Lazarus was sick).

2. Therefore his sisters sent unto him saying, Lord, behold he whom thou lovest is sick. When Jesus heard that, he said, This sickness is not unto death, but that the glory of God might be manifest in him. Now Jesus loved Mary and her sister and Lazarus.

3. When he heard that he was sick, he abode two days still in the same place where he was. Then after that, saith he to his disciples, Let us go into Judea again.

4. His disciples said unto him, Master, the Jews of late sought to stone thee and goest thou thither again? Jesus answered, Are there not twelve hours in the day? If any man walketh in the day he stumbleth not, because he seeth the light of this world.

5. But if a man walk in the night, he stumbleth, because there is no light in him. These things said he, and after that he saith unto them, Our friend Lazarus sleepeth, but I go that I may awake him out of sleep.

6. Then said his disciples, Lord if he sleep, he shall do well. And a messenger came unto him saying, Lazarus is dead. 7. Now when Jesus came, he found that he had lain in the grave four days already (Bethany was nigh unto Jerusalem, about fifteen furlongs off). And many of the Jews came to Martha and Mary to comfort them concerning their brother.

8. Then Martha, as soon as she heard that Jesus was coming, went and met him, but Mary sat still in the house. Then said Martha unto Jesus, Lord if thou hadst been here my brother had not died. But I know that even now, whatsoever thou wilt ask of God, God will give it thee.

9. Jesus saith unto her, Thy brother sleepeth, and he shall rise again. Martha said unto him, I know that he shall rise again, at the resurrection at the last day.

10. Jesus said unto her, I am the resurrection and the life, he that believeth in me, though he were dead yet shall he

live. I am the Way, the Truth and the Life, and whosoever liveth and believeth in me shall never die.

11. She saith unto him, Yea, Lord: I believe that thou art the Christ, the Son of God, which should come into the world. And when she had so said she went her way and called Mary her sister secretly saying, The Master is come and calleth for thee. As soon as she heard that she arose quickly and came unto him.

12. Now Jesus was not yet come into the town, but was in that place where Martha met him. The Jews then which were with her in the house and comforted her, when they saw Mary that she arose up hastily and went out, followed her saying, She goeth unto the grave to weep there.

13. Then when Mary was come to where Jesus was, and saw him she fell down at his feet, saying unto him, Lord if thou hadst been here my brother had not died. When Jesus therefore saw her weeping and the Jews also weeping that came with her, he groaned in the spirit and was troubled. And said, Where have ye laid him? They said unto him, Lord, come and see, and Jesus wept.

14. Then said the Jews, Behold, how he loved him! And some of them said, Could not this man which opened the eyes of the blind, have caused that even this man should not have died? Jesus therefore groaning again in himself (for he feared that he might be already dead) cometh to the grave. It was a cave and a stone lay upon it.

15. Jesus said, Take ye away the stone. Martha, the sister of him supposed to be dead, saith unto him, Lord by this time he stinketh, for he hath been dead four days. Jesus saith unto her, Said I not unto thee, that if thou wouldest believe thou shouldst see the glory of God? Then they took away the stone from the place where Lazarus was laid.

16. And Jesus lifted up his eyes and chanting, invoked the great Name, and said, My Parent, I thank Thee that thou has heard me. And I know that Thou hearest me always, but because of the people which stand by I call upon Thee

that they may believe that Thou hast sent me. And when he had thus spoken he cried with a loud voice, Lazarus come forth.

17. And he that was as dead came forth bound hand and foot with graveclothes, and his face was: bound about with a napkin.

18. Jesus said unto them, Loose him and let him go. When the thread of life is cut indeed, it cometh not again, but when it is whole there is hope. Then many of the Jews which came to Mary and had seen the things which Jesus did, believed on him.

Lection LVII
Concerning Little Children
The Forgiveness Of Others
Parable Of The Fishes

1. AT the same time came the disciples unto Jesus, saying, who is the greatest in the kingdom of Heaven? And Jesus called a little child unto him and set him in the midst of them and said, Verily I say unto you, except ye be converted and become innocent and teachable as little children, ye shall not enter into the kingdom of Heaven.

2. Whosoever therefore shall humble himself as this little child, the same is the greatest in the kingdom of Heaven. And whoso shall receive one such little child in my name receiveth me.

3. Woe unto the world because of offenses! for it must needs be that offences come, but woe to that man by whom the offence cometh. Wherefore if thy lust, or thy pleasure do offend others, cut them off and cast them from thee, it is better for thee to enter into life without, rather than having that which will be cast into everlasting fire.

4. Take heed that ye neglect not one of these little ones, for I say unto you, That in heaven their angels do always behold the Face of God. For the Son of man is come to save

that which was lost.

5. How think ye? if a man have a hundred sheep, and one of them be gone astray, doth he not leave the ninety and nine and go into the mountains and seek that which is gone astray? And if so be that he find it, verily I say unto you, he rejoiceth more over that sheep than over the ninety and nine which went not astray.

6. Even so it is not the will of your Parent, Who is in heaven, that one of these little one should perish.

7. AND there were certain men of doubtful mind, came unto Jesus, and said unto him: Thou tellest us that our life and being is from God, but we have never seen God, nor do we know of any God. Canst thou shew us Whom thou callest the Father-Mother, one God? We know not if there be a God.

8. Jesus answered them, saying, Hear ye this parable of the fishes. The fishes of a certain river communed with one another, saying, They tell us that our life and being is from water, but we have never seen water, we know not what water is. Then some among them, wiser than the rest, said: We have heard there dwelleth in the sea a wise and learned Fish, who knoweth all things. Let us journey to him, and ask him to shew us what water is.

9. So several of them set out to find this great and wise Fish and they came at last to the sea wherein the wise Fish dwelt, and they asked of him.

10. And when he heard them he said unto them, O ye foolish fish that consider not! Wise are ye, the few, who seek. In the water ye live, and move, and have your being; from the water ye came, to the water ye return. Ye live in the water, yet ye know it not. In like manner, ye live in God, and yet ye ask of me, "Shew us God." God is in all things, and all things are in God.

11. AGAIN Jesus said unto them, If thy brother or sister shall trespass against thee, go and declare the fault between thee and thy brother or sister alone; if they shall

hear thee, thou hast gained them. But if they will not hear thee, then take with thee one or two more, that in the mouth of two or three witnesses every word may be established.

12. And if they shall neglect to hear them, tell it unto the church, but if they neglect to hear the church, let them be unto thee as those that are outside the church. Verily I say unto you, Whatsoever ye shall justly bind on earth, shall be bound in heaven, and whatsoever ye shall justly loose in earth, shall be loosed in heaven.

13. Again I say unto you, That if seven, or even if three of you shall agree on earth as touching anything that they ask, it shall be done for them of my Father-Mother Who is in heaven. For where even three are gathered together in my name there I am in the midst of them, and if there be but one, I am in the heart of that one.

14. THEN came Peter to him and said, Lord, how oft shalt my brother sin against me and I forgive him? till seven times? Jesus saith unto him, I say not unto thee, Until seven times, but until seventy times seven. For in the Prophets likewise unrighteousness was found, even after they were anointed by the Holy Spirit.

15. And he spake this parable, saying, There was a certain king who would take account of his servants, and when he had begun to reckon, one was brought unto him which owed him ten thousand talents. But forasmuch as he had not to pay, his lord commanded him to be sold, and his wife and children and all that he had, and payment to be made.

16. The servant therefore, fell down and worshipped him, saying, Lord, have patience with me and I will pay thee all. Then the lord of that servant was moved with compassion and loosed him, and forgave him his debt.

17. But the same servant went out and found one of his fellow-servants which owed him a hundred pence, and he laid hands on him and took him by the throat, saying, Pay

me that thou owest.

18. And his fellow-servant fell down at his feet and besought him, saying, Have patience with me and I will pay thee all. And he would not, but went and cast him into prison till he should pay the debt.

19. So when his fellow-servants saw what he had done they were very sorry, and came and told unto their lord all that was done.

20. Then his lord, after he had called him, said unto him, O thou wicked servant, I forgave thee all that debt because thou desiredst me; shouldst not thou also have had compassion on thy fellow-servant, even as I had pity on thee. And his lord was wroth, and delivered him to the tormentors, till he should pay all that was due unto him.

21. So likewise shall the heavenly Parent judge you, if ye from your hearts forgive not every one, his brother or sister, their trespasses. Nevertheless, let every man see that he pay that which he oweth, for God loveth the just.

Lection LVIII
Divine Love To The Repentant

1. Jesus said unto the disciples and to the multitude around them, Who is the son of God? Who is the daughter of God? Even the company of them who turn from all evil and do righteousness, love mercy and walk reverently with their God. These are the sons and the daughters of man who come up out of Egypt, to whom it is given that they should be called the sons and the daughters of God.

2. And they are gathered from all tribes and nations and peoples and tongues, and they come from the East and the West and the North and the South, and they dwell on Mount Zion, and they eat bread and they drink of the fruit of the vine at the table of God. and they see God face to face.

3. Then drew near unto him all the taxgatherers and sinners for to hear him. And the Pharisees and Scribes mur-

mured, saying, This man receiveth sinners and eateth with them.

4. AND he spake this parable unto them, saying, What man of you having an hundred sheep, if he lose one of them doth not leave the ninety and nine in the wilderness, and go after that which is lost, until he find it? And when he hath found it he layeth it on his shoulders, rejoicing.

5. And when he cometh home, he calleth together his friends and neighbours, saying unto them, Rejoice with me, for I have found my sheep which was lost. I say unto you, that likewise joy shall be in heaven over one sinner that repenteth, more than over ninety and nine just persons which need no repentance.

6. Either what woman having ten pieces of silver, if she lose one piece doth not light a candle and seek diligently till she find it? And when she hath found it she calleth her friends and her neighbours together, saying, Rejoice with me, for I have found the piece of silver which I had lost. Likewise, I say unto you, there is joy in the presence of the angels of God over one sinner that repenteth.

7. AND he also spake this parable, A certain man had two sons, and the younger of them said to his parents, Give me the portion of goods that falleth to me. And they divided unto him their living. And not many days after the younger son gathered all together and took his journey into a fair country, and there wasted his substance with riotous living.

8. And when he had spent all, there arose a mighty famine in that land, and he began to be in want. And he went and joined himself to a citizen of that country, and he sent him into his fields to feed swine. And he would fain have filled his body with the husks that the swine did eat, and no man gave unto him.

9. And when he came to himself he said, How many hired servants of my father's have bread enough and to spare, and I perish with hunger! I will arise and go to my father

and mother, and will say unto them. My father and my mother, I have sinned against Heaven and before you, and am no more worthy to be called your son, make me as one of your hired servants.

10. And he arose and came to his parents. But when he was a great way off, his mother and his father saw him and had compassion, and ran and fell on his neck and kissed him. And the son said unto them, My father and my mother, I have sinned against Heaven and in your sight, and am no more worthy to be called your son.

11. But the father said to his servants, Bring forth the best robe, and put it on him, and put a ring on his hand and shoes on his feet, and bring hither the best ripe fruits, and the bread and the oil and the wine, and let us eat and be merry; for this my son was dead and is alive again, he was lost and is found. And they began to be merry.

12. Now his elder son was in the field, and as he came and drew nigh to the house he heard music and dancing. And he called one of the servants and asked what these things meant. And he said unto him, Thy brother who was lost is come back, and thy father and thy mother have prepared the bread and the oil and the wine and the best ripe fruits, because they have received him safe and sound.

13. And he was angry and would not go in, therefore came his father out and entreated him. And he answering, said to his father, Lo, these many years have I served thee, neither transgressed I at any time thy commandments, and yet thou never gavest me such goodly feast that I may make merry with my friends.

14. But as soon as this thy son is come, which hath devoured thy living with harlots, thou preparest for him a feast of the best that thou hast.

15. And his father said unto him, Son, thou art ever with me, and all that I have is thine. It was meet, therefore, that we should be merry and be glad, for this thy brother was dead and is alive again, and was lost and is found.

Lection LIX
Iesus Forewarneth His Disciples
Glad Tidings to Zaccheus

1. AND Jesus went up into a mountain and there he sat with his disciples and taught them, and he said unto them, Fear not, little flock, for it is your Father's good pleasure to give you the kingdom.

2. Sell that ye have and do that which is good, for them which have not; provide yourselves bags which wax not old, a treasure in the heavens that faileth not, where no thief approacheth, neither moth corrupteth. For where your treasure is, there will your heart be also.

3. Let your loins be girded about, and your lights burning, and ye yourselves like unto men that wait for their lord, when he will return from the wedding that when he cometh and knocketh they may open unto him immediately.

4. Blessed are those servants whom the lord, when he cometh, shall find watching; verily I say unto you that he shall gird himself and make them to sit down at his table, and will come forth and serve them.

5. And if he shall come in the second watch, or come in the third watch and find them so, blessed rare those servants.

6. And this know, that the guardian of the house not knowing what hour the thief would come, would have watched and not have suffered his house to have been broken through. Be ye therefore ready also, for the Son of man cometh at an hour when ye think not.

7. Then Peter said unto him, Lord, speakest thou this parable unto us, or even to all? And the Lord said, Who then is that faithful and wise steward, whom his lord shall make ruler over his household, to give them who serve their portion in due season?

8. Blessed is that servant whom his lord when he cometh shall find so doing. Of a truth I say unto you, that he will make him ruler over all that he hath.

9. But and if that servant say in his heart, My lord delayeth his coming and shall begin to beat the menservants and maidservants and to eat and drink and to be drunken, the lord of that servant will come in a day when he looketh not for him, and at an hour when he is not aware and will appoint him his portion with the unfaithful.

10. And that servant which knew his lord's will and prepared not himself, neither did according to his will, shall be beaten with many stripes. But he that knew not, and did commit things worthy of stripes, shall be beaten with few stripes. For unto whomsoever much is given, of him shall they much require the less.

11. For they who know the Godhead, and have found in the way of Life the mysteries of light and then have fallen into sin, shall be punished with greater chastisements than they who have not known the way of Life.

12. Such shall return when their cycle is completed and to them will be given space to consider, and amend their lives, and learning the mysteries, enter into the kingdom of light.

13. AND Jesus entered and passed through Jericho. And, behold, there was a man named Zaccheus, which was the chief among the collectors of tribute, and he was rich.

14. And he sought to see Jesus who he was; and could not for the press, because he was little of stature. And he ran before, and climbed up into a sycamore tree to see him: for he was to pass that way.

15. And when Jesus came to the place, he looked up, and saw him, and said unto him, Zacheus, make haste, and come down; for to day I must abide at thy house. And he made haste and came down, and received him joyfully.

16. And when they saw it, they all murmured, saying, That he was gone to be guest with a man that is a sinner.

17. And Zachaeus stood, and said unto the Lord, Behold, Lord, the half of my goods I give to the poor; and if I have taken anything from any man by false accusation, I restore him fourfold.

18. And Jesus said unto him, This day is salvation come to thine house, forsomuch as thou art a just man, thou also art a son of Abraham. For the Son of man is come to seek and to save that which ye deem to be lost.

Lection LX
Iesus Rebuketh Hyprocrisy

1. THEN spake Jesus to the multitude, and to his disciples, saying. The scribes and the Pharisees sit in Moses's seat. All therefore whatsoever they bid you observe, that observe and do; but do not ye after their works: for they say and do not. For they bind heavy burdens and grievous to be borne, and lay them on men's shoulders; but they themselves will not move them with one of their fingers.

2. But all their works they do for to be seen of men; they make broad their phylacteries, and enlarge the borders of their garments, and love the uppermost rooms at feasts, and the chief seats in the synagogues, and greetings in the markets, and to be called of men, Rabbi, Rabbi.

3. But desire not ye to be called Rabbi: for one is your Rabbi, even Christ; and all ye are brethren. And call not any one father on earth, for on earth are fathers in the flesh only; but in Heaven there is One Who is your Father and your Mother, Who hath the Spirit of truth, Whom the world cannot receive.

4. Neither desire ye to be called masters, for one is your Master, even Christ. But they that are greatest among you shall be your servants. And whosoever shall exalt themselves shall be abased; and they that are humble in themselves shall be exalted.

5. Woe unto you, scribes and Pharisees, hypocrites! for ye shut up the kingdom of Heaven against men: for ye neither go in yourselves neither suffer ye them that are entering, to go in.

6. Woe unto you, scribes and Pharisees, hypocrites" for ye

298

devour widows' houses, and for a pretence make long prayer; therefore ye shall receive the greater damnation.

7. Woe unto you, scribes and Pharisees, hypocrites! for ye compass sea and land to make one proselyte; and when he is made, ye make him twofold more the child of hell than yourselves.

8. Woe unto you, ye blind guides, who say, Whosoever shall swear by the Temple, it is nothing, but whosoever shall swear by the gold of the Temple, he is a debtor! Ye fools and blind; for whether is greater, the gold, or the Temple that sanctifieth the gold?

9. And, Whosoever shall swear by the altar, it is nothing; but whosoever sweareth by the gift that is upon it, he is guilty. Ye fools and blind: for whether is greater, the gift, or the altar, that sanctifieth the gift?

10. Whoso therefore shall swear by the altar, sweareth by it, and by all things thereon. And whoso shall swear by the Temple, sweareth by it, and by him that dwelleth therein. And he that shall swear by Heaven sweareth by the throne of God, and by the Holy One that sitteth thereon.

11. Woe unto you, scribes and Pharisees, hypocrites! for ye pay tithe of mint and anise and cummin, and have omitted the weightier matters of the law, judgment, mercy, and faith: these ought ye to have done, and not to leave the other undone. Ye blind guides! for ye strain out a gnat, and swallow a camel.

12. Woe unto you, scribes and Pharisees, hypocrites! for ye make clean the outside of the cup and of the platter, but within they are full of extortion and excess. Thou blind Pharisee, cleanse first that which is within the cup and platter, then the outside of them that they may be clean also.

13. Woe unto you, scribes and Pharisees, hypocrites! for ye are like unto whited sepulchres, which indeed appear beautiful outward, but are within full of the bones of the dead and of all uncleanness. Even so ye also outwardly

appear righteous unto men, but within ye are full of hypocrisy and make believe.

14. Woe unto you, scribes and Pharisees, hypocrites! because ye build the tombs of the prophets, and garnish the sepulchres of the righteous, and say, If we had been in the days of our fathers, we would not have been partakers with them in the blood of the prophets.

15. Wherefore ye be witness unto yourselves, that ye do as the children of them which killed the prophets. Fill ye up then the measure of your fathers.

16. Wherefore saith holy Wisdom, behold I send unto you prophets, and wise men, and scribes: and some of them ye shall kill and crucify; and some of them shall ye scourge in your synagogues, and persecute them from city to city. And upon you shall come all the righteous blood shed upon the earth, from the blood of righteous Abel unto the blood of Zacharias son of Barachias, who was slain between the temple and the altar. Verily I say unto you, All these things shall come upon this generation.

17. O Jerusalem, Jerusalem, thou that killest the prophets, and stonest them which are sent unto thee, how often would I have gathered thy children together, even as a hen gathereth her chickens under her wings, and ye would not! 18. Behold, now your house is left unto you desolate. For I say unto you, Ye shall not see me henceforth, till ye shall say, Holy, Holy, Holy, Blessed are they who come in the Name of the Just One.

Lection LXI
Iesus Foretelleth The End

1. AND as Jesus sat upon the Mount of Olives, the disciples came unto him privately, saying, Tell us, when shall these things be? and what shall be the sign of thy coming, and of the end of the world? And Jesus answered and said unto them, Take heed that no man deceive you. For many

shall come in my Name, saying, I am Christ; and shall deceive many.

2. And ye shall hear of wars and rumours of wars; see that ye be not troubled; for all these things must come to pass, but the end is not yet. For nation shall rise against nation, and kingdom against kingdom; and there shall be famines, and pestilences, and earthquakes, in divers places. All these are the beginning of sorrows.

3. And in those days those that have power shall gather to themselves the lands and riches of the earth for their own lusts, and shall oppress the many who lack and hold them in bondage, and use them to increase their riches, and they shall oppress even the beasts of the field, setting up the abominable thing. But God shall send them his messenger and they shall proclaim his laws, which men have hidden by their traditions, and those that trangress shall die.

4. Then shall they deliver you up to be afflicted, and shall kill you; and ye shall be hated of all nations for my Name's sake. And then shall many be offended, and shall betray one another, and shall hate one another. And many false prophets shall rise, and shall deceive many.

5. And because iniquity shall abound, the love of many shall wax cold. But he that shall endure unto the end, the same shall be saved. And this gospel of the kingdom shall be preached in all the world for a witness unto all nations; and then shall the end come.

6. When ye therefore shall see the abomination of desolation, spoken of by Daniel the prophet, stand in the holy place, (whoso readeth, let him understand) then let them which be in Judea flee to the mountains. Let them which are on the housetop not come down to take anything out of the house; neither let them who are in the field return back to take their clothes.

7. And woe unto them that are with child, and to them that give suck in those days! But pray ye that your fight be not

in the winter, neither on the Sabbath day; for there shall be great tribulation, such as was not since the beginning of the world to this time, no, nor ever shall be. And except those days be shortened, there should no flesh be saved; but for the elect's sake those days shall be shortened.

8. Then if any man shall say unto you, Lo, here is Christ, or there; haste not to believe. For there shall arise false Christs, and false prophets, who shall shew great signs and wonders; insomuch that, if it were possible, they shall deceive the very elect. Behold, I have told you before.

9. Wherefore if they shall say unto you, Behold, he is in the desert; go not forth: behold, he is in the secret chambers; haste not to believe. For as the lightening cometh out of the east, and shineth even unto the west; so shall also the coming of the Son of man be. For wheresoever the carcase is, there will the eagles be gathered together.

10. Immediately after the tribulation of those days shall the sun be darkened, and the moon shall not give her light, and the stars shall fall from Heaven, and the powers of the Heavens shall be shaken.

11. And then shall appear the sign of the Son of man in Heaven; and then shall all the tribes of the earth mourn, and they shall see the Son of man coming in the clouds of Heaven with power and great glory. And he shall send his angels with a great sound as of a trumpet, and they shall gather together his elect from the four winds, from one end of Heaven to the other.

12. Now learn a parable of the fig tree; When its branch is yet tender, and putteth forth leaves, ye know that summer is nigh. So likewise ye, when ye shall see all these things, know that it is near, even at the doors. Verily I say unto you, this generation shall not pass till all these things be fulfilled. Heaven and earth shall pass away, but my words shall not pass away.

13. But of that day and hour knoweth no man, no, not the angels of Heaven, but the All Parent only. For as the days

of Noe were, so shall also the comming of the Son of man be.

14. For as in the days that were before the flood, they were eating and drinking, marrying and giving in marriage, until the day that Noe entered into the ark and knew not until the flood came, and took them all away; so shall also the coming of the Son of man be.

15. Then shall two be in the field; the one shall be taken, and the other left. Two women shall be grinding at the mill; the one shall be taken, and the other left. Watch therefore: for ye know not what hour your Lord doth come.

16. But know this, that if the guardian of the house had known in what watch the thief would come, he would have watched, and would not have suffered his house to be broken up. Therefore be ye also ready: for in such an hour as ye think not, the Son of man cometh.

17. Who then is a faithful and wise servant, whom his lord hath made ruler over his household, to give them meat in due season?

18. Blessed be that servant, whom his lord when he cometh shall find so doing. Verily I say unto you, That he shall make him ruler over all his goods.

19. But and if that evil servant shall say in his heart, My lord delayeth his coming, and shall begin to smite his fellow servants, and to eat with the glutton, and drink with the drunken.

20. The lord of that servant shall come in a day when he looketh not for him, and in an hour that he is not aware of. And shall appoint him his portion with the hypocrites in the outer darkness with the cruel, and them that have no love, no pity: there shall be weeping and gnashing of teeth.

Lection LXII
The Parable Of The Ten Virgins

1. THEN shall the kingdom of Heaven be like unto ten virgins, which took their lamps, and went forth to meet the

bridegroom. And five of them were wise, and five were foolish.

2. They that were foolish took their lamps, and took no oil with them: But the wise took oil in their vessels with their lamps.

3. While the bridegroom tarried, they all slumbered and slept. And at midnight there was a great cry made, Behold, the bridegroom cometh; go ye out to meet him. Then all those virgins arose, and trimmed their lamps.

4. And the foolish said unto the wise, Give us of your oil; for our lamps are gone out. But the wise answered, saying, Not so, lest there be not enough for us and you: but go ye rather to them that sell, and buy for yourselves.

5. And while they went to buy, the bridegroom came; and they that were ready went in with him to the marriage, and the door was shut.

6. Afterwards came also the other virgins, saying Lord, Lord, open to us. But he answered and said, Verily I say unto you, I know you not.

7. Watch therefore, for ye know neither the day nor the hour wherein the Son of man cometh. Keep your lamps burning.

Lection LXIII
Parable Of The Talents

1. He also said: The kingdom of Heaven is as a man travelling into a far country, who called his own servants, and delivered unto them his goods. And unto one he gave five talents, to another two, and to another one; to every man according to his several ability; and straightway took his journey.

2. Then he that had received the five talents went and traded with the same, and made them other five talents. And likewise he that had received two, he also gained another two. But he that had received one went and digged in the earth,

and hid his lord's money.

3. After a long time, the lord of those servants cometh, and reckoneth with them. And so he that had received five talents came and brought other five talents, saying, Lord, thou deliveredst unto me five talents; behold, I have gained beside them five talents more. His lord said unto him, Well done, thou good and faithful servant: thou hast been faithful over a few things, I will make thee ruler over many things; enter thou into the joy of thy lord.

4. He also that had received two talents came and said, Lord, thou deliveredst unto me two talents; behold, I have gained two other talents beside them. His lord said unto him, Well done, good and faithful servant; thou hast been faithful over a few things, will make thee ruler over many things; enter thou into the joy of thy lord.

5. Then he which had received the one talent came and said, Lord, I knew thee that thou art an hard man, reaping where thou hast not sown, and gathering where thou hast not strawed. And I was afraid, and went and hid thy talent in the earth; lo, there thou hast that is thine.

6. His lord answered and said unto him, Thou wicked and slothful servant, dost thou tell me that I reap where I sowed not, and gather where I have not strawed? Thou oughtest therefore to have put thy talents to use, with profit, and then at my coming I should have received mine own with usury.

7. Take therefore the talent from him, and give it unto him who hath two talents. For unto every one that hath improved shall be given, and he shall have abundance, but from him that hath not improved, shall be taken away, even that which he hath. And cast yet out the unprofitable servant into outer darkness, for that is the portion he hath chosen.

8. Jesus also said unto his disciples, Be ye approved moneychangers of the kingdom, rejecting the bad and the false, and retaining the good and the true.

9. AND Jesus sat over against the Treasury and beheld how the people cast money into the Treasury.

10. And there came a certain poor widow and she threw in two mites, which make a farthing.

11. And He called His disciples unto him and said, Verily I say unto you, that this poor widow hath cast more in than all they which have cast into the Treasure.

12. For all they did cast in of their abundance, but she of her poverty did cast in all that she had, even all her living.

Lection LXIV
Iesus Teacheth In The Palm Circle
The Divine Life And Substance

1. JESUS came to a certain fountain near Bethany, around which grew twelve palm trees, where he often went with his disciples to teach them of the mysteries of the kingdom, and there he sat beneath the shade of the trees and his disciples with him.

2. And one of them said, Master, it is written of old, The Alohim made man in Their own image, male and female created They them. How sayest thou then that God is one? And Jesus said unto them, Verily, I said unto you, In God there is neither male nor female and yet both are one, and God is the Two in One. He is She and She is He. The Alohim—our God—is perfect, Infinite, and One.

3. As in the man, the Father is manifest, and the Mother hidden; so in the woman, the Mother is manifest, and the Father hidden. Therefore shall the name of the Father and the Mother be equally hallowed, for They are the great Powers of God, and the one is not without the other, in the One God.

4. Adore ye God, above you, beneath you, on the right hand, on the left hand before you, behind you, within you, around you. Verily, there is but One God, Who is All in All, and in Whom all things do consist, the Fount of all Life

and all Substance, without beginning and without end.

5. The things which are seen and pass away are The manifestations of the unseen which are eternal, that from the visible things of Nature ye may reach to the invisible things of the Godhead; and by that which is natural, attain to that which is spiritual.

6. Verily, the Alohim created man in the divine image male and female, and all nature is in the Image of God, therefore is God both male and female, not divided, but the Two in One, Undivided and Eternal, by Whom and in Whom are all things, visible and invisible.

7. From the Eternal they flow, to the Eternal they return. The spirit to Spirit, soul to Soul, mind to Mind, sense to Sense, life to Life, form to Form, dust to Dust.

8. In the beginning God willed and there came forth the beloved Son, the divine Love, and the beloved Daughter, the holy Wisdom, equally proceeding from the One Eternal Fount; and of these are the generations of the Spirits of God, the Sons and Daughters of the Eternal.

9. And These descend to earth, and dwell with men and teach them the ways of God, to love the laws of the Eternal, and obey them, that in them they may find salvation.

10. Many nations have seen their day. Under divers names have they been revealed to them, and they have rejoiced in their light; and even now they come again unto you, but Israel receiveth them not.

11. Verily I say unto you, my twelve whom I have chosen, that which hath been taught by them of old time is true—though corrupted by the foolish imaginations of men.

12. Again, Jesus spake unto Mary Magdalene saying, It is written in the law, Whoso leaveth father or mother, let him die the death. Now the law speaketh not of the parents in this life, but of the Indweller of light which is in us unto this day.

13. Whoso therefore forsaketh Christ the Saviour, the Holy

law, and the body of the Elect, let them die the death. Yea, let them be lost in the outer darkness, for so they willed and none can hinder.

Lection LXV
The Last Anointing by Mary Magdalene
Neglect Not The Present Time

1. NOW, on the evening of the Sabbath before the Passover, as Jesus was in Bethany he went to the house of Simon the leper, and there they made him a supper, and Martha served while Lazarus was one of them that sat at table with him.

2. And there came Mary called Magdalene, having an alabaster box of ointment of spikenard, very precious and costly, and she opened the box and poured the ointment on the head of Jesus, and anointed his feet, and wiped them with the hair of her head.

3. Then said one among his disciples, Judas Iscariot, who was to betray him, Why is this waste of ointment which might have been sold for three hundred pence and given to the poor? And this he said not that he cared for the poor but because he was filled with jealousy and greed, and had the bag, and bare what was put therein. And they murmured against her.

4. And Jesus said, Let her alone, why trouble ye her? for she hath done all she could; yea, she hath wrought a good work on me. For ye have the poor always with you, but me ye have not always. She hath anointed my body for the day of my burial.

5. And verily, I say unto you, wheresoever this Gospel shall be preached in the whole world there shall also be told this that she hath done for a memorial of her.

6. Then entered Satan into the heart of Judas Iscariot and he went his way and communed with the chief priests and captains how he might betray him. And they were glad

and covenanted with him for thirty pieces of silver, the price of a slave, and he promised them, and after that sought opportunity to betray him.

7. And at that time Jesus said to his disciples Preach ye unto all the world, saying, Strive to receive the mysteries of Light, and enter into the Kingdom of Light, for now is the accepted time and now is the day of Salvation.

8. Put ye not off from day to day, and from cycle to cycle and eon to eon, in the belief, that when ye return to this world ye will succeed in gaining the mysteries, and entering into the Kingdom of Light.

9. For ye know not when the number of perfected souls shall be filled up, and then will be shut the gates of the Kingdom of Light, and from hence none will be able to come in thereby, nor will any go forth.

10. Strive ye that ye may enter while the calls is made, until the number of perfected souls shall be sealed and complete, and the door is shut.

Lection LXVI
Iesus Again Teacheth His Disciples Concerning The Nature Of God The Two In One

1. AGAIN Jesus taught them saying, God hath raised up witnesses to the truth in every nation and every age, that all might know the will of the Eternal and do it, and after that, enter into the kingdom, to be rulers and workers with the Eternal.

2. God is Power, Love and Wisdom, and these three are One. God is Truth, Goodness and Beauty, and these three are One.

3. God is Justice, Knowledge and Purity, and these three are One. God is Splendour, Compassion and Holiness, and these three are One.

4. And these four Trinities are One in the hidden Deity,

309

the Perfect, the Infinite, the Onely.

5. Likewise in every man who is perfected, there are three persons, that of the son, that of the spouse, and that of the father, and these three are one.

6. So in every woman who is Perfected are there three persons, that of the daughter, that of the bride, and that of the mother and these three are one; and the man and the woman are one, even as God is One.

7. Thus it is with God the Father-Mother, in Whom is neither male nor female and in Whom is both, and each is threefold, and all are One in the hidden Unity.

8. Marvel not at this, for as it is above so it is below, and as it is below so it is above, and that which is on earth is so, because it is so in Heaven.

9. Again I say unto you, I and My Bride are one, even as Maria Magdalena, whom I have chosen and sanctified unto Myself as a type, is one with Me; I and My Church are One. And the Church is the elect of humanity for the salvation of all.

10. The Church of the first born is the Maria of God. Thus saith the Eternal, She is My Mother and she hath ever conceived Me, and brought Me forth as Her Son in every age and clime. She is My Bride, ever one in Holy Union with Me her Spouse. She is My Daughter, for she hath ever issued and proceeded from Me her Father, rejoicing in Me.

11. And these two Trinities are One in the Eternal, and are strewn forth in each man and woman who are made perfect, ever being born of God, and rejoicing in light, ever being lifted up and made one with God, ever conceiving and bringing forth God for the salvation of the many.

12. This is the Mystery of the Trinity in Humanity, and moreover in every individual child of man must be accomplished the mystery of God, ever witnessing to the light, suffering for the truth, ascending into Heaven, and sending forth the Spirit of Truth, And this is the path of salva-

tion, for the kingdom of God is within.

13. And one said unto him, Master, when shall the kingdom come? And he answered and said, When that which is without shall be as that which is within, and that which is within shall be as that which is without, and, the male with the female, neither male nor female, but the two in One. They who have ears to hear, let them hear.

Lection LXVII
The Last Entry Into Jerusalem
The Sheep And The Goats

1. NOW on the first day of the week when they came nigh to Jerusalem, unto Bethage and Bethany, at the Mount of Olives, he sendeth forth two of his disciples, and saith unto them, Go your way into the village over against you, and as soon as you be entered into it, ye shalt find an ass tied, whereon never man sat, loose him and bring him.

2. And if any say unto you, Why do ye this? say ye that the Lord hath need of him, and straightway they will send him hither.

3. And they went their way and found the ass tied without in a place where two ways met, and they loosed him. And certain of them that stood there said unto them, What do ye, loosing the colt? And they said unto them, even as Jesus had commanded. And they let them go.

4. And they brought the ass to Jesus, and cast their garments upon him, and he sat upon the ass. And many spread their garments in the way, and others cut down branches off the trees and strewed them in the way.

5. And they that went before, and they that followed cried, saying, Hosanna, Blessed art thou who comest in the name of Jova: Blessed be the Kingdom of our ancestor David, and blessed be thou that comest in the name of the Highest: Hosanna in the highest.

6. AND Jesus entered into Jerusalem and into the Temple,

and when he had looked round about upon all things, he spake this parable unto them, saying—

7. When the Son of man shall come in his glory and all the holy angels with him, then shall he sit upon the throne of his glory. And before him shall be gathered all nations, and he shall separate them one from another, as a shepherd divideth his sheep from the goats. And he shall set the sheep on his right hand, but the goats on the left.

8. Then shall the King say unto them on his right hand, Come ye blessed of my Parent, inherit the kingdom prepared for you from the foundation of the world. For I was an hungered and ye gave me food, was thirsty and ye gave me drink. I was a stranger and ye took me in. Naked and ye clothed me. I was sick and ye visited me. I was in prison and ye came unto me.

9. Then shall the righteous answer him, saying, Lord, when saw we thee an hungered and fed thee? Or thirsty and gave thee drink? when saw we thee a stranger and took thee in? or naked and clothed thee? Or when saw we thee sick, or in prison and came unto thee ?

10. And the King shall answer and say unto them, Behold, I manifest myself unto you, in all created forms; and verily I say unto you, Inasmuch as ye have done it unto the least of these my brethren, ye have done it unto me.

11. Then shall he say also unto them on his left hand, Depart from me ye evil souls into the eternal fires which ye have prepared for yourselves, till ye are purified seven times and cleansed from your sins.

12. For I was an hungered and ye gave me no food, I was thirsty and ye gave me no drink. I was a stranger and ye took me not in, naked and ye clothed me not, sick and in prison and ye visited me not.

13. Then shall they also answer him, saying, Lord, when saw we thee an hungered, or athirst, or a stranger, or naked, or in prison, and did not minister unto thee ?

14. Then shall he answer them, saying, Behold I manifest

myself unto you, in all created forms, and Verily I say unto you, Inasmuch as ye did it not to the least of these, my brethren, ye did it not unto me.

15. And the cruel and the loveless shall go away into chastisement for ages, and if they repent not, be utterly destroyed; but the righteous and the merciful, shall go into life and peace everlasting.

Lection LXVIII
The Householder And The Husbandmen Order Out Of Disorder

1. AND Jesus said, Hear another parable: There was a certain householder, who planted a vineyard, and hedged it round about and digged a winepress in it, and built a tower, and let it out to husbandmen and went into a far country.

2. And when the time of the ripe fruits drew near, he sent his servants to the husbandmen that they might receive the fruits of it. And the husbandmen took his servants and beat one, and stoned another, and killed another.

3. Again he sent other servants, more honourable than the first, and they did unto them likewise. But last of all he sent unto them his son, saying, They will reverence my son.

4. But when the husbandmen saw the son, they said among themselves. This is the heir, come let us kill him, and let us seize on his inheritance. And they caught him and cast him out of the vineyard and slew him.

5. When the lord of the vineyard cometh what will he do unto those husbandmen? They say unto him, He will miserably destroy those wicked men and will let out his vineyard to other husbandmen, which shall render him the fruits in their seasons.

6. Jesus saith unto them, Did ye never read in the scriptures, The Stone which the builders rejected, the same is

become the head of the Pyramid? this is the Lord's doing and it is marvellous in our eyes?

7. Therefore say I unto you, The kingdom of God shall be taken from you and given to a nation bringing forth the fruits thereof. And whosoever shall fall on this Stone shall be broken, but on whomsoever it shall fall, it will grind them to powder.

8. And when the chief priests and Pharisees had heard his parables, they perceived that he spake of them. But when they sought to lay hands on him they feared the multitude, because they took him for a prophet.

9. And the disciples asked him afterwards the meaning of this parable, and he said unto them, The vineyard is the world, the husbandmen are your priests, and the messengers are the servants of the good Law, and the Prophets.

10. When the fruits of their labour are demanded of the priests, none are given, but they evilly treat the messengers who teach the truth of God, even as they have done from the beginning.

11. And when the Son of Man cometh, even the Christ of God, they gather together against the Holy One, and slay him, and cast him out of the vineyard, for they have not wrought the things of the Spirit, but sought their own pleasure and gain, rejecting the holy Law.

12. Had they accepted the Anointed One, who is the corner stone and the head, it would have been well with them, and the Building would have stood, even as the Temple of God inhabited by the Spirit.

13. But the day will come when the Law which they reject shall become the head stone, seen of all, and they who stumble on it shall be broken, but they who persist in disobedience shall he ground to pieces.

14. For to some of the angels God gave dominion over the course of this world, charging them to rule in wisdom. in justice and in love. But they have neglected the commands of the Most High, and rebelled against the good order of

God. Thus cruelty and suffering and sorrow have entered the world, till the time the Master returns, and taketh possession of all things, and calleth his servants to account.

15. AND he spake another parable, saying: A certain man had two sons, and he came to the first and said, Son, go work today in my vineyard, and he answered and said, I will not, but afterwards he repented and went. And he came to the second and said likewise, and he answered and said, I go, sir, and went not. Whether of them twain did the will of his father?

16. They say unto him, The first, and Jesus saith unto them, Verily I say unto you, That the publicans and harlots go into the kingdom of God before you. For John came unto you in the way of righteousness and ye believed him not, but the taxgatherers and the harlots believed him, and ye, when ye had seen it, repented not afterwards, that ye might believe him.

17. AND the Lord gathered together all his disciples in a certain place. And he said unto them, Can ye make perfection to appear out of that which is imperfect? Can ye bring order out of disorder? And they said, Lord, we cannot.

18. And he placed them according to the number of each in a four-square order, each side lacking one of twelve (and this he did, knowing who should betray him, who should be counted one of them by man, but was not of them).

19. The first in the seventh rank from above in the middle, and the last in the seventh from below, and him that was neither first nor last did he make the Centre of all, and the rest according to a Divine order did he place them, each finding his own place, so those which were above, were even as those which were below, and the left side was equal to the right side, and the right side to the left, according to the sum of their numbers.

20. An he said, See you how ye stand? I say unto you, In like manner is the order of the kingdom, and the One who

ruleth all is in your midst, and he is the centre, and with him are the hundred and twenty, the elect of Israel, and after them cometh the hundred and forty and four thousand, the elect of the Gentiles, who are their brethren.

Lection LXIX
The Christ Within The Soul
The Resurrection And The Life
Salome's Question

1. As Jesus sat by the west of the Temple with his disciples, behold there passed some carrying one that was dead to burial, and a certain one said unto him, Master, if a man die, shall he live again?

2. And he answered and said, I am the resurrection and the life, I am the Good, the Beautiful, the True, if a man believe in me he shall not die, but live eternally. As in Adam all die, so in the Christ shall all be made alive. Blessed are the dead who die in me, and are made perfect in my image and likeness, for they rest from their labours and their works do follow them. They have overcome evil, and are made Pillars in the Temple of my God, and they go out no more, for they rest in the Eternal.

3. For them that have done evil there is no rest, but they go out and in, and suffer correction for ages, till they are made perfect. But for them that have done good and attained unto perfection, there is endless rest and they go into life everlasting. They rest in the Eternal.

4. Over them the repeated death and birth have no power, for them the wheel of the Eternal revolves no more, for they have attained unto the Centre, where is eternal rest, and the centre of all things is God.

5. AND one of the disciples asked him, How shall a man enter into the Kingdom? And he answered and said, If ye make not the below as the above, and the left as the right, and the behind as the before, entering into the Centre

316

and passing into the Spirit, ye shall not enter into the Kingdom of God.

6. And he also said, Believe ye not that any man is wholly without error for even among the prophets, and those who have keen initiated into the Christhood, the word of error has been found. But there are a multitude of error which are covered by love.

7. AND now when the eventide was come, he went out unto Bethany with the twelve. For there abode Lazarus and Mary and Martha whom he loved.

8. And Salome came unto him, and asked him, saying, Lord, how long shall death hold sway? And, he answered, So long as ye men inflict burdens and ye woman bring forth, and for this purpose I am come, to end the works of the heedless.

9. And Salome saith unto him, Then I have done well in not bringing forth. And the Lord answered and said Eat of every pasture which is good, but of that which hath the bitterness of death, eat not.

10. And when Salome asked when those things of which she enquired should be known, the Lord said, When ye shall tread upon the vesture of shame and rise above desire; when the two shall be one, and the male with the female shall be neither male nor female.

11. And again, to another disciple who asked, When shall all obey the law? Jesus said, When the Spirit of God shall fill the whole earth and every heart of man and of woman.

12. I cast the law into the earth and it took root and bore in due time twelve fruits for the nourishment of all. I cast the law into the water and it was cleansed from all defilements of evil. I cast the law into the fire, and the gold was purged from all dross. I cast the law into the air, and it was made alive by the Spirit of the Living One that filleth all things and dwelleth in every heart.

13. And many other like sakings he spake unto them who had ears to hear, and an understanding mind. But to the

multitude they were dark sayings.

Lection LXX
Iesus Rebukes Peter For His Haste

1. NOW on the morrow as they were coming from Bethany, Peter was hungry, and perceiving a fig tree afar off having leaves thereon, he came if happily he might find fruit thereon, and when he came he found nothing but leaves, for the time of figs was not yet.

2. And Peter was angry and said unto it, Accursed tree, no man eat fruit of thee hereafter for ever. And some of the disciples heard of it.

3. And the next day as Jesus and his disciples passed by, Peter said unto Jesus, Master, behold, the fig tree which I cursed is green and flourishing, wherefore did not my word prevail?

4. Jesus said unto Peter, Thou knowest not what spirit thou art of. Wherefore didst thou curse that which God hath not cursed? And Peter said, Behold Lord I was a hungered, and finding leaves and no fruit, I was angry, and I cursed the tree.

5. And Jesus said, Son of Jonas knewest thou not that the time of figs was not yet? Behold the corn which is in the field which groweth according to its nature first the green shoot, then the stalk, then the ear—would thou be angry if thou camest at the time of the tender shoot or the stalk, and didst not find the corn in the ear? And wouldst thou curse the tree which, full of buds and blossoms, had not yet ripe fruit?

6. Verily Peter I say unto thee, one of my twelve will deny me thrice in his fear and anger with curses, and swear that he knows me not, and the rest will forsake me for a season.

7. But ye shall repent and grieve bitterly, because in your heart ye love me, and ye shall be as an Altar of twelve hewn stones, and a witness to my Name, and ye shall be as the Servants of servants, and the keys of the Church will I give

318

unto you, and ye shall feed my sheep and my lambs and ye shall be my vice-gerents upon earth.

8. But there shall arise men amongst them that succeed you, of whom some shall indeed love me even as thou, who being hotheaded and unwise, and void of patience, shall curse those whom God hath not cursed, and persecute them in their ignorance, because they cannot yet find in them the fruits they seek.

9. And others being lovers of themselves shall make alliance with the kings and rulers of the world, and seek earthly power, and riches, and domination, and put to death by fire and sword those who seek the truth, and therefore are truly my disciples.

10. And in their days I Jesus shall be crucified afresh and put to open shame, for they will profess to do these things in my Name. And Peter said, Be it far from thee Lord.

11. And Jesus answered, As I shall be nailed to the cross, so also shall my Church in those days, for she is my Bride and one with me. But the day shall come when this darkness shall pass away, and true Light shall shine.

12. And one shall sit on my throne, who shall be a Man of Truth and Goodness and Power, and he shall be filled with love and wisdom beyond all others, and shall rule my Church by a fourfold twelve and by two and seventy as of old, and that only which is true shall he teach.

13. And my Church shall be filled with Light, and give Light unto all nations of the earth, and there shall be one Pontiff sitting on his throne as a King and a Priest.

14. And my Spirit shall be upon him and his throne shall endure and not be shaken, for it shall be founded on love and truth and equity, and light shall come to it, and go forth from it, to all the nations of the earth, and the Truth shall make them free.

Lection LXXI
The Cleansing Of The Temple

1. AND the Jews' Passover was at hand, and Jesus went up again from Bethany into Jerusalem. And he found in the temple those that sold oxen and sheep and doves, and the changers of money sitting.

2. And when he had made a scourge of seven cords, he drove them all out of the temple and loosed the sheep and the oxen, and the doves, and poured out the changers' money, and overthrew the tables;

3. And said unto them, Take these things hence; make not my Father's House an House of merchandise. Is it not written, My House is a House of prayer, for all nations? but ye have made it a den of thieves, and filled it with all manner of abominations.

4. And he would not suffer that any man should carry any vessel of blood through the temple, or that any animals should be slain. And the disciples remembered that it was written, Zeal for thine house hath eaten me up.

5. Then answered the Jews, and said unto him, What sign shewest thou unto us, seeing that thou doest these things? Jesus answered and said unto them, Again I say unto you, Destroy this temple, and in three days I will raise it up.

6. Then said the Jews, Forty and six years was this temple in building and wilt thou rear it up in three days? But he spake of the temple of his Body.

7. When therefore he was risen from the dead, his disciples remembered that he had said this unto them; and believed the scripture and the word which Jesus had said.

8. But the scribes and the priests saw and heard, and were astonished and sought how they might destroy him, for they feared him, seeing that all the people were attentive to his doctrines.

9. And when even was come he went out of the city. For by day he taught in the Temple and at night he went out and

abode on the Mount of Olives, and the people came early in the morning to hear him in the Temple courts.

10. Now when he was in Jerusalem at the passover, many believed in his Name, when they saw the miracles which he did.

11. But Jesus did not commit himself unto them, because he knew all men. And needed not that any should testify of man; for he knew what was in man.

12. And Jesus seeing the passover night was at hand, sent two of his disciples, that they should prepare the upper room where he desired to eat with his twelve, and buy such things as were needful for the feast which he purposed thereafter.

Lection LXXII
The Many Mansions In The One House

1. AND as Jesus sat with his disciples in the Garden of Gethsemane he said unto them: Let not your heart be troubled; ye believe in God, believe also in me. In my parent's house are many mansions: if it were not so, I would have told you. I go to prepare a place for you. And if I go and prepare a place for you, I will come again, and receive you unto myself; that where I am, there ye may be also. And whither I go ye know, and the way ye know.

2. Thomas said unto him, Lord, we know not whither thou goest; and how can we know the way? Jesus saith unto him, I am the Way, the Truth, and the Life: no man cometh unto the All Parent but by me, If ye had known me, ye should have known my Parent also: and from henceforth ye know and have seen my Parent.

3. Philip saith unto him, Lord, shew US the All-Parent and it sufficeth us. Jesus saith unto him, Have I been so long time with you, and yet hast thou not known me, Philip? he that hath seen me hath seen the All-Parent; and how sayest

thou then, Shew us the All-Parent? Believest thou not that I am in the All-Parent, and the All-Parent in me? the words that I speak unto you I speak not of myself: but the All-Parent who dwelleth in me doeth the works.

4. Believe me, that I am in the All-Parent and the All-Parent in me: or else, believe me for the very works' sake. Verily, verily, I say unto you, They who believe on me, the works that I do shall they do also; and greater works than these shall they do; because I go unto my Parent.

5. And whatsoever ye shall ask in my Name, that will I do, that the All-Parent may be glorified in the Son and Daughter of Man. If ye shall ask anything in my Name, I will do it.

6. If ye love me, keep my commandments. And I will pray the All-Parent, Who shall give you another Comforter, to abide with you for ever; even the Spirit of truth, whom the world cannot receive, because it seeth not, neither knoweth, but ye know; for the Spirit dwelleth with you, and shall be in you.

7. They who have my commandments, and keep them, these are they who love me; and they that love me shall be loved of my Parent, and I will love them and will manifest myself to them.

8. Judas saith unto him, Lord, how is it that thou wilt manifest thyself unto us, and not unto the world? Jesus answered and said unto him, If any love me, they will keep my words: and the Holy One will love them and we will come unto them, and make our abode with them.

9. They that love me not keep not my sayings: and the word which ye hear is not mine, but the All-Parent's who sent me. These things have I spoken unto you, being yet present with you. But the Comforter, who is my Mother, Holy Wisdom, whom the Father will send in my name, she shall teach you all things, and bring all things to your remembrance, whatsoever I have said unto you.

10. Peace I leave with you, my peace I give unto you: not as the world giveth, give I unto you. Let not your heart be

troubled, neither let it be afraid. Ye have heard how I said unto you, I go away, and come again unto you. If ye loved me ye would rejoice, because I said, I go unto the All-Parent: for the All-Parent is greater than I.

11. And now I have told you before it come to pass, that, when it is come to pass, ye may believe. Hereafter I will not talk much with you; for the prince of this world cometh, and hath nothing in me.

12. But that the world may know that I love the All-Parent; as the All-Parent gave me commandment, even so I do. Even unto the end.

Lection LXXIII
Christ The True Vine

1. AFTER these things Jesus spake saying unto them: I am the true vine, and my Parent is the vinedresser. Every branch in me that beareth not fruit is taken away: and every branch that beareth fruit, is purged that it may bring forth more fruit.

2. Abide in me, and I in you. As the branch cannot bear fruit of itself, except it abide in the vine; no more can ye, except ye abide in me. I am the tree, ye are the branches: Whoso abide in me and I in them, the same bring forth much fruit; for without me ye do nothing.

3. If any abide not in me, they are cast forth as useless branches, and they wither away; and men gather them, and cast them into the fire, and they are burned. If ye abide in me, and my words abide in you, ye shall ask what ye will, and it will be done unto you.

4. Verily, I am the true Bread which cometh down out of Heaven, even the Substance of God which is one with the Life of God. And, as many grains are in one bread, so are ye, who believe, and do the will of my Parent, one in me. Not as your ancestors did eat manna and are dead; but they who eat this Bread shall live for ever.

5. As the wheat is separated from the chaff, so must ye be

separated from the falsities of the world; yet must ye not go out of the world, but live separate in the world, for the life of the world.

6. Verily, verily, the wheat is parched by fire, so must ye my disciples pass through tribulations. But rejoice ye: for having suffered with me as one body ye shall reign with me in one body, and give life to the world.

7. Herein is my Parent glorified, that ye bear much fruit; so shall ye be my disciples. As the All-Parent hath loved me, so have I loved you: continue ye in my love. If ye keep my commandments, ye shall abide in my love; even as I have kept my Parent's commandments, and abide in the spirit of love.

8. These things have I spoken unto you, that my joy might remain in you, and that your joy might be full. This is my commandment, That ye love one another, as I have loved you. Greater love hath no man than this, that a man lay down his life for his friend Ye are my friends, if ye do whatsoever I command you.

9. Henceforth I call you not servants; for the servant knoweth not what his lord doeth: but I have called you friends; for all things that I have heard of my Parent I have made known unto you. Ye have not chosen me, but I have chosen you, and ordained you, that ye should remain: that whatsoever ye shall ask of the All-Parent in my Name, ye may receive.

10. These things I command you, that ye love one another and all the creatures of God. If the world hate you, ye know that it hated me before it hated you. If ye were of the world, the world would love its own: but because ye are not of the world, but I have chosen you out of the world' therefore the world hateth you.

11. Remember the word that I said unto you, The servant is not greater than his lord. If they have persecuted me, they will also persecute you; if they have kept my saying, they will keep yours also. But all these things will they do unto you for my Name's sake, because they know not him

that sent me.

12. If I had not come and spoken unto them, they had not had sin: but now they have no cloke for their sin. He that hateth me hateth my Parent also. If I had not done among them the works which none other man did, they had not had sin: but now have they, have seen and hated both me and my Parent. But this cometh to pass, that the word might be fulfilled that is written in their law, They hated me without a cause.

13. But when the Comforter is come, Whom I will send unto you from the All Parent, even the Spirit of truth, which proceedeth from the Father and the Mother the same shall testify of me: And ye also shall bear witness, because ye have been with me from the beginning.

Lection LXXIV
Iesus Foretelleth Persecutions

1. THESE things have I spoken unto you that ye should be forewarned, They shall put you out of the synagogues; yea, the time cometh, that whosoever killeth you will think that they do God's service. And these things will they do unto you, because they have not known the All Parent, nor me.

2. But these things have I told you, that when the time shall come, ye may remember that I told you of them. And these things I said not unto you at the beginning, because I was with you. But now I go my way to my Parent that sent me; and none of you asketh me, Whither goest thou? But because I have said these thing unto you, sorrow hath filled your heart.

3. Nevertheless I tell you the truth; It is expedient for you that I go away; for if I go not away, the Comforter will not come unto you; but if I depart, I will send my Spirit unto you. And when the Spirit is come, the world shall be reproved of sin and of righteousness, and of judgement.

4. Of sin, because they believe not on me; of righteous-

ness, because I go to my Father, and ye see me no more; of judgement, because the prince of this world is judged.

5. I have yet many things to say unto you, but ye cannot bear them now. Howbeit when the Spirit of Truth is come, she will guide you into all truth: and the same will shew you things to come and shall glorify me: for the same shall receive of mine, and shall shew it unto you.

6. All things that my Parent hath are mine: therefore said I, that the Comforter shall take of mine and shall shew it unto you. A little while, and ye shall not see me: and again, a little while, and ye shall see me, because I go to the All-Parent. Then said some of his disciples among themselves, What is that he saith unto us, A little while, and ye shall not see me: and again, a little while, and ye shall see me; and, Because I go to the All-Parent?

7. Now Jesus knew that they were desirous to ask him, and said unto them, Do ye enquire among yourselves of that I Said, A little while, and ye shall see me? Verily, verily, I say unto you, That ye shall weep and lament, but the world shall rejoice: and ye shall be sorrowful, but your sorrow shall be turned into joy.

8. A woman when she is in travail hath sorrow, because her hour is come: but as soon as she is delivered of the child, she remembereth no more the anguish, for joy that a man is born into the world. And ye now therefore have sorrow; but I will see you again, and your heart shall rejoice, and your joy no man taketh from you.

9. And in that day ye shall ask me nothing. Verily, verily, I say unto you, Whatsoever ye shall ask my Parent in my name, ye will receive. Hitherto have ye asked nothing in my name: ask and ye shall receiveth that your joy may be full. These things have I spoken unto you in proverbs; but the time cometh, when I shall no more speak unto you in a mystery, but I shall shew you plainly of the All-Parent.

10. At that day ye shall ask in my name: and I say not unto

you, that I will pray my Parent for you; For the All-Parent in truth loveth you, because ye have loved me, and have believed that I came out from God. I came forth from God, and am come into the world; again, I leave the world, and go unto my God.

11. His disciples said unto him, Lo, now speakest thou plainly, and speakest no mystery. Now are we sure that thou knowest all things, and needest not that any man should ask thee: by this we believe that thou comest forth from God.

12. Jesus answered them, Do ye now believe? Be hold, the hour cometh, yea, is now come, that ye shall be scattered, every man to his own home, and shall leave me alone: and yet I am not alone, because the Father is with me.

13. These things I have spoken unto you, that in me ye might have peace. In the world ye shall have tribulation: but be of good cheer; I have overcome the world. Arise, let us go hence.

Lection LXXV
The Last Paschal Supper

1. AND at evening the Master cometh into the house, and there are gathered with him the Twelve and their fellows; Peter and Jacob and Thomas and John and Simon and Matthew and Andrew and Nathanael and James and Thaddeus and Jude and Philip and their companions (and there was also Judas Iscariote, who by men was numbered with the twelve, till the time when he should be manifested).

2. And they were all clad in garments of white linen, pure and clear, for linen is the righteousness of the saints; and each had the colour of his tribe. But the Master was clad in his pure white robe, over all, without seam or spot.

3. And there arose contention among them as to which of them should be esteemed the greatest, wherefore he said

unto them, He that is greatest among you let him be as he that doth serve.

4. And Jesus said, With desire have I desired to eat this Passover with you before I suffer, and to institute the Memorial of my Oblation for the service and salvation of all. For behold the hour cometh when the Son of man shall be betrayed into the hands of sinners.

5. And one of the twelve said unto him, Lord, is it I ? And he answered, He to whom I give the sop the same is he.

6. And Iscariot said unto him, Master, behold the unleaven bread, the mingled wine and the oil and the herbs, but where is the lamb that Moses commanded? (for Judas had bought the lamb, but Jesus had forbidden that it should be killed).

7. And John spake in the Spirit, saying, Behold the Lamb of God, the good Shepherd which giveth his life for the sheep. And Judas was troubled at these words, for he knew that he should betray him. But again Judas said, Master, is it not written in the law that a lamb must be slain for the passover within the gates?

8. And Jesus answered, If I am lifted up on the cross then indeed shall the lamb be slain; but woe unto him by whom it is delivered into the hands of the slayers; it were better of him had he not been born.

9. Verily I say unto you, for this end have I come into the world, that I may put away all blood offerings and the eating of the flesh of the beasts and the birds that are slain by men.

10. In the beginning, God gave to all, the fruits of the trees, and the seeds, and the herbs, for food; but those who loved themselves more than God, or their fellows, corrupted their ways, and brought diseases into their bodies, and filled the earth with lust and violence.

11. Not by shedding innocent blood, therefore, but by living a righteous life, shall ye find the peace of God. Ye call me the Christ of God and ye say well, for I am the Way, the

Truth and the Life.

12. Walk ye in the Way, and ye shall find God. Seek ye the Truth, and the Truth shall make you free. Live in the Life, and ye shall see no death. All things are alive in God, and the Spirit of God filleth all things.

13. Keep ye the commandments. Love thy God with all thy heart, and love thy neighbour as thyself. On these hang all the law and the prophets. And the sum of the law is this— Do not ye unto others as ye would not that others should do unto you. Do ye unto others, as ye would that others should do unto you.

14. Blessed are they who keep this law, for God is manifested in all creatures. All creatures live in God, and God is hid in them.

15. After these things, Jesus dipped the sop and gave it to Judas Iscariot, saying, What thou doest, do quickly. He then, having received the sop, went out immediately, and it was light.

16. And when Judas Iscariot had gone out, Jesus said, Now is the Son of man glorified among his twelve, and God is glorified in him. And verily I say unto you, they who receive you receive me, and they who receive me receive the Father-Mother Who sent me, and ye who have been faithful unto the truth shall sit upon twelve thrones, judging the twelve tribes of Israel.

17. And one said unto him, Lord, wilt thou at this time restore the kingdom unto Israel? And Jesus said, My kingdom is not of this world, neither are all Israel which are called Israel.

18. They in every nation who defile not themselves with cruelty, who do righteousness, love mercy, and reverence all the works of God, who give succour to all that are weak and oppressed—the same are the Israel of God.

Lection LXXVI
The Washing Of Feet
The Eucharistic Oblation

1. AND the Paschal Supper being ended, the lights were kindled, for it was even. And Jesus arose from the table and laid aside his garment, and girded himself with a towel, and pouring water into a basin, washed the feet of each of the fourfold Twelve, and wiped them with the towel with which he was girded.

2. And one of them said, Lord, thou shalt not wash my feet. And Jesus said, If I wash thee not thou hast no part with me. And he answered, Lord, wash not my feet only, but my head and my hands.

3. And he said unto him, They who have come out of the bath, need not but to wash their feet, and they are clean every whit.

4. AND then putting on the overgarment of pure white linen without spot or seam, he sat at the table and said unto them, Know ye what I have done unto you? Ye call me Lord and Master, and if then your Lord and Master have washed your feet, ye ought also to wash one another's feet. For I have given this example, that as I have done unto you, so also should ye do unto others.

5. A new commandment I give unto you, that ye love one another and all the creatures of God. Love is the fulfilling of the law. Love is of God, and God is love. Whoso loveth not, knoweth not God.

6. Now ye are clean through the word which I have spoken unto you. By this shall all men know that ye are my disciples if ye have love one to another and shew mercy and love to all creatures of God, especially to those that are weak and oppressed and suffer wrong. For the whole earth is filled with dark places of cruelty, and with pain and sorrow, by the selfishness and ignorance of man.

7. I say unto you, Love your enemies, bless them that curse you, and give them light for their darkness and let the spirit of love dwell within your hearts, and abound unto all. And again I say unto you, Love one another, and all the creation of God And when he had finished, they said, Blessed be God.

8. Then he lifted up his voice, and they joined him, saying, As the hart panteth after the water brooks, so panteth my soul after thee, O God. And when they had ended, one brought unto him a censer full of live coals, and he cast frankincense thereon even the frankincense which his mother had given him in the day of his manifestation, and the sweetness of the odour filled the room.

9. Then Jesus, placing before him the platter, and behind it the chalice, and lifting up his eyes to heaven, gave thanks for the goodness of God in all things and unto all, and after that he took in his hands the unleavened bread, and blessed it; the wine likewise mingled with water and blessed it; chanting the Invocation of the Holy Name the Sevenfold, calling upon the thrice Holy Father-Mother in Heaven to send down the Holy Spirit and make the bread to be his body, even the Body of the Christ, and the fruit of the vine to be his Blood, even the Blood of the Christ, for the remission of sins and everlasting life, to all who obey the gospel.

10. Then lifting up the Oblation towards heaven, he said, The Son who is also the Daughter of man is lifted up from the earth, and I shall draw all men unto me; then it shall be known of the people that I am sent from God.

11. These things being done, Jesus spake these words, lifting his eyes to heaven. Abba Amma, the hour is come, Glorify thy Son that Thy Son may be glorified in thee.

12. Yea, Thou hast glorified me, Thou hast filled my heart with fire, Thou hast set lamps on my right hand and on my left, so that no part of my being should be without light. Thy Love shineth on my right hand and on my left, so that no part of my being should be without light. Thy Love

shineth on my right hand, and Thy Wisdom on my left. Thy Love, Thy Wisdom, Thy Power are manifest in me.

13. I have glorified Thee on earth, I have finished the work Thou gavest me to do. Holy One, keep through Thy Name the Twelve and their fellows whom Thou hast given me, that they may be One even as we are One. Whilst I was with them in the world I kept them in Thy Name, and none of them is lost, for he who went out from us, was not of us, nevertheless, I pray for him that he may be restored. Father-Mother, forgive him, for he knoweth not what he doeth.

14. And now come I to Thee, and these things I speak in the world that they may have my joy fulfilled in themselves. I give them Thy word, and the world hath them, because they are not of the world, even as I am not of the world.

15. I pray not that Thou shouldst take them out of the world, but that Thou shouldst keep them from evil, whilst yet in the world, Sanctify them through Thy truth. Thy word is Truth. As thou sendest me into the world, so also I send them into the world, and for their sakes I sanctify myself, that they also may be sanctified through the Truth.

16. Neither pray I for these alone, but for all that shall be added to their number, and for the Two and Seventy also whom I sent forth, yea, and for all that shall believe in the Truth through Thy word, that they also may be one as Thou Most Holy art in me and I in Thee, that they may also be one in Thee, that the world may know that Thou hast sent me.

17. Holy Parent, I will also, that they whom Thou hast given me, yea all who live, be with me where I am, that they may partake of my glory which thou givest me, for Thou lovest me in all, and all in me, from before the foundations of the world.

18. The world hath not known Thee in Thy righteousness, but I know Thee, and these know that Thou hast sent me.

19. And I have declared unto them Thy Name that the love wherewith Thou hast loved me may be in them, and that

from them it may abound, even unto all Thy creatures, yea, even unto all These words being ended, they all lifted up their voices with him, and prayed as he taught them, saying:

20. Our Father-Mother: Who art above and within. Hallowed be Thy sacred Name, in Biune Trinity. In Wisdom, Love and Equity Thy Kingdom come to all. Thy holy Will be done always, as in Heaven, so on Earth. Give us day by day to partake of Thy holy Bread, and the fruit of Thy living Vine. As we seek to perfect others, so perfect us in Thy Christ. Shew upon us Thy goodness, that to others we many shew the same. In the hour of trial, deliver us from evil.

21. For Thine are the Kingdom, the Power and the Glory: From the Ages of ages, Now, and to the Ages of ages. Amun.

22. THEN our Master taketh the holy Bread and breaketh it, and the Fruit of the Vine also, and mingleth it, and having blessed and hallowed both, and casting a fragment of the Bread into the Cup, he blessed the holy Union.

23. Then he giveth the bread which he had hallowed to his disciples saying, Eat ye, for this is my Body, even the Body of the Christ, which is given for the Salvation of the body and the soul.

24. Likewise he giveth unto them the fruit of the Vine which he had blessed saying unto them, Drink ye, for this is my Blood, even the Blood of the Christ which is shed for you and for many, for the Salvation of the Soul and the Body.

25. And when all had partaken, he said unto them, As oft as ye assemble together in my Name, make this Oblation for a Memorial of me, even the Bread of everlasting life and the Wine of eternal salvation' and eat and drink thereof with pure heart, and ye shall receive of the Substance and the Life of God, which dwelleth in me.

26. And when they had sung a hymn, Jesus stood up in the midst of his apostles, and going to him who was their Centre, as in a solemn dance, they rejoiced in him. And then he went out to the Mount of Olives, and his disciples followed him.

27. Now Judas Iscariot had gone to the house of Caiaphas and said unto him, Behold he has celebrated the Passover, within the gates, with the Mazza in place of the lamb. I indeed bought a lamb, but he forbade that it should be killed, and lo, the man of whom I bought it is witness.
28. And Caiaphas rent his clothes and said, Truly this is a Passover of the law of Moses. He hath done the deed which is worthy of death, for it is a weighty transgression of the law. What need of further witness? Yea, even now two robbers have broken into the Temple and stolen the book of the law, and this is the end of his teaching. Let us tell these things to the people who follow him, for they will fear the authority of the law.
29. And one that was standing by as Judas came out, said unto him, Thinkest thou that they will put him to death?
30. And Judas said, Nay, for he will do some mighty work to deliver himself out of their hands, even as when they of the synagogue in Capernaum rose up against him, and brought him to the brow of the hill that they might throw him down headlong, and did he not pass safely through their midst? He will surely escape them now also, and proclaim himself openly and set up the Kingdom whereof he spake.

Lection LXXVII
The Agony In The Gethsemane

1. AND as they went to the Mount of Olives, Jesus said unto them, All ye shall be offended because of me this night; for it is written, I will smite the shepherd, and the sheep of the flock shall be scattered abroad. But after I am risen again, I will go before you into Galilee.
2. Simon answered and said unto him, Though all men shall be offended because of thee, yet will I never be offended. And the Lord said, Simon, Simon, behold Satan hath desired to have you, that he may sift you as wheat. But I have prayed for thee that thy faith fail not; and when

thou art converted, strengthen thy brethren.

3. And he said unto him, Lord, I am ready to go with thee, both unto prison and unto death. And Jesus said, I tell thee, Simon, the cock shall not crow this night, before that thou shalt thrice deny that thou knowest me.

4. Then cometh Jesus with them, having crossed the brook Kedron, unto the garden called Gethsemane, and saith unto the disciples, Sit ye here while I go and pray yonder. (Judas also, which betrayed him, knew the place, for Jesus ofttimes resorted thither with his disciples.)

5. Then saith he unto them, My soul is exceeding sorrowful, even unto death; tarry ye here, and watch with me.

6. And he went little farther and fell on his face and prayed, saying, O my Father-Mother, if it be possible, let this cup pass from me; nevertheless not as I will, but as Thou wilt.

7. And there appeared an angel unto him, from heaven strengthening him. And he cometh unto the disciples and finding them asleep, saith unto Peter, What, could ye not watch with me one hour?

8. Watch and pray that ye enter not into temptation: the spirit indeed is willing, but the flesh is weak.

9. He went away again a second time and prayed, saying, O my Father-Mother, if this cup may not pass away from me, except I drink it, Thy will be done.

10. And being in an agony he prayed more earnestly: and his sweat was as it were great drops of blood falling to the ground.

11. And he came and found them asleep again, for their eyes were heavy.

12. And he left them and went away again and prayed a third time, saying, O my Father-Mother, not my will but Thine be done, in earth as it is in heaven.

13. Then cometh he unto his disciples and saith unto them, Sleep on now, and take your rest; behold, the hour is at hand, and the Son of man is betrayed into the hands of sinners. Rise, let us be going: behold, he is at hand that doth betray me.

Lection LXXVIII
The Betrayal

1. AND it came to pass while Jesus yet spake, behold there came a multitude, and Judas that was called Iscariot went before them. For Judas, having received a band of men and officers from the chief priests and Pharisees, came thither with lanterns and torches and weapons.

2. Jesus therefore, knowing all things that should come upon him, went forth and said unto them, Whom seek ye? They answered him, Jesus of Nazareth. Jesus saith unto them, I am he.

3. As soon then as he had said unto them, I am he, they went backward and fell to the ground. And when they arose, then asked he them again, Whom seek ye? And they said, Jesus of Nazareth. And Jesus answered, I have told you, I am he; if therefore ye seek me let these go their way.

4. Now he that betrayeth him gave them a sign, saying, Whomsoever I shall kiss, that same is he: hold him fast.

5. And forthwith he came to Jesus and said, Hail, Master; and kissed him. And Jesus said unto him. Friend, wherefore art thou come? Is it with a kiss that thou betrayest the Son of man?

6. Then Jesus said unto the chief priests and captains of the temple and the elders, which were come to him, Why ye come out as against a thief, with swords and staves? When I was daily with you in the temple, ye stretched forth no hands against me; but this is your hour, and the power of darkness.

7. Then came they and laid hands on Jesus. And Simon Peter stretched forth his hand, and drew his sword and struck a servant of the high priest's and smote off his ear.

8. Then said Jesus unto him, Put up again thy sword into its place; all they that take the sword shall perish by the sword. And Jesus touched his ear and healed him.

9. And he said unto Peter, Thinkest thou that I cannot now pray to my Parent, and He shall presently give me more than twelve legions of angels? But how then shall the scriptures be fulfilled, that thus it must be?

10. Then all the disciples forsook him and fled. And they that had laid hands on Jesus led him away to Caiaphas, the high priest. But they brought him to Annas first because he was father-in-law to Caiaphas, who was the high priest for that same year.

11. Now Caiaphas was he who gave council to the Jews that it was expedient that one man should die for the sins of the people.

12. And the scribes and the elders were assembled together, but Peter and John and Simon and Jude followed far off unto the high priest's palace, and they went in and sat with the servants to see the end.

13. And they had kindled a fire in the midst of the hall, and when they were set down together, Peter sat down among them and warmed himself, and Simon also sat by him.

14. But a certain maid beheld him as he sat by the fire, and earnestly looked upon him and said, This man was also with him. And he denied him, saying, Woman, I know him not.

15. And after a little while, another saw him and said, Thou art also of them. And Simon said, Man, I am not.

16. And about the space of one hour another confidently affirmed, saying, Of a truth this fellow was with Jesus of Nazareth for his speech betrayeth him.

17. And Simon denied the third time with an oath, saying, I know not the man. And immediately, while he yet spake, the cock crew.

18. And the Lord turned and looked upon Simon. And Simon remembered the word of the Lord, how he had said unto him, Before the cock crow this day thou shalt deny me thrice. And Simon went out and wept bitterly.

Lection LXXIX
The Hebrew Trial Before Caiaphas

1. THE high priest then asked Jesus of his disciples and of his doctrine, saying, How old art thou? Art thou he that said that our father Abraham saw thy day?

2. And Jesus answered, Verily before Abraham was I am. And the high priest said, Thou are not yet fifty years old. How sayest thou that thou hast seen Abraham? Who art thou? Whom makest thou thyself to be? What dost thou teach?

3. And Jesus answered him, I spake openly to the world; I even taught in the synagogue and in the temple, whither the Jews always resort; and in secret have I said nothing. Why asketh thou me? Ask them which heard me, what I have said unto them; behold, they know what I said.

4. And when he had thus spoken, one of the officers which stood by, struck Jesus with the palm of his hand, saying, Answerest thou the high priest so? Jesus answered him, If I have spoken evil, bear witness of the evil, but if well why smitest thou me?

5. Now the chief priests and elders, and all the council sought false witnesses against Jesus to put him to death; but found none; yea, many false witnesses came, yet they agreed not together.

6. At the last came two false witnesses. And one of them said, This fellow said, I am able to destroy the temple of God and to build it in three days. And the other said, This man said I will destroy this temple and build up another.

7. And the high priests arose and said unto him, Answerest thou nothing? What is it which these witnesses speak against thee? But Jesus held his peace. Now it was unlawful among the Hebrews to try a man by night.

8. And they said unto him, Art thou the Christ? tell us. And he said unto them, If I tell you, ye will not believe; and

if I also ask you, ye will not answer me, nor let me go.

9. And they asked him further saying, Dost thou abolish the sacrifices of the law, and the eating of flesh as Moses commanded? And he answered, Behold, a greater than Moses is here.

10. And the high priest answered and said unto him, I adjure thee by the living God, that thou tell us whether thou be the Christ, the Son of God. Jesus saith unto him, thou hast said; and I say unto you, Hereafter shall ye see the Son of man sitting on the right hand of power and coming in the clouds of Heaven.

11. Then the high priest rent his clothes, saying, He hath spoken blasphemy; what further need have we of witnesses? Behold, now ye have heard his blasphemy. What think ye? They answered and said, He is worthy of death.

12. Then did they spit in his face and buffeted him; and others smote him with the palms of their hands, saying, Prophesy unto us, thou Christ, Who is he that smote thee?

13. Now when morning was come all the chief priests and the elders of the people, even the whole council held a consultation, and took council against Jesus to put him to death.

14. And they gave forth their sentence against Jesus, that he was worthy of death, and that he should be bound and carried away, and delivered unto Pilate.

Lection LXXX
The Sorrow and Penance Of Judas

1. NOW Judas, who had betrayed him, when he saw that he was condemned, repented himself, and brought again the thirty pieces of silver to the chief priests and elders, saying, I have sinned in that I have betrayed the innocent blood.

2. And they said, What is that to us? See thou to that. And he cast down the pieces of silver in the temple and de-

parted and went out and hanged himself.

3. And the chief priests took the pieces of silver and said, It is not lawful for to put them into the treasury, because it is the price of blood.

4. And they took council and bought with them the potter's field, to bury strangers in. Wherefore that field was called Aceldama, that is, the field of blood, unto this day.

5. Then was fulfilled that which was spoken by Zachariah, the prophet, saying, They weighed for my price thirty pieces of silver. And they took the thirty pieces of silver, the price of him that was valued, whom they of the children of Israel did value, and gave them for the potteries field, and cast them to the potter in the House of the Lord.

6. Now, Jesus had said to his disciples, Woe unto the man who receiveth the mysteries, and falleth into sin thereafter.

7. For such there is no place of repentance in this cycle, seeing they have crucified afresh the Divine Offspring of God and man, and put the Christ within them to an open shame.

8. Such are worse than the beasts, whom ye ignorantly affirm to perish, for in your Scriptures it is written, That which befalleth the beast befalleth the sons of men.

9. All live by one breath, as the one dieth so dieth the other, so that a man hath no preeminence over a beast, for all go to the same place—all come from the dust and return to the dust together.

10. These things spake Jesus concerning them which were not regenerate, not having received the Spirit of Divine Love, who, once having received the Light, crucified the Son of God afresh, putting him to an open shame.

Lection LXXXI
The Roman Trial Before Pilate

1. THEN led they Jesus from Caiaphas unto the hall of

judgment, to Pontius Pilate, the Governor, and it was early, and they themselves went not into the judgment hall, lest they should be defiled; but that they might keep the feast.

2. Pilate therefore went out unto them and said, What accusation bring ye against this man? They answered and said unto him, If he were not a malefactor, we would not have delivered him up unto thee. We have a law and by our law he ought to die, because he would change the customs and rites which Moses delivered unto us, yea, he made himself the Son of God.

3. Then said Pilate unto them, Take ye him, and Judge him according to your law. For he knew that for envy they had delivered him.

4. The Jews therefore said unto him, It is not lawful for us to put any man to death. So the saying of Jesus was fulfilled, which he spake, signifying what death he should die. 5. And they further accused him saying, We found this fellow perverting the nation, and forbidding to give tribute to Caesar, saying that he himself is Christ a King.

6. Then Pilate entered into the judgment hall again and called Jesus and said unto him, Art thou the King of the Jews? Jesus answered him, Sayest thou this thing of thyself, or did others tell it thee of me?

7. Pilate answered, Am I a Jew ? Thine own nation and the chief priests have delivered thee unto me; what hast thou done? Jesus answered, My kingdom is not of this world, if my kingdom were of this world, then would my servants fight, that I should not be delivered to the Jews; but now is my kingdom not from hence.

8. Pilate therefore said unto him, Art thou a King then? Jesus answered, Thou sayest that I am, yea, a King I am. To this end was I born and for this cause came I unto the world, that I should bear witness unto the truth. Every one that is of the truth heareth my voice.

9. Pilate said unto him, What is truth? Jesus said, Truth is from heaven. Pilate said, Then truth is not on earth. Jesus

said unto Pilate, Believe thou, that truth is on earth amongst those who receive and obey it. They are of the truth who judge righteously.

10. And when he had heard this, he went out again unto the Jews and saith unto them, I find in him no fault at all. And when he was accused of the chief priests and elders he answered them nothing.

11. Then said Pilate unto him, Hearest thou not, how many things they witness against thee?

12. And he answered him never a word, insomuch that the governor marvelled greatly, and again he said unto them, I find no fault in this man.

13. And they waxed the more fierce saying, He stirreth up the people, teaching throughout all Jewry, beginning from Galilee to this place. When Pilate heard of Galilee he asked, whether the man were a Galilean.

14. AND as soon as he knew that he belonged unto Herod's jurisdiction, he sent him to Herod, who himself also, was at Jerusalem at the time.

15. And when Herod saw Jesus he was exceedingly glad, for he was desirous to see him of a long season, because he had heard many things of him, and he hoped to have seen some miracle done by him.

16. Then he questioned with him in many words, but he answered him nothing. And the chief priests and scribes stood and vehemently accused him, and many false witnesses rose up against him, and laid to his charge things that he knew not.

17. And Herod with his men of war set him at nought, and mocked him, and arrayed him in a gorgeous robe and sent him again to Pilate. And the same day Pilate and Herod were made friends together, for before they were at enmity between themselves.

18. And Pilate went again into the Judgment Hall and saith unto Jesus, Whence art thou? But Jesus gave him no answer. Then saith Pilate unto him, Speakest thou not unto

me? knowest thou not that I have power to crucify thee, and have power to release thee?

19. Jesus answered, Thou couldest have no power at all against me, except it were given thee from above, therefore he that delivered me unto thee hath the greater sin.

20. And from thenceforth Pilate sought to release him; but the Jews cried out, saying, If thou let this man go thou art no Caesar's friend, whosoever maketh himself a king speaketh against Caesar.

21. And Pilate called together the chief priests and rulers of the people. When he was set down on the judgement seat his wife sent unto him, saying. Have thou nothing to do with that just man, for I have suffered many things this day in a dream, because of him.

22. And Pilate said unto them, Ye have brought this man unto me, as one that perverteth the people, and behold I have examined him before you, and have found no fault in this man touching those things: whereof ye accuse him. No, nor yet Herod, for I sent you to him, and lo nothing worthy of death was found in him.

23. But ye have a custom that I should release unto you one at the Passover, will ye therefore that I release unto you the King of the Jews?

24. Then cried they all again, saying, Not this man, but Barabbas. Now Barabbas was a robber. And, for sedition made in the city, and for murder, was cast into prison.

25. Pilate therefore, willing to release Jesus, spake again to them. Whether of the twain will ye that I release unto you; Jesus Barabbas, or Jesus which is called the Christ? They said, Barabbas.

26. Pilate said unto them, What then shall I do with Jesus which is called the Christ? They all say unto him, Let him be crucified.

27. And the Governor said, Why what evil hath he done? But they cried out all the more saying, Crucify him, crucify him.

28. Pilate therefore went forth again and said unto him, Behold, again, I bring him forth to you, that ye may know that I find no fault in him, and again they cried out, Crucify him, crucify him.

29. And Pilate said unto them, the third time, Why, what evil hath he done? I have found no cause of death in him: I will therefore chastise him, and let him go.

30. And they were instant with loud voices, requiring that he might be crucified. And the voices of them and of the chief priests prevailed.

31. When Pilate saw that he could prevail nothing, but that rather a tumult was made, he took water, and washed his hands before the multitude, saying, I am innocent of the blood of this just person: see ye to it.

32. Then answered all the people, and said, His blood be on us and on our children. And Pilate gave sentence that it should be as they required. And he delivered Jesus to their will.

Lection LXXXII
The Crucifixion

1. THEN released he Barabbas unto them, and when he had scourged Jesus he delivered him to be crucified. Then the soldiers of the governor took Jesus to the common hall and gathered unto him the whole band of soldiers.

2. And they stripped him and put on him a purple robe. And when they had plaited a crown of thorns they put it upon his head and a reed in his right hand, and they bowed the knee before him and mocked him, saying, Hail, King of the Jews!

3. Then came Jesus forth, wearing the crown of thorns, and the purple robe. And Pilate saith unto them, Behold

the man!

4. When the chief priests therefore and officers saw him, they cried out, saying, Crucify him, crucify him. And Pilate saith unto them, Take ye him and crucify him, for I find no fault in him.

5. And they spit upon him, and took the reed and smote him on the head. And after that they had mocked him they took the robe off from him, and put his own raiment on him, and led him away to crucify him.

6. And as they led him away, they laid hold upon one Simon, a Cyrenian, coming out of the county, and on him they laid the cross that he might bear it after Jesus. And there followed him a great company of people and of women, which also bewailed and lamented him.

7. But Jesus, turning unto them, said, Daughters of Jerusalem, weep not for me, but weep for yourselves and for your children. For behold the days are coming in which they shall say, Blessed are the barren, and the wombs that never bare, and the paps which never gave suck.

8. Then shall they begin to say to the mountains, Fall on us; and to the hills, Cover us. For it they do these things in a green tree, what shall be done in the dry.

9. And there were also two other malefactors led with him to be put to death. And when they were come unto a place called Calvary, and Golgotha, that is to say a place of a skull, there they crucified him; and the malefactors, one on the right hand, and other on the left.

10. And it was the third hour when they crucified him, and they gave him vinegar to drink mingled with gall, and when he had tasted thereof, he would not drink. And Jesus said, Abba Amma, forgive them, for they know not what they do.

11. Then the soldiers, when they had crucified Jesus, took his raiment and made four parts, to every soldier a part; and also his vesture. Now the vesture was without seam, woven from the top throughout. They said therefore among themselves, Let us not rend it, but cast lots for it, whose it

shall be.

12. That the scripture might be fulfilled, which saith, They parted my raiment among them, and for my vesture they did cast lots. These things therefore the soldiers did. And sitting down they watched him there.

13. And a superscription was also written over him in letters of Greek, and Latin, and Hebrew, This is the King of the Jews.

14. This title then read many of the Jews, for the place where Jesus was crucified was nigh to the city, and it was written in Hebrew and Greek and Latin. then said the chief priests of the Jews to Pilate, Write not, The King of the Jews, but that, he said, I am the King of the Jews. Pilate answered, What I have written, I have written.

15. And one of the malefactors which were hanged railed on him, saying, If thou be the Christ, save thy self and us. But the other answering rebuked him, saying, Dost not thou fear God, seeing thou art in the same condemnation? And we indeed justly, for we receive the due reward of our deeds, but this man hath done nothing amiss.

16. And he said unto Jesus, Lord remember me when thou comest into thy kingdom. And Jesus said unto him, Verily I say unto thee, to day shalt thou be with me in Paradise.

17. And they that passed by reviled him, wagging heir heads and saying, Thou that wouldst destroy the temple, and build it in three days, save thyself. If thou be the Son of God, come down from the Cross.

18. Likewise also the chief priests mocking him, while the scribes and elders said, He saved a lamb, himself he cannot save. If he be the King of Israel, let him now come down from the cross and we will believe him. He trusted in God, let Him deliver him now, if He will have him, for he said, I am the Son of God.

19. The usurers and the dealers in beasts and birds also cast the like things into his teeth, saying, Thou who drivest from the temple the traders in oxen and sheep and doves,

art thyself but a sheep that is sacrificed.

20. Now from the Sixth hour there was darkness over all the land unto the Ninth hour, and some standing around, lighted their torches, for the darkness was very great. And about the Sixth hour Jesus cried with a loud voice, Eli, Eli, lame sabachthani? that, is to say, My God, My God, why hast Thou forsaken me ?

21. Some of them that stood there, when they heard that, said, This man calleth for Elias; others said, He calleth on the Sun. The rest said, Let be, let us see whether Elias will come to save him.

22. Now there stood by the cross of Jesus his mother and his mother's sister, Mary, the wife of Cleophas, and Mary Magdalene.

23. When Jesus therefore saw his mother, and the disciple standing by whom he loved, he saith unto his mother, Woman, behold thy son! And he said to the disciple, Behold thy mother! And from that hour that disciple took her into his own home.

24. After this, Jesus knowing that all things were now accomplished, that the scripture might be fulfilled, saith, I am athirst. And from a vessel they filled a sponge with vinegar and put it upon hyssop and put it to his mouth.

25. And Jesus cried with a loud voice, saying, Abba Amma, into Thy hand I commend my spirit.

26. When Jesus had therefore received the vinegar, he cried aloud, It is finished; and he bowed his head and gave up the ghost. And it was the ninth hour.

27. And behold there was great thunder and lightning, and the partition wall of the Holy place, from which hung the veil, fell down, and was rent in twain, and the earth did quake, and the rocks also were rent.

28. Now when the centurion and they that were with him watching Jesus, saw the earthquake and those things that

were done, they feared greatly, saying, Truly this was a Son of God.

29. And many women were there, which followed from Galilee, ministering unto them, and among them were Mary the mother of James and Joses, and the mother of Zebedee's children and they lamented, saying, The light of the world is hid from our eyes, the Lord our Love is crucified.

30. Then the Jews, because it was the preparation, that the bodies should not remain upon the cross on the Sabbath, for that was a Paschal Sabbath, besought Pilate that their legs might be broken, and that they might be taken away.

31. Then came the soldiers, and brake the legs of the two who were crucified with him. But when they came to Jesus, and saw that he was dead already, they brake not his legs, but one of the soldiers with a spear pierced his heart and forthwith came there out blood and water.

32. And he that saw it bare record and his record is true, and he knoweth that he saith true, that ye might believe. For these things were done that the Scriptures might be fulfilled—A bone of him shall not be broken, and again—In the midst of the week the Messiah shall be cut off.

Lection LXXXIII
The Burial Of Iesus

1. NOW, when the even was come, Joseph of Arimathea, an honourable councillor, who also waited for the Kingdom of God, came and went in boldly unto Pilate and craved the body of Jesus. (He was a good man and just, and had not consented to the council and deed of them).

2. And Pilate marvelled if he were already dead, and calling unto him the centurion, he asked him whether he had been any while dead. And when he knew it of the centurion, he gave the body to Joseph. He came therefore, and took the body of Jesus.

3. And there came also Nicodemus, who at the first came to Jesus by night, and brought a mixture of myrrh and aloes, about an hundred weight. Then took they the body of Jesus and wound it in linen clothes with the spices, as the manner of the Jews is to bury.

4. Now in the place where he was crucified there was a garden, and in the garden a new sepulchre, wherein was never man yet laid. There laid they Jesus therefore, and it was about the beginning of the second watch when they buried him, because of the Jews' preparation day, for the sepulchre was nigh at hand.

5. And Mary Magdalene and the other Mary, and Mary the mother of Joses beheld where he was laid. There at the tomb they kept watch for three days and three nights.

6. And the women also, who came with him from Galilee, followed after, bearing lamps in their hands and beheld the sepulchre and how his body was laid, and they made lamentation over him.

7. And they returned and rested the next clay, being a high day, and on the day following they bought and prepared spices and ointments and waited for the end of the Sabbath.

8. Now the next day that followed, the chief priests and Pharisees came together unto Pilate, saying, Sir we remember that deceiver said, while he was yet alive, After three days I will rise again.

9. Command therefore that the sepulchre be made sure until the third day be past, lest his disciples come by night and steal him away, and say unto the people, He is risen from the dead, so the last error shall be worse than the first.

10. Pilate said unto them, Ye have a watch, go your way, make it as sure as you can. So they went and made the sepulchre sure, sealing the stone and setting a watch till the third day should be past.

Lection LXXXIV
The Resurrection Of Iesus

1. NOW after the Sabbath was ended and it began to dawn, on the first day of the week, came Mary Magdalene to the sepulchre, bearing the spices which she had prepared, and there were others with her.

2. And as they were going, they said among themselves, who shall roll away the stone from the door of the sepulchre? For it was great. And when they came to the place and looked, they saw that the stone was rolled away.

3. For behold there was a great earthquake; and the angel of the Lord descended from heaven, and rolled back the stone from the door, and sat upon it. His countenance was like lighting and his raiment white as snow: And for fear of him the keepers did shake and became as dead men.

4. And the angel answered and said unto the women, Fear not ye, for I know that ye seek Jesus, which was crucified. He is not here: for he is risen, as he said.

5. Come, see the place where the Lord lay. And go quickly and tell his disciples that he is risen from the dead; and, behold he goeth before you into Galilee; there shall ye see him; lo, I have told you.

6. And they entered in and found not the body of Jesus. Then she ran and came to Simon Peter and the other disciple whom Jesus loved, and said unto them, They have taken away the Lord out of the sepulchre, and we know not where they have laid him.

7. And they ran and came to the scpulchre, and looking in, they saw the linen clothes lying, and the napkin that had been about his head not lying with the linen clothes, but wrapped up in a place by itself.

8. And it came to pass as they were much perplexed, behold, two angels stood by them in glistening garments of white, and said unto them, Why seek ye the living among the dead? He is not here, he is risen, and, behold, he goeth

before you into Galilee, there shall we see him.

9. Remember ye not how he spake unto you, when he was yet in Galilee, that the Son of Man should be crucified and that he would rise again after the third day? And they remembered his words. And they went out quickly and fled from the sepulchre, for they trembled with amazement, and they were afraid.

10. NOW at the time of the earthquake, the graves were opened; and many of the saints which slept arose, and came out of the graves after his resurrection, and went into the city and appeared unto many.

11. But Mary stood without at the sepulchre weeping, and as she wept she again stooped down, and looked into the sepulchre and saw two angels in white garments, the one at the head, and the other at the feet, where the body of Jesus had lain. And they said unto her, Woman, why weepest thou?

12. She saith unto them, Because they have taken away my Lord, and I know not where they have laid him. And when she had thus said, she turned herself back, and saw Jesus standing, and knew not that it was Jesus.

13. Jesus saith unto her, Woman, why weepest thou? Whom seekest thou? She, supposing him to be the gardener, saith unto him, Sir, if thou have borne him hence, tell me where thou hast laid him, and I will take him away. Jesus said unto her, Mary, She turned herself and saith unto him, Rabboni; which is to say, Master.

14. Jesus saith unto her, Touch me not, for I am not yet ascended to my Father One with my Mother, but go to my brethren, and say unto them, I ascend unto my Parent and your Parent; to my God and your God.

15. And Mary Magdalene came and told the disciples that she had seen the Lord, and that he had spoken these things unto her, and commanded her to announce his resurrection from the dead.

Lection LXXXV
Iesus Appeareth To Two At Emmaus

1. AND behold, two of them went that same day to a village called Emmaus, which was from Jerusalem about three-score furlongs. And they talked together of all these things which had happened.

2. And it came to pass, that, while they communed together and reasoned, Jesus himself drew near, and went with them. But their eyes were holden that they should not know him.

3. And he said unto them, What manner of communications are these that ye have one with another, as ye walk and are sad?

4. And the one of them, whose name was Cleophas, answering, said unto him, Art thou only a stranger in Jerusalem and hast not known the things which are come to pass there in these days? And he said unto them, What things?

5. And they said unto him, Concerning Jesus of Nazareth who was a Prophet mighty in deed and word before God and all the people; and how the chief priests and our rulers delivered him to be condemned to death, and have crucified him. But we trusted that it had been he which should have redeemed Israel; and beside all this three days have passed since these things were done.

6. Yea, and certain women also of our company made us astonished, which were early at the sepulchre; and when they found not his body, they came saying, that they had also seen a vision of angels, who said that he was alive.

7. And certain of them who were with us went to the sepulchre, and found it even so as the women had said; but him they saw not.

8. Then he said unto them, O fools and slow of heart to believe all that the prophets have spoken; Ought not Christ to have suffered these things, and then to enter into his glory?

9. And beginning at Moses and all the prophets, he expounded unto them in all the scriptures, the things concerning himself.

10. And they drew nigh unto the village whither they went; and he made as though he would have gone further. But they constrained him, saying, Abide, with us, for it is toward evening, and the day is far spent. And he went in to tarry with them.

11. And it came to pass as he sat at table with them, he took bread and the fruit of the vine, and gave thanks, blessed, and brake, and gave to them. And their eyes were opened, and they knew him; and he vanished out of their sight.

12. And they said one to another, Did not our hearts burn within us while he talked with us by the way, and while he opened to us the scriptures? And they rose up the same hour and returned to Jerusalem, and found the twelve gathered together, and them that were with them, saying, The Lord is risen indeed, and hath appeared to Simon.

13. And they told what things were done in the way and how he was known of them in breaking of bread.

14. Now while they had been going to Emmaus, some of the watch came into the city, and showed unto Caiaphas what things had been done.

15. And they assembled with the elders and took council and said, Behold, while the soldiers slept, some of his disciples came and took his body away; and is not Joseph of Arimathea one if his disciples?

16. For this cause then did he beg the body from Pilate that he might bury it in his garden in his own tomb. Let us therefore give money to the soldiers, saying, say ye, His disciples came by night and stole him away while we slept. And if this come to the ears of the governor we will persuade him, and secure you.

Lection LXXXVI
Iesus Appeareth In The Temple
Blood Sacrifices Cease

1. THE same day, at the time of sacrifice in the Temple there appeared among the dealers in beasts and in birds, One clothed in white raiment, bright as light, and in his hand a whip of seven cords.

2. And at the sight of him, those who sold and bought fled in terror, and some of them fell as dead men, for they remembered how before his death Jesus had driven them away from the Temple enclosure, in like manner.

3. And some declared that they had seen a spirit. And others that they had seen him who was crucified and that he had risen from the dead.

4. And the sacrifices ceased that day in the Temple, for all were in fear, and none could be had to sell or to buy, but, rather, they let their captives go free.

5. And the priests and elders caused a report to be spread, That they who had seen it were drunken, and had seen nothing. But many affirmed that they had seen him with their own eyes, and felt on their backs the scourge, but were powerless to resist, for when some of the bolder among them put forth their hands, they could not seize the form which they beheld, nor grasp the whip which chastised them. 6. And from that time, these believed in Jesus, that he was sent from God, to deliver the oppressed, and free those that were bound. And they turned from their ways and sinned no longer.

7. To others he also appeared in love and mercy and healed them by his touch, and delivered them from the hands of the persecutor. And many like things were reported of him, and many said, Of a truth the Kingdom is come.

8. And some of those who had slept and risen, when Jesus rose from the dead appeared, and were seen by many in the holy City, and great fear fell upon the wicked, but light

and gladness came to the righteous in heart.

Lection LXXXVII
Iesus Appeareth To The Twelve

1. THEN the same day at evening, being the first day of the week, when the doors were shut where the disciples were assembled for fear of the Jews, came Jesus and stood in the midst, and saith unto them, Peace be unto you. But they were affrighted and supposed that they had seen a spirit.
2. And he said unto them, Behold, it is I myself, like as ye have seen me aforetime. A spirit can in deed appear in flesh and bones as ye see me have. Behold my hands and my feet, handle and see.
3. And when he had so said, he shewed unto them his hands and his Heart. Then were the disciples glad, when they saw the Lord.
4. For Thomas, called Didymus, one of the disciples, had said unto them, Except I shall see in his hands the print of the nails, and thrust my hand into his heart, I will not believe. Then saith he to Thomas, Behold my hands, my heart, and my feet; reach hither thy hands, and be not faithless but believing.
5. And Thomas answered and said unto him, My Lord and my God! And Jesus saith unto him, Thomas, because thou hast seen me, thou hast believed; blessed are they that have not seen and yet have believed.
6. Then saith Jesus unto them again, Peace be unto you, as Abba Amma hath sent me, even so send I you. And when he had said this he breathed on them and said unto them, Receive ye the Holy Ghost; preach the Gospel, and anounce ye unto all nations; the resurrection of the Son of Man.
7. Teach ye the holy law of love which I have delivered unto you. And whosoever forsake their sins, they are remitted

unto them, and whosoever continue in their sins they are retained unto them.

8. Baptise them who believe and repent, bless and anoint them, and offer ye the pure Oblation of the fruits of the earth, which I have appointed unto you for a Memorial of me.

9. Lo, I have given my body and my blood to be offered on the Cross, for the redemption of the world from the sin against love, and from the bloody sacrifices and feasts of the past.

10. And ye shall offer the Bread of life, and the Wine of salvation, for a pure Oblation with incense, as it is written of me, and ye shall eat and drink thereof for a memorial, that I have delivered all who believe in me from the ancient bondage of your ancestors.

11. For they, making a god of their belly, sacrificed unto their god the innocent creatures of the earth, in place of the carnal nature within themselves.

12. And eating of their flesh and drinking of their blood to their own destruction, corrupted their bodies and shortened their days, even as the Gentiles who knew not the truth, or who knowing it, have changed it into a lie.

13. As I send you, so send ye others also, to do these things in my Name, and he laid his hands upon them.

14. In the like manner as the Apostles, so also be ordained Prophets and Evangelists and Pastors, a Holy Priesthood, and afterwards he laid his hand upon those whom they chose for Deacons, one for each of the fourfold twelve.

15. And these are for the rule and guidance of the Church Universal, that all may be perfected in their places in the Unity of the Body of the Christ.

Lection LXXXVIII
The Eighth Day After The Resurrection

1. AND after seven days again, his disciples were within

the Upper Room; then came Jesus, the doors being shut, and stood in their midst and said, Peace be unto you, and he was known unto them in the holy Memorial.

2. And he said unto them. Love ye one another and all the creatures of God. Yet I say unto you, not all are men, who are in the form of man. Are they men or women in the image of God whose ways are ways of violence, of oppression and wrong, who choose a lie rather than the truth?

3. Nay, verily, till they are born again, and receive the Spirit of Love and Wisdom within their hearts. Then only are they sons and daughters of Israel, and being of Israel they are children of God, And for this cause came I into the world, and for this I have suffered at the hands of sinners.

4. These are the words which I spake unto you, while I was yet with you, that all things must be fulfilled which were written in the law of Moses and in the prophets, and in the psalms, concerning me.

5. And Jesus said, I stood in the midst of the world, and in the flesh was I seen and heard, and I found all men glutted with their own pleasures, and drunk with their own follies, and none found I hungry or athirst for the wisdom which is of God. My soul grieveth over the sons and daughters of men because they are blind in their heart, and in their soul are they deaf and hear not my voice.

6. Then opened he their understanding, that they might understand the scriptures. And said unto them, Thus it is written, and thus it behooved the Christ to suffer, and to rise from the dead after the third day. And that repentance and remission of sins should be preached in my name among all nations, beginning at Jerusalem. And ye are witnesses of these things.

7. And, behold, I send the promice of my Parent upon you, even of my Father One with my Mother, Whom ye have not seen on the earth. For I say unto you of a truth, as the whole world have been ruined by the sin and vanity of woman, so by the simplicity and truth of woman shall it be

saved, even by you shall it be saved.

8. Rejoice therefore and be ye glad, for ye are more blessed than all who are on earth, for it is ye, my twelve thousand who shall save the whole world.

9. Again I say unto you when the great tyrant and all the seven tyrants began to fight in vain against the Light, they knew not with Whom or What they fought.

10. For they saw nothing beyond a dazzling Light, and when they fought they expended their strength one against another, and so it is.

11. For this cause I took a fourth part of their strength, so that they might not have such power, and prevail in their evil deeds.

12. For by involution and evolution shall the salvation of all the world be accomplished: by the Descent of Spirit into matter, and the Ascent of matter into Spirit, through the ages.

Lection LXXXIX
Iesus Appeareth At The Sea Of Tiberias

1. AFTER these things Jesus shewed himself again to the disciples at the sea of Tiberias, and on this wise shewed he himself. There were together Simon, Peter, and Thomas, called Didymus, and Nathanael of Cana in Galilee, and James and John and two other of his disciples.

2. And Peter saith unto them, I go a fishing. They say unto him, We also go with thee. They went forth and entered into a ship immediately, and that night they caught nothing. And when the morning was now come, Jesus stood on the shore, but the disciples knew not that it was Jesus.

3. Then Jesus said unto them, Children, have ye any meat? They answered him, Nay, Lord, not enough for all; there is naught but a small loaf, a little oil, and a few dried fruits. And he said unto them, Let these suffice; come and dine.

4. And he blessed them, and they ate and were filled, and

there was a pitcher of water also, and he blessed it likewise, and lo, it was the fruit of the vine.

5. And they marvelled, and said. It is the Lord. And none of the disciples dost ask him. Who art thou? knowing it was the Lord.

6. This is now the sixth time that Jesus shewed himself to his disciples, after that he was risen from the dead. So when they had dined, Jesus saith to Peter, son of Jonas, lovest thou me more than these? He saith unto him, Yea, Lord, thou knowest that I love thee. He saith unto him, Feed my lambs. He saith unto him again the second time, Peter, son of Jonas, lovest thou me? He saith unto him, Yea, Lord thou knowest that I love thee. He said unto him. Feed my sheep.

7. He saith unto him the third time, Peter, son of Jonas, lovest thou me? Peter was grieved because he said unto him the third time, Lovest thou me ? And he said unto him, Lord, thou knowest all things; thou knowest that I love thee.   8. Jesus saith unto him, Feed my Flock. Verily verily, I say unto thee, thou art a rock from the Rock, and on this rock will I build my Church, and I will raise thee above my twelve to be my vicegerent upon earth for a centre of Unity to the twelve, and another shall be called and chosen to fill thy place among the twelve, and thou shalt be the Servant of servants and shalt feed my rams, my sheep and my lambs.   9. And yet another shall arise and he shall teach many things which I have taught you already, and he shall spread the Gospel among the Gentiles with great zeal. But the keys of the Kingdom will I give to those who succeed thee in my Spirit and obeying my law.

10. And again I say unto thee. When thou wast young thou girdedst thyself and walketh whither thou wouldst, but when thou shalt be old, thou shalt stretch forth thy hands and another shall gird thee and carry thee whither thou wouldst not. This spake he, signifying by what death he should glorify God.

11. And when he had spoken this he saith unto him, Follow me. Then Peter, turning about, seeth the disciple whom Jesus loved following. Peter seeing him, saith to Jesus, Lord and what shall this man do? Jesus saith unto him, If I will that he tarry till I come, what is that to thee? follow thou me.

12. Then went this saying abroad among the brethren that disciple should not die: yet Jesus said not unto him, He shall not die, but, if I will that he tarry till I come, what is that to thee.

Lection XC
What Is Truth?

1. AGAIN the twelve were gathered together in the Circle of palm trees, and one of them even Thomas said to the other, What is Truth? for the same things appear different to different minds, and even to the same mind at different times.What, then, is Truth?

2. And as they were speaking Jesus appeared in their midst and said, Truth, one and absolute, is in God alone, for no man, neither any body of men, knoweth that which God alone knoweth, who is the All in All. To men is Truth revealed, according to their capacity to understand and receive.

3. The One Truth hath many sides, and one seeth one side only, another seeth another, and some see more than others, according as it is given to them.

4. Behold this crystal: how the one light its manifest in twelve faces, yea four times twelve, and each face reflecteth one ray of light, and one regardeth one face, and another another, but it is the one crystal and the one light that shineth in all.

5. Behold again, When one climbeth a mountain and attaining one height, he saith, This is the top of the mountain, let us reach it, and when they have reached that

height, lo, they see another beyond it until they come to that height from which no other height is to be seen, if so be they can attain it.

6. So it is with Truth. I am the Truth and the Way and the Life, and have given to you the Truth I have received from above. And that which is seen and received by one, is not seen and received by another. That which appeareth true to some, seemeth not true to others. They who are in the valley see not as they who are on the hill top.

7. But to each, it is the Truth as the one mind seeth it, and for that time, till a higher Truth shall be revealed unto the same: and to the soul which receiveth higher light, shall be given more light. Wherefore condemn not others, that ye be not condemned.

8. As ye keep the holy Law of Love, which I have given unto you, so shall the Truth be revealed more and more unto you, and the Spirit of Truth which cometh from above shall guide you, albeit through many wanderings, into all Truth, even as the fiery cloud guided the children of Israel through the wilderness.

9. Be faithful to the light ye have, till a higher light is given to you. Seek more light, and ye shall have abundantly; rest not, till ye find.

10. God giveth you all Truth, as a ladder with many steps, for the salvation and perfection of the soul, and the truth which seemeth to day, ye will abandon for the higher truth of the morrow. Press ye unto Perfection.

11. Whoso keepeth the holy Law which I have given, the same shall save their souls, however differently they may see the truths which I have given.

12. Many shall say unto me, Lord, Lord, we have been zealous for thy Truth. But I shall say unto them, Nay, but, that others may see as ye see, and none other truth beside. Faith without charity is dead. Love is the fulfilling of the Law.

13. How shall faith in what they receive profit them that

hold it in unrighteousness? They who have love have all things, and without love there is nothing worth. Let each hold what they see to be the truth in love, knowing that where love is not, truth is a dead letter and profiteth nothing.

14. There abide Goodness, and Truth, and Beauty, but the greatest of these is Goodness. If any have hatred to their fellows, and harden their hearts to the creatures of God's hands, how can they see Truth unto salvation, seeing their eyes are blinded and their hearts are hardened to God's creation?

15. As I have revieved the Truth, so have I given it to you. Let each receive it according to their light and ability to understand, and persecute not those who receive it after a different interpretation.

16. For Truth is the Might of God, and it shall prevail in the end over all errors. But the holy Law which I have given is plain for all, and just and good. Let all observe it for the salvation of their souls.

Lection XCI
The Order of the Kingdom (Part I)

1. In that time after Jesus had risen from the dead he tarried ninety days with Mary his mother and Mary Magdalene, who anointed his body, and Mary Cleophas and the twelve, and their fellows, instructing them and answering questions concerning the kingdom of God.

2. And as they sat at supper—when it was even— Mary Magdalene asked him, saying, Master, wilt thou now declare unto us the Order of the Kingdom?

3. And Jesus answered and said, Verily I say unto thee, O Mary, and to each of any disciples, The kingdom of Heaven is within you. But the time cometh when that which is within shall be made manifest in the without, for the sake of the world.

4. Order indeed is good, and needful, but before all things is love. Love ye one another and all the creatures of God, and by this shall all men know that ye are my disciples.

5. AND one asked him saying, Master, wilt thou that infants be received into the congregation in like manner as Moses commanded by circumcision? And Jesus answered, For those who are in Christ there is no cutting of the flesh, nor shedding of blood.

6. Let the infant of eight clays be Presented unto the Father-Mother, who is in Heaven, with prayer and thanksgiving, and let a name be given to it by its parents, and let the presbyter sprinkle pure water upon it, according to that which is written in the prophets, and let its parents see to it that it is brought up in the ways of righteousness, neither eating flesh, nor drinking strong drink, nor hurting the creatures which God hath given into the hands of man to protect. .

7. AGAIN one said unto him, Master, how wilt thou when they grow up? And Jesus said, After seven years, or when they begin to know the evil from the good, and learn to choose the good, let them come unto me and receive the blessing at the hands of the presbyter or the angel of the church with prayer and thanksgiving, and let them be admonished to keep from flesheating and strong drink, and from hunting the innocent creatures of God, for shall they be lower than the horse or the sheep to whom these things are against nature?

8. And again he said, If there come to us any that eat flesh and drink strong drink, shall we receive them? And Jesus said unto him, Let such abide in the outer court till they cleanse themselves from these grosser evils; for till they perceive, and repent of these, they are not fit to receive the higher mysteries.

9. AND another asked him saying, When wilt thou that they receive Baptism? And Jesus answered, After another seven years, or when they know the doctrine, and do that

which is good, and learn to work with their own hands, and choose a craft whereby they may live, and are stedfastly set on the right way. Then let them ask for initiation, and let the angel or presbyter of the church examine them and see if they are worthy, and let him offer thanksgiving and prayer, and bury them in the waters of separation, that they may rise to newness of life, confessing God as their Father and Mother, vowing to obey the Holy Law, and keep themselves separate from the evil in the world.

10. AND another asked him, Master, at what time shall they receive the Anointing? And Jesus answered, When they have reached the age of maturity, and manifested in themselves the sevenfold gifts of the Spirit, then let the angel offer prayer and thanksgiving and seal them with the seal of the Chrism. It is good that all be tried in each degree seven years. Nevertheless let it be unto each according to their growth in the love, and the wisdom of God.

Lection XCII
The Order of the Kingdom (Part II)

1. AND another asked him saying, Master, wilt thou that there be marriages among us as it is among the nations of earth? And Jesus answered, saying, Among some it is the custom that one woman may marry several men, who shall say unto her, Be thou our wife and take away our reproach. Among others it is the custom, that one man may marry several women, and who shall say unto him, Be thou our husband and take away our reproach, for they who love feel it is a reproach to be unloved.

2. But unto you my disciples, I shew a better and more perfect way, even this, that marriage should be between one man and one woman, who by perfect love and sympathy are united, and that while love and life do last, howbeit in perfect freedom. But let them see to it that they have perfect health, and that they truly love each other in all

purity, and not for worldly advantage only, and then let them plight their troth one to another before witnesses.

3. Then, when the time is come, let the angel or presbyter offer prayer and thanksgiving and bind them with the scarlet cord, if ye will, and crown them, and lead them thrice around the altar and let them eat of one bread and drink of one cup. Then holding their hands together, let him say to them in this wise, Be ye two in one, blessed be the holy union, you whom God doth join together let no man put asunder, so long as life and love do last.

4. And if they bear children, let them do so with discretion and prudence according to their ability to maintain them. Nevertheless to those who would be perfect and to whom it is given, I say, let them be as the angels of God in Heaven, who neither marry nor are given in marriage, nor have children, nor care for the morrow, but are free from bonds, even as I am, and keep and store up the power of God within, for their ministry, and for works of healing, even as I have done. But the many cannot receive this saying, only they to whom it is given.

5. AND another asked him saying, Master, in what manner shall we offer the Holy Oblation? And Jesus answered, saying, The oblation which God loveth in secret is a pure heart. But for a Memorial of worship offer ye unleavened bread, mingled wine, oil and incense. When ye come together in one place to offer the Holy Oblation, the lamps being lighted, let him who presideth, even the angel of the church, or the presbyter, having clean hands and a pure heart, take from the things offered, unleavened bread and mingled wine with incense.

6. And let him give thanks over them and bless them, calling upon the Father-Mother in Heaven to send their Holy Spirit that it may come upon and make them to be the Body and Blood, even the Substance and Life of the Eternal, which is ever being broken and shed for all.

7. And let him lift it up toward Heaven and pray for all,

even for those who are gone before, for those who are yet alive, and for those who are yet to come As I have taught you, so pray ye, and after this let him break the bread and put a fragment in the cup, and then bless the holy union, and then let him give unto the faithful, saying after this manner, This is the body of the Christ even the substance of God (ever being broken and shed, for you and for all), unto eternal life. As ye have seen me do, so do ye also, in the spirit of love, for the words I speak unto you, they are spirit and they are life.

Lection XCIII
The Order of the Kingdom (Part III)

1. AND another spake, saying, Master, if one have committed a sin, can a man remit or retain his sin? And Jesus said, God forgiveth all sin to those who repent, but as ye sow, so also must ye reap; Neither God nor man can remit the sins of those who repent not nor forsake their sins; nor yet retain the sins of those who forsake them. But if one being in the spirit seeth clearly that any repent and forsake their sins, such may truly say unto the penitent, Thy sins are forgiven thee, for All sin is remitted by repentance and amendment and they are loosed from it, who forsake it and bound to it, who continue it.

2. Nevertheless the fruits of the sin must continue for a season, for as we sew so must we reap, for God is not mocked, and they who sow to the flesh shall reap corruption, they who sow to the spirit shall reap life, everlasting. Wherefore if any forsake their sins and confess them, let the presbyter say unto such in this wise, May God forgive thee thy sins, and bring thee to everlasting life. All sin against God is forgiven by God, and sin against man by man.

3. AND another asked him, saying, If any be sick among us, shall we have power to heal even as thou dost? And

Jesus answered, This power cometh of perfect chastity and of faith. They who are born of God keep their seed within them.

4. Nevertheless if any be sick among you, let them send for the presbyters of the church that they may anoint them with oil of olive in the Name of the Lord, and the prayer of faith, and the going out of power, with the voice of thanksgiving, shall raise them up, if they are not detained by sin, of this, or a former life.

5. AND another asked him saying, Master, how shall the holy assembly be ordered and who shall minister therein? And Jesus answered. When my disciples are gathered in my name let them choose from among themselves true and faithful men and women, who shall be ministers and counsellors in temporal things and provide for the necessities of the poor, and those who cannot work, and let these look to the ordering of the goods of the church, and assist at the Oblation, and let these be your deacons, with their helps.

6. And when these have given proof, of their ministry, let them choose from them, those who have spiritual gifts, whether of guidance, or of prophecy, or of preaching and of teaching and healing, that they may edify the flock, offer the holy Oblation and minister the mysteries of God and let these be your presbyter, and their helps.

7. And from these who have served well in their degree let one be chosen who is counted most worthy, and let him preside over all and he shall be your Angel. And let the Angel ordain the deacons and consecrate the presbyters— anoint them and laying their hands upon them and breathing upon them that they may receive the Holy Spirit for the office to which they are called. And as for the Angel let one of the higher ministry anoint and consecrate him, even one of the Supreme Council.

8. For as I send Apostles and Prophets so also I send Evangelists And Pastors—the eight and forty pillars of the tab-

ernacle—that by the ministry of the four I may build up and perfect my Church, and they shall sit in Jerusalem a holy congregation, each with his helper and deacon, and to them shall the scattered congregations refer in all matters pertaining to the Church. And as light cometh so shall they rule and guide and edify and teach my holy Church. They shall receive light from all, and to all shall they give more light.

9. And forget not with your prayers and supplications intercessions and giving of thanks, to offer the incense, as it is written in the last of your prophets, saying, From the rising of the sun unto the setting of the same incense shall be offered unto My Name in all places with a pure oblation, for My Name shall be great among the Gentiles.

10. For verily I say unto you, incense is the memorial of the intercession of the saints within the veil, with words that cannot be uttered.

Lection XCIV
The Order of the Kingdom (Part IV)

1. AND another asked him, saying, Master, how wilt thou that we bury our dead? And Jesus answered, Seek ye council of the deacons in this matter, for it concerneth the body only. Verily, I say, unto you there is no death to those who believe in the life to come. Death, as ye deemed it, is the door to life, and the grave is the gate to resurrection, for those who believe and obey. Mourn ye not, nor weep for them that have left you, but rather rejoice for their entrance into life.

2. As all creatures come forth from the unseen into this world, so they return to the unseen, and so will they come again till they be purified. Let the bodies of them that depart be committed to the elements, and the Father-Mother, who reneweth all things, shall give the angels charge over them, and let the presbyter pray that their bodies may rest

in peace, and their souls awake to a joyful resurrection.

3. There is a resurrection from the body, and there is a resurrection in the body. There is a raising out of the life of the flesh, and there is a falling into the life of the flesh. Let prayer be made For those who are gone before, and For those that are alive, and For those that are yet to come, for all are One family in God. In God they live and move and have their being.

4. The body that ye lay in the grave, or that is consumed by fire, is not the body that shall be, but they who come shall receive other bodies, yet their own, and as they have sown in one life, so shall they reap in another. Blessed are they who have worked righteousness in this life, for they shall receive the crown of life.

5. AND another asked him, saying, Master, under the law Moses clad the priests with garments of beauty for their ministration in the Temple. Shall we also clothe them to whom we commit the ministry of sacred things as thou hast taught us? And Jesus answered, White linen is the righteousness of the Saints, but the time truly cometh when Zion shall be desolate, and after the time of her affliction is past, she shall arise and put on her beautiful garments as it is written.

6. But seek ye first the kingdom of righteousness, and all these things shall be added unto you. In all things seek simplicity, and give not occasion to vain glory. Seek ye first to be clothed with charity, and the garment of salvation and the robe of righteousness.

7. For what doth it profit if ye have not these? As the sound of brass and tinkling of cymbal are ye, if ye have not love. Seek ye righteousness and love and peace, and all things of beauty shall be added to you.

8. AND yet another asked him, saving, Master, how many of the rich and mighty will enter into life and join us who are poor and despised. How, then, shall we carry on the work of God in the regeneration of mankind? And Jesus

said, This also is a matter for the deacons of the church in council with the elders.

9. But when my disciples are come together on the Sabbath, at even, or in the morning of the first day of the week, let them each bring an offering of a tithe, or the tithe of a tithe of their increase, as God doth prosper them, and put it in the treasury, for the maintenance of the church and the ministry, and the works thereof. For I say unto you, it is more blessed to give than to receive.

10. So shall all things be done, decently and in order, And the rest will the Spirit set in order who proceedeth from the Father-Mother in heaven. I have instructed you now in first principles, and, lo, I am with you always, even unto the end of the Age.

Lection XCV
The Ascension Of Christ

1. AND Jesus after he had shewed himself alive to his disciples after his resurrection, and sojourned with them for ninety days, teaching and speaking of the Kingdom, and the things pertaining to the Kingdom of God, and had finished all things that he had to do, led forth the twelve with Mary Magdalene, and Joseph his father and Mary his mother, and the other holy women as far as Bethany to a mountain called Olivet, where he had appointed them.

2. And when they saw him as he stood in the midst of them, they worshipped him, but some doubted. And Jesus spake unto them, saying, Behold, I have chosen you from among men, and have given you the Law, and the Word of truth. 3. I have set you as the light of the world, and as a city that cannot be hid. But the time cometh when darkness shall cover the earth, and gross darkness the people, and the enemies of truth and righteousness shall rule in my Name, and set up a kingdom of this world, and oppress the peoples, and cause the enemy to blaspheme, putting

for my doctrines the opinions of men, and teaching in my Name that which I have not taught, and darkening much that I have taught by their traditions.

4. But be of good cheer, for the time will also come when the truth they have hidden shall be manifested, and the light shall shine, and the darkness shall pass away, and the true kingdom shall be established which shall be in the world, but not of it, and the Word of righteousness and love shall go forth from the Centre, even the holy city of Mount Zion, and the Mount which is in the land of Egypt shall be known as an altar of witness unto the Lord.

5. And now I go to my Parent and your Parent, my God and your God. But ye, tarry in Jerusalem, and abide in prayer, and after seven days ye shall receive power from on high, and the promise of the Holy Spirit shall be fulfilled unto you, and ye shall go forth from Jerusalem unto all the tribes of Israel, and to the uttermost parts of the earth.

6. And having said these things, he lifted up his pure and holy hands and blessed them. And it came to pass that while he blessed them, he was parted from them, and a cloud, as the sun in brightness, received him out of their sight, and as he went up some held him by the feet and others worshipped him, falling to the earth on their faces.

7. And while they gazed steadfastly into heaven, behold two stood by them in white apparel, and said, Ye men of Israel, why stand ye gazing into thee, heaven; this same Jesus who is taken from you in a cloud, and as ye have seen him go into heaven, so shall he come again to the earth.

8. Then returned they unto Jerusalem from the Mount of Olives, which is from the city a Sabbath day's journey. And as they returned they missed Mary Magdalene, and they looked for her, but found her not. And some of the disciples said, The Master hath taken her, and they marvelled and were in great awe.

9. Now it was midsummer when Jesus ascended into

heaven, and he had not yet attained his fiftieth year, for it was needful that seven times seven years should be fulfilled in his life.

10. Yea, that he might be perfected by the suffering of all experiences, and be an example unto all, to children and parents, to the married and the celibates, to youth and those of full age, yea, and unto all ages and conditions of mortal life.

Lection XCVI
The Pouring Out Of The Spirit
The Taking of Mary And Joseph

1. AND as the disciples were gathered together in the upper room when they returned from the Mount, they all continued with one accord in prayer and supplication, and their number was about one hundred and twenty.

2. And in that day James stood up and said; Men and brethren, it is known unto you how the Lord, before he left us, chose Peter to preside over us and watch over us in his Name; and how it must needs be that one of those who have been with us and a witness to his resurrection be chosen and appointed to take his place.

3. And they chose two called Barsabas and Matthias, and they prayed and said, Thou lord, who knowest the hearts of all men, shew which of these two thou hast chosen to take part in this Apostleship from which thou dost raise thy servant Peter to preside over us.

4. And they gave forth their lots, and the lot fell upon Matthias, and the Twelve received him, and he was numbered among the Apostles.

5. Then John and James separated Peter from their number by laying on of hands, that he might preside over them in the Name of the Lord, saying, Brother be thou as a hewn stone, sixsquared. Even thou, Petros, which art Petra, bearing witness to the Truth on every side.

6. And to the Apostles were given staves to guide their steps in the ways of truth, and crowns of glory withal; and to the Prophets burning lamps to shew light on the path and censers with fire; and to the Evangelists the book of the holy law to recall the people to the first principles; and to the Pastors were given the cup and platter to feed and nourish the flock.

7. But to none was given aught that was not given to all, for all were one priesthood under the Christ as their Master Great High Priest in the Temple of God; and to the Deacons were given baskets that they might carry therein the things needful for the holy worship. And the number was about one hundred and twenty, Peter presiding over them.

8. AND when the third day had fully come they were all with one accord in the one place, and as they prayed there came a sound from heaven as of a rushing mighty wind, and the room in which they were assembled was shaken, and it filled the place.

9. And there appeared cloven tongues of flame like fire, and sat upon the head of each of them. And they were all filled with the Holy Spirit and began to speak with tongues as the Spirit gave them utterance. And Peter stood up and preached the Law of Christ unto the multitude of all nations and tongues who were gathered together by the report of what had been seen and heard, each man hearing in his own tongue wherein he was born.

10. And of them that listened there were gathered unto the Church that day, three thousand souls, and they received the Holy Law, repented of their sins, and were baptized and continued stedfastly in the Apostles' fellowship and worship, and the Oblation and prayers.

11. And they who believed gave up their possessions, and had all things in common and abode together in one place, shewing the love and the goodness of God to their brothers and sisters and to all creatures, and working with their hands for the common weal.

12. And from these there were called twelve to be Prophets with the Apostles, and twelve to be Evangelists and twelve to be Pastors, and their Helps were added unto them, and Deacons of the Church Universal, and they numbered one hundred and twenty. And thus was the Tabernacle of David set up, with living men filled with goodness, even as the Master had shewn unto them.

13. And to the Church in Jerusalem was given James the Lord's brother for its president and Angel, and under him four and twenty priests in a fourfold ministry, and helpers and deacons also. And after six days many came together, and there were added six thousand men and women who received the holy Law of Love, and they received the word with gladness.

14. AND as they gathered together on the Lord's Day after the Sabbath was past, and were offering the holy Oblation, they missed Mary and Joseph, the parents of Jesus. And they made search but found them not.

15. And some of them said, Surely the Lord hath taken them away, as he did Magdalene. And they were filled with awe, and sung praises to God.

16. And the Spirit of God came upon the Apostles and the Prophets with them and, remembering what the Lord had taught them, with one voice they confessed and praised God, saying.

17. We believe in One God: the Infinite, the Secret Fount, the Eternal Parent: Of Whom are all things invisible and visible. The ALL in all, through all around all. The holy Twain, in whom all things consist; Who hath been, Who is, Who shall be.

18. We believe in one Lord our Lady, the perfect holy Christ: God of God, Light of light begotten. Our Lord, the Father, Spouse and Son. Our Lady, the Mother, Bride and Daughter. Three Modes in one Essence undivided: One Biune Trinity. That God may be manifest as the Father, Spouse and Son of every soul: and that every soul may be per-

fected as the Mother, Bride and Daughter of God.

19. And this by ascent of the soul into the spirit and the descent of the spirit into the soul. Who cometh from heaven, and is incarnate of the Virgin ever blessed, in Jesu-Maria and every Christ of God: and is born and teacheth the way of life and suffereth under the world rulers, and is crucified, and is buried and descendeth into Hell. Who riseth again and ascendeth into glory; from thence giving light and life to all.

20. We believe in the Sevenfold Spirit of God, the Life-Giver: Who proceedeth from the holy Twain. Who cometh upon Jesu-Maria and all that are faithful to the light within: Who dwelleth in the Church, the Israel elect of God. Who cometh ever into the world and lighteth every soul that seeks. Who giveth the Law which judgeth the living and the dead, Who speaketh by the Prophets of every age and clime.

21. We believe in One Holy Universal and Apostolic Church: the Witness to all truth, the Receiver and Giver of the same. Begotten of the Spirit and Fire of God: Nourished by the waters, seeds and fruits of earth. Who by the Spirit of Life, her twelve Books and Sacraments, her holy words and works: knitteth together the elect in one mystical communion and atoneth humanity with God. Making us partakers of the Divine Life and Substance: betokening the same in holy Symbols.

22. And we look for the coming of the Universal Christ: and the Kingdom of Heaven wherein dwelleth righteousness. And the holy City whose gates are Twelve: wherein are the Temple and Altar of God. Whence proceed three Orders in fourfold ministry: to teach all truth and offer the daily sacrifice of praise.

23. As in the inner so in the outer: as in the great so in the small. As above, so below: as in heaven so in earth. We believe in the Purification of the soul: through many births and experiences. The Resurrection from the dead: and the

Life everlasting of the just. The Ages of Ages: and Rest in God for ever.—Amun.

24. And as the smoke of the incense arose, there was heard the sound as of many bells, and a multitude of the heavenly host praising God and saying:

25. Glory, honour, praise and worship be to God; the Father, Spouse, and Son: One with the Mother, Bride and Maid: From Whom proceedeth the Eternal Spirit: By whom are all created things. From the Ages of Ages. Now: and to the Ages of Ages—Amun—Alleluia, Alleluia, Alleluia.

26. And if any man take from, or add, to the words of this Gospel, or hide, as under a bushel, the light thereof, which is given by the Spirit through us, the twelve witnesses chosen of God, for the enlightenment of the world unto salvation: Let him be Anathema Maranatha, until the coming of Christ Jesu-Maria, our Saviour, with all the Holy Saints.

27. For them that believe, these things are true. For them that believe not, they are as an idle tale. But to those with perceiving minds and hearts, regarding the spirit rather than the letter which killeth, they are spiritual verities.

28. For the things that are written are true, not because they are written, but rather they are written because they are true, and these are written that ye may believe with your hearts, and proclaim with your mouths to the salvation of many. Amen.

Here endeth the Holy Gospel of the Perfect Life of Jesu-Maria, the Christ, the Son of David after the Flesh, the Son of God after the Spirit. Glory be to God by Whose power and help it has been written.

ORDER FORM:

The Holy Virus

1) Secure Internet site: http://www.holyvirus.net
   Mastercard / Visa / Discover / Paypal

2) Via "snail mail" - check or money order only

Quantity 1 - 5 ....29.95 ea
Quantity 6- 10 ....27.95 ea
Quantity 11 - 15 ....24.95 ea
Quantity 16 - 50 ....21.95 ea

Price all books: _____
Shipping: _____
Sales Tax: _____
Total: _____

Shipping and handling: $5 first book
add $2 for each additional book.

UPS: add $4.00 to shipping total.
Canada: add $5.00 to shipping total.
(No UPS to Canada).
Idaho residents add 6% sales tax.

Total quantity books _____

Name: _____

Street: _____

City: _____ **State:** _____ **ZIP:** _____

Phone No: (____) _____

Make Checks Payable to:
Grapevine Publications   **P.O. Box 45057**   **Boise, Idaho**   **83711**